Conversations with T

Literary Conversations Series

Peggy Whitman Prenshaw
General Editor

APPOMATTOX REGIONAL LIBRARY
HOPEWELL,VIRGINIA 23860
07/90

Charles Ford

Conversations
with Tom Wolfe

Edited by
Dorothy M. Scura

University Press of Mississippi
Jackson and London

818
Con
c.1

Copyright © 1990 by the University Press of Mississippi
All rights reserved
Manufactured in the United States of America
93 92 91 90   4 3 2 1
The paper in this book meets the guidelines for permanence and durability
of the Committee on Production Guidelines for Book Longevity of the Council
on Library Resources.

Library of Congress Cataloging-in-Publication Data

Conversations with Tom Wolfe / edited by Dorothy M. Scura.
    p.   cm. — (Literary conversations series)
   ISBN 0-87805-426-X (alk. paper). — ISBN 0-87805-427-8 (alk. paper
: pbk.)
  1. Wolfe, Tom—Interviews.   2. Authors, American—20th century—
Interviews.   I. Scura, Dorothy McInnis.   II. Series.
PS3573.0526Z63   1990
818'.5409—dc20   89-25046
                        CIP

British Library Cataloging-in-Publication data available

Books by Tom Wolfe

The Kandy-Kolored Tangerine-Flake Streamline Baby. New York: Farrar, Straus and
  Giroux, 1965.
The Pump House Gang. New York: Farrar, Straus and Giroux, 1968.
The Electric Kool-Aid Acid Test. New York: Farrar, Straus and Giroux, 1968.
Radical Chic & Mau-Mauing the Flak Catchers. New York: Farrar, Straus and
  Giroux, 1970.
The Painted Word. New York: Farrar, Straus and Giroux, 1975.
Mauve Gloves & Madmen, Clutter & Vine. New York: Farrar, Straus and Giroux,
  1976.
The Right Stuff. New York: Farrar, Straus and Giroux, 1979.
In Our Time. New York: Farrar, Straus and Giroux, 1980.
From Bauhaus to Our House. New York: Farrar, Straus and Giroux, 1981.
The Bonfire of the Vanities. New York: Farrar, Straus and Giroux, 1987.

Contents

Introduction

For more than a quarter of a century Tom Wolfe has chronicled our time—from the Californian car customizers and Ken Kesey's Merry Pranksters of the sixties to the ambition-driven inhabitants of New York City in the eighties. Along the way he has focused on surfers, bikers, car racers, radical chic liberals, modern painting and architecture, the astronauts, and many other subjects. And he has followed no one in his career. His style is new, distinctive, singular; his choice of topics is unpredictable and unexpected; his genre—in both fiction and nonfiction—is a hybrid of reporting and ficiton-writing. Toby Thompson points out in 1987 that Wolfe "has received more applause than any other literary journalist of our time. An author who has truly influenced his era, he's perhaps the best and best-known nonfictionist in America." And then that same year Wolfe published his first major work of fiction, *Bonfire of the Vanities*, which was widely reviewed and stayed on top of the bestseller lists for over a year.

And so Tom Wolfe has both brought us the news and made the news in the period during which these interviews were first published. The first interview takes place in London in 1966, with talk about his first book, *The Kandy-Kolored Tangerine-Flake Streamline Baby* (1965). The last interview is with *Time* in 1989, and Wolfe talks about his most recent book, *The Bonfire of the Vanities* (1987). In the twenty-two years between publication of those books, Wolfe published eight others. During that time Wolfe has talked openly with interviewers about a wide range of subjects including his own work. Articulate, literate, knowledgeable, and witty, Wolfe is an excellent subject for the interviewer.

He talks to many interviewers about his own writing and the way he writes. A disciplined artist, he sets a daily goal of 10 pages, about 2,000 words, and he works from an outline. Much of his work was written easily; *The Electric Kool-Aid Acid Test* took only six months, the period Wolfe claims is sufficient for writing a book. He does, however, suffer writing blocks, and he tells a number of interviewers of his problem in writing an article on car customizers in 1965 for *Esquire*, his first national assignment. Unable to write and facing a deadline, he typed his notes in the form of a memo to the editor. *Esquire* published these notes, and Tom Wolfe's distinctive writing style was born. Wolfe also tells of his problem in writing *The Bonfire of the Vanities*, a problem he solved by agreeing to write the novel in installments for *Rolling Stone,* thus producing the work serially. He then performed a major rewrite for book publication.

In these interviews Wolfe also talks about the writers who have influenced him and the writers he admires. He tells Joe David Bellamy that he was impressed by certain Russian writers—Yevgeni Zamyatin and Boris Pilniak, to name two—whom he discovered (in translation) in the library stacks when he was a graduate student at Yale. And he tells Martin Levine that he admires Dostoevski, Dickens, and Zola—each of whom wrote about material outside themselves. He is a champion of realism, in both reporting and fiction, and he tells Joe David Bellamy that the great novelists are often those who perform a "news-bearing function." Wolfe seems to identify with Dickens and Balzac, who were not as highly regarded in their own times as they are now. He points out that Balzac was never inducted into the French Academy. He likes the work of such contemporary writers as Henry Miller, Jack Kerouac, Michael Herr, Calder Willingham, Jimmy Breslin, and others. The contemporary writer he most often names as admirable is Philip Roth, whom he calls a social historian.

Because Tom Wolfe has written satirically and fearlessly about controversial subjects, interviewers often question him about his response to criticism as well as his own politics. He first stirred up controversy with a parody of the *New Yorker* published in *New York Magazine* in 1965. That piece outraged William Shawn, Muriel Spark, Murray Kempton, Walter Lippman, and even J. D. Salinger. Wolfe tells Mary V. McLeod that the *New Yorker* debacle made him "fireproof" with respect to criticism of his work.

With the publication of *Radical Chic & Mau-Mauing the Flak Catchers,* interviewers became more interested in Wolfe's politics.

Wolfe tells Martin L. Gross in 1980, "I have never been very much interested in politics. I'm much more interested in intellectual fashions." He goes on to explain that he has a "contrary streak" and was liberal as an undergraduate when others were conservative, conservative in graduate school when others were liberal. However, in an interview with Ron Reagan he does talk about the nuclear dilemma and Cambodia as well as his own lack of sympathy with "the idea that there is something wonderful about socialism. . . . " Wolfe observes that socialism "leads only to extermination camps."

Many interviewers are struck by the contrast between the acerbic tone of Tom Wolfe's work and Tom Wolfe in person. William Overend points out that "almost everything Wolfe has written, the very way he writes, has been controversial. But in conversation he comes across as soft-spoken, slightly remote without rubbing that Yale background in, and possibly just a little bit on guard, having played the game himself so many times from the other side." In 1981, Joshua Gilder observes that "in contrast to his exclamatory, whammo prose, the 50-year-old Wolfe is surprisingly soft-spoken and gentlemanly in manner." Lori Simmons Zelenko describes Wolfe as a "dandy vision in chocolate-brown and ivory" with a "matching fedora." She finds his "demeanor" a contrast "to the biting tone of his social satires of the art world, the architects, and the astronauts." Elaine Dundy calls his style "hyperbolic, rhapsodic, and colloquial," and she describes him as "the mildest of men with amiable if absentminded good manners" and "a soft voice gently dipped in the South"; Dundy characterizes him as "Tom Sawyer drawn by Beardsley."

Interviewers seem unable to ignore Wolfe's distinctive mode of dress—his white suit, high shirt collar, spats, broad-brimmed hat, white umbrella. He talks frequently about how he came to dress in this unusual style, telling Martin Levine that he has "thirty or forty feet" of custom-made suits. John Taylor points out that "Wolfe's gaudiness" is termed " 'counterbohemian' " by Wolfe himself. Toby Thompson talks with Wolfe's good friend, the painter Richard Merkin, about Wolfe's dress: " 'Dandyism is a mask,' he [Merkin] observes, 'but underneath, Tom's not flashy. He does it for effect. . . . ' "

These interviews, most importantly, serve as a record of many of the subjects that have been on Tom Wolfe's mind for the past twenty-five years. He expresses clearly what he has been trying to do—"to show the world 'life in our times'," he explains to Joe David Bellamy in 1972. Wolfe tells Bellamy that Balzac thought of himself as ' "the secretary of French society'," and Wolfe repeatedly echoes Balzac's words in describing the nature of his own work. He tells William F. Buckley, for example, that he is "a lowly social historian." And in discussing morality with Bill Moyers, he insists, "I'm just a social secretary. I just take notes on what I see going on. I have no agenda." For the last question in this collection of interviews, Bonnie Angelo of *Time* asks Wolfe to assess himself as a writer, and he responds, "I am just a chronicler. My passion is to discover, and to write about it." These interviews show Tom Wolfe talking outside the covers of his books about his writing and about this time he has chronicled so well.

As with all books published in the Literary Conversations series, these interviews are presented chronologically and reproduced in full as first printed or broadcast. In the thirty-two interviews selected for this collection, there are, of course, questions which are asked a number of times, but it is interesting to follow Wolfe's answers through the years. Because the context is always different, the answers to similar questions often reveal new information. The most important literary journalist of our time, Wolfe is now also a novelist. His views on his work and on the world are important adjuncts to his publications. These interviews provide material for the student and scholar as well as lively and provocative reading.

My sincere appreciation is extended to Tom Wolfe and to all of the interviewers who created these interviews as well as the publishers, editors, and agents who granted permission to reprint the material. For various kinds of assistance I'd like to thank Joan Kalyan, Wanda Giles, Lisa Lance, Carla McDonough, Margaret Goergen, and Phyllis Etzler. For granting me a semester's leave at the beginning of a new job, I thank Dean Lorman Ratner of the College of Liberal Arts, University of Tennessee. For support in obtaining permissions, I acknowledge the John Hodges Better English Fund in the English Department, University of Tennessee.

This book is for Wynne, who loves reporting as much as Tom Wolfe does, and for Caroline, whose future is all possibility.

DMS
August 1989

Chronology

1931   2 March, Thomas Kennerly Wolfe, Jr., born in Richmond, Virginia, son of Helen Hughes and Thomas Kennerly Wolfe, agronomist and editor of *The Southern Planter*

1947   Graduates from St. Christopher's, Richmond

1951   Graduates *cum laude* from Washington and Lee University where he was one of the founders of *Shenandoah*

1951-57   Attends Yale University where he takes a Ph.D. in American Studies, writing a dissertation on *The League of American Writers: Communist Activity Among American Writers, 1929-1942*

1956-59   Works as reporter for the *Springfield* (Massachusetts) *Union*

1959-62   Works as reporter and Latin American correspondent for the *Washington Post*

1962-66   Works as magazine writer and reporter for the *New York Herald Tribune;* November 1965, one-man exhibition of drawings at the Maynard Walker Gallery in New York City; 1965, publication of *The Kandy-Kolored Tangerine-Flake Streamline Baby*

1966-67   Joins *New York World Journal Tribune* as a magazine writer

1968   Becomes contributing editor for *New York* magazine
        (until 1976); publication of *The Pump House Gang* and
        The Electric Kool-Aid Acid Test

1970   Publication of *Radical Chic & Mau-Mauing the Flak
        Catchers*

1973   Publication of *The New Journalism* (introductory essay by
        Wolfe and an anthology of 23 essays selected by Wolfe
        and E. W. Johnson)

1974   One-man show of drawings at the Tunnel Gallery, New
        York City

1975   Publication of *The Painted Word*

1976   Publication of *Mauve Gloves & Madmen, Clutter & Vine*

1978   27 May, marries Sheila Berger, art director of *Harper's
        Magazine*

1979   Publication of *The Right Stuff*

1980   Birth of daughter, Alexandra Kennerly; Publication of *In
        Our Time*

1981   Publication of *From Bauhaus to Our House*

1985   Birth of son, Thomas

1987   Publication of *The Bonfire of the Vanities*

Conversations with Tom Wolfe

How to Wolfe a Tangerine at a Tangent

Terry Coleman/1966

From *Manchester Guardian Weekly*, 94 (10 March 1966), 12.
Reprinted with permission.

Good old Tom Wolfe was a pitcher. He had curves, he had
screwballs, he had a great glider, he was 21, and he was going to play
pro-ball. He went to a try-out camp with the old New York Giants.
For three days he pitched, for three days no one took any notice, so
he asked them, give it to me straight. Well son, they said.

Well, he remembered he had a bachelor's degree in English from
Washington and Lee, so off he went to Yale for four years to do a
doctorate in American studies. He is always happy to explain what
American studies are. He was supposed to teach but couldn't face it,
so wasn't it a good idea to go all proletarian and bohemian, you
know, with a turtle-neck sweater. He'd read Jack London, so there
was Wolfe, down and out in New Haven.

Great insights were to be gotten by close association with the
working classes. He drove a truck and drank ten cent beer. And there
he was at four in the afternoons in this shanty drinking this ten cent
beer and watching the girls dancing (bopping as it then was) and
watching their pleated skirts go up, and that was what working-class
life was adding up to.

So he thought of newspapers. He went to New York. It was a
matter of whether they'd give him Washington, or maybe he'd be
chief of bureau in Paris. He tried the *Times*, UPI, and AP. The *Daily
News* offered Dr. Wolfe $40 a week as copy boy, but he could hear
them grinning. They never had a Ph.D. copy boy before, though they
have them all the time at the *Times*.

Anyway, he went off to the Springfield (Mass.) *Union* at $55 a
week as a reporter of meetings and sewer committees. Who, what,
when, where, why—and write short sentences. After three years he
went to the *Washington Post*. Anything light, he wrote it.

Then it was 1960, and Wolfe had five years of Spanish though
he couldn't speak a word of it, so they sent him to Cuba. Just keep

it straight, none of your writing. He got an award for his Cuban reporting.

Then he went to the *New York Herald Tribune*. Light pieces again, by Thomas Wolfe. He'd never written anything longer than 750 words: 1,000 words was a whole column, a long long story. But a writer on the *Trib* has some freedom. On the *Times* you get the classic crime story full of allegeds, and you don't even begin to think it won't ever happen to you. On the *Trib* there's a columnist who writes as if it might.

In 1963 there was a four-month newspaper strike in New York. Wolfe was out of a job, so he went to *Esquire* and offered them a piece on the people who make and buy custom-built cars, with fins, and chrome, and hopped-up engines, and chopping and channelling. Chopping is lowering the top of the car, bringing it nearer the bonnet line. Channelling is lowering the body itself down between the wheels.

Esquire paid his expenses, and in California he found a new young society. The kids have money and impose their own style of life. "Practically every style recorded in art history is the result of the same thing," he says, "a lot of attention to form plus the money to make monuments to it."

It was a good piece—the trouble was he couldn't write it. He sent his notes in a letter, which just said what he had seen, and they used it as it was. It was the first Tom Wolfe piece. In the next year he wrote another 40 pieces like that. He uses the occasional "pow," strings of dots, disjointed dialogue: he gives impressions, catches atmosphere. It is his way of expressing what people are thinking, without taking the liberty, as he puts it, of going inside their minds. It's nothing that half a dozen novelists haven't done before, but it's new in journalism. It sounds, as I say, as if it really happened.

Now Wolfe is in London for the publication of *The Kandy-Kolored Tangerine-Flake Streamline Baby* (reviewed by Stanley Reynolds on the preceding page.) The baby is a custom-built car, and the title that of his first *Esquire* piece.

The other day he sat in the writing room at Brown's Hotel off Piccadilly, talking softly against the racket of electric drills tearing up a road somewhere, and chatted about his baseball, and his reporting.

About Utopia, the way Utopists saw the English working family

watching BBC-2, reading economics, listening to the choir of King's
Cambridge, with dad sitting in a blue suit with lapels a bit too wide
but clean and pressed: but they don't, he says, do they? About James
Joyce: the man could write (says Wolfe), pity he's incomprehensible.

Wolfe is not merely the in-writer of the blurbs. In his pieces about a
Sunday king of love in New York, or about commissionaires who hate
Volkswagens, or about Junior Johnson, the American stock-car hero,
he is something rarer than that. With his bit of Gregg, and his Wolfe
shortforms, he is a good reporter.

He's in England now for some weeks. I'd like to see him let loose
on the general election. He might, as I say, make it sound as if it was
really happening.

Tom Wolfe . . . But Exactly, Yes!

Elaine Dundy/1966

From *Vogue*, 147 (15 April 1966), 124, 152-55. This article was originally published in *Vogue*. Reprinted with permission.

"I Shall Revolt," wrote Tom Wolfe under the name of Jocko Thor when he was twenty-five years old and studying for his Ph.D. at Yale:

> I shall burst this placid pink shell
> I shall wake up slightly hungover,
> Favoured, adored, worshiped and clamoured for.
> I shall raise Hell and be a real
> Cut-up.

Ten years later, almost to the day (one is tempted to say), It All Came True, with the publication and public acclaim of his book *The Kandy-Kolored Tangerine-Flake Streamline Baby,* a collection of articles he had written over a fifteen-month period. The book hit the best-seller lists right off the bat, went into its fourth printing a month after publication, and parties were given for him everywhere from New York to Boston, from Richmond, Virginia, to San Diego, California, at which he appeared in a white-on-white suit kissing the ladies' hands, and when he wasn't at these parties being favoured and adored, he was at some radio or television studio being worshipped and clamoured for. How did he like it? He *loved* it. On this level he is one of your simple, barefoot American boys of letters, sharing in common with them all their simple hopes and fears and determination to Make Out. What is uncommon about his celebrity is that it was won in the field of journalism rather than the novel or the play, for everyone knows that the only proper stance to assume towards journalism (especially by its practitioners) is to look down upon it—or at least sideways. Yet here was Tom Wolfe (and with that *name,* too) flinging himself at it as if he'd never even heard it was Number One on Cyril Connolly's list of Enemies of Promise, taking journalism like a walnut, cracking it wide open and getting down to the meat of what was really going on inside all those facts. And with

6

the excitement of his discoveries came an entirely communicable rush of words, all saying—Look at what I've found and wait till I tell you about it! His style is hyperbolic, rhapsodic, and colloquial— American, that is, as opposed to English, his satire devastating, his intentions serious, and his innovation to project himself with a novelist's omniscience into his subjects so that they seem to become his own creations.

That his pieces bear rereading is attested to by the fact that every one of those in *The Kandy-Kolored* et cetera has formerly appeared in large-circulation newspapers or magazines—some of them have made four trips including in the hard-cover edition; by the fact that they collect well, that they don't become too much of a muchness all bunched together; by the fact that each one has a rhythm and drive peculiar to itself and yet they seem organically related so that the whole book adds up to more than the sum of its parts: The American Scene, Mid-Sixties.

Tom Wolfe, the new Wild Man of American literature, is, upon first acquaintance, the mildest of men with amiable if absentminded good manners, a soft voice gently dipped in the South (he comes from Virginia), "afred" for *afraid,* for instance—a voice that is hesitant and full of pauses unless he is "putting you on"—or "lying," as it used to be called—which is quite often, at which point it becomes firm, clear, and fluent. He has fair, floppy blond hair, a sensitive, sharp, bony nose—a nose for news—and big, powerful-looking hands. A largish young man in his pink placid shell with a country air about him in spite of his dandified clothes—Tom Sawyer drawn by Beardsley—he exudes at most times a calmness, cool and loose, if not exactly a sanity—the giveaway being the pale-blue eyes that widen in panic, delight, or suspicion from time to time. This interesting mixture of phlegm and sensibility has been in his time a semiprofessional baseball player and a lorry loader before he became what he is today: the New Journalist.

In typecasting he is suited to his role of observer. What the people he is going to write about are confronted with is an easygoing chap in crazy clothes who never gets their backs up, who is willing to go along with any and all plans, who nevertheless always has a notebook in plain sight in which he jots things down in shorthand. Doesn't the notebook put people off? Not at all, he claims, as we are all victims of what he calls "information compulsion"—*i.e.*, the desire to unload whatever is currently on our minds.

Tom's new flat is on Beekman Place, one of New York's swankier addresses. ("When I came up North, I didn't come here to fool around, you know.") It has taken him just three months to turn it into a Chelsea pad: a four-room Chelsea pad the outlines of which are still fighting desperately to retain their original individual status but have lost. "It's *all* apartment," he said enthusiastically at the time he moved in. "Nothing has been converted from one thing into something else. The dining room was *always* a dining room, the kitchen *always* a kitchen!"

Besides the kitchen which is still a kitchen and the bathroom which is still a bathroom, the dining room is a Chelsea pad, the living room is a Chelsea pad, and the bedroom is a Chelsea pad. And the fourth room has no function whatsoever. And no furniture. The largest of these Chelsea pads has improvised curtains in its windows; some (three differently coloured layers of gauze) with more ingenuity than others (bedsheets).

There are no carpets, and in the packing cases the books still lie unpacked. There is a pretty handpainted screen done by a girl friend and one painting—a self-portrait of a friend of his going off to the Draft Board with an inward look on his face.

There are four white chairs with a matching white table, "fake Saarinen," a drawing board, two divans with cushions and covers— also loosely improvised, and an improvised lighting fixture covered with gauze hanging from the ceiling. For the rest, it is filled (if that's the word) with piles of his own drawings collected for his one-man exhibition at the Maynard Walker Gallery last November, piles of newspaper clippings, and piles of just . . . *things*. A sign over the telephone reads:

Hello, Baby,
Just try this little
game one more time.

As if on cue, the phone comes to life with long, blasting, heart-attacking alarm-clock peals through the empty rooms, and Tom, although bestowing a look of hatred upon it, makes no attempt to still it. His fear of telephones is pathological. Originally, it was his editors and overshot deadlines he was hiding from; nowadays, with his celebrity, it is just about everyone he needs to avoid if he's going to get any work done. He would like to rent a room with a telephone out in New Jersey, give out that number as his, and then sit back in New York thinking about it ringing and ringing and ringing.

Tom Wolfe arrives for his interview at Sardi's East a surprising five minutes early wearing a pale-grey sharkskin suit and a tie twice as wide as usual with a lot of whorly clowns dancing about on it. It is a vintage tie from a line which was abruptly discontinued in about 1946, landing the shop with about ten thousand of these obsolete numbers which Tom is doing his best to get moving again.

It is necessary to refer to his clothes because he ascribes almost magical properties to them. "If that shirt and that shirt were running a race," he will say, pointing to what appear to be two identical shirts, "*that* shirt would win." *Or,* "What's the matter with people, don't they realize that *everything's* wrong with my coat? Too wide lapels, too much shoulder padding, and more buttons than a policeman's uniform?" He plans his wardrobe for what might be considered oddly disparate purposes: to look well in while simultaneously giving offense to his viewers—to "shake 'em up" as he puts it.

The interview takes place over iced tea, beer, and finally champagne in an effort to placate the hovering waiter longing to turf us out for the dinner crowd, and begins, portentously enough with (deep breath):

What do you feel is the function of journalism?

The idea of what *is* news today—what people in power are doing—is still a nineteenth-century concept. (Actually, sitting there at the table in his pale-grey suit and fancy shirt and gold watch chain, Tom himself looks very like a nineteenth-century concept.) I don't think that's the news. I like to give people news they didn't know was news.

Not the big subjects such as the latest war wherever it may be. Stock-car racing, on the other hand, I find a significant subject and one that never got written about. Perfect journalism would deal constantly with one subject: Status. And every article written would be devoted to discovering and defining some new status.

What about the charge that you are exploiting the factual authority of journalism and the atmospheric license of fiction?

That again is a nineteenth-century orientation. First implication: Anything serious has to be ponderous. Second implication: All journalism should sound as if it's been lifted off the blotter of the police reports. To write from the 'outside' point of view is immediately to have about thirty-five people on your back. All you old teachers, all your literary peers—that sort of thing. 'Watch out for excess,' they all seem to be saying.

Do you remember when you first discovered yourself wandering around the minds of your subjects? You have Phil Spector, the Tycoon of Teen, sitting on a plane and looking out at the rain and thinking, "All these raindrops are high on something. . . . Schizoid raindrops."

I don't remember when I started doing that, but it isn't exactly what I'm doing. Those 'wanderings' are based on things Phil Spector said to me—he described that scene to me—and couched in his way of talking. What I try to do is re-create a scene from a triple point of view: the subject's point of view, my own, and that of the other people watching—often within a single paragraph. Incidentally, I always use the present-tense.

Is there a literary precedent that you are aware of for this type of writing?

The Serapion Brothers group of Soviet writers in the twenties.

Hey—if you're going to start lying this early in the—

Brother Serapion is a character in one of Hoffmann's tales. Apparently this group of writers . . .

All right—name some.

Eugene Zamyatin, Boris Pilnyak. Anyway, this group of writers was finally asked by the Commissars, look, are you for or against us? And they said we are neither for nor against. They fooled around with multiple points of view. I stumbled across these writers in the Yale stacks while reading Gogol, who fascinated me. I learned he influenced this Serapion Brothers group, so I read them.

"With Wolfe for the Defense you don't need a Prosecutor," is the way someone described your supposedly "ambivalent" attitude towards your subjects. Isn't it necessary to have a moral attitude towards them?

No! You can't approach a subject with a moral commitment and come up with something *new*. As soon as any approach has reached the stage that it takes on a moral tone it is already out of date—it's frozen. Popular moral attitudes are at least fifty years out of date. Academia knows this. In journalism we have the moral concept of One World, but any sociologist knows that Europe today—never mind the Common Market—is actually more fragmented in terms of nationalism than it was before the second World War.

But when you find yourself liking or disliking certain people you write about, doesn't it influence the way you write?

I've often disliked people at the outset, but I can't think of a soul, if they turn out to be worth writing about. . . . I've never finished a story disliking them. There are some, however, that I never get through to—Cassius Clay, for instance. And I missed the important story about him: that he was getting involved with the Black Muslims at the time I was seeing him.

I should have been aware of this from various things he said. Anyway, writing about people—it's not a friendship situation. I'm always interested in the different responses I get to my articles. Some people think I'm attacking the subject and some that it's a great boost. In fact, they're attributing to me their own feelings. It's good. It means I've been more or less scholarly. Rocket Scholarship.

Explain certain calculated mannerisms that reoccur in your work: "and everything," "or some other place," et cetera, and certain odd favourite words that are repeated: "arteriosclerotic," for instance. And your idiosyncratic use of punctuation and expletives.

Repeating words means that they have become for me inseparable from the meaning I want. Eventually I get over them. Arteriosclerotic—I was obsessed for awhile with people's blood vessels getting stiffer and stiffer without them knowing it. 'And everything' et cetera because that's the way people talk. 'Or some other place' to indicate there are other places but not to be distracting, to keep the thing moving when I want it to. The exact opposite of this is *The New Yorker* style which requires that whenever you mention, say, an actor's name, you give the play he was in at the time, the cast, the theatre, and the length of time it ran, and you get a fact-stuffed sentence that's quite beside the point.

I don't mind repetitions—three blues in the same sentence is O.K. It goes faster than another word meaning just the same thing. What I like is a tension going between colloquial speech and precise and

even scholarly ways of thinking. I'm trying to restore punctuation to
its rightful place. Dots, dashes, exclamation points were dropped out
of prose because they 'reeked of sentiment.' But an ! is someone
getting carried away. Why not? The writer carefully not using this
punctuation doesn't bother to convey what's exciting to the reader.
Sure, dots and dashes slow down the eye. That's good. That's the
best thing that can happen. It's reproducing the abruptness that
occurs in your mind when you're thinking.

People only *write* in careful flowing sentences; they don't think that
way and they don't talk that way. Take Hemingway. People always
think that the reason he's easy to read is that he's concise. He isn't. I
hate conciseness—it's too difficult. The reason Hemingway is easy to
read is that he repeats himself all the time, using 'and' for padding. I
use expletives to indicate an atmosphere in a non-literal way. You get
to a point where you have to use a word with no literal meaning. You
can indicate a lot that way.

Which contemporary writers do you most admire?

There are so few writers nowadays you can have any admiration
for. They are already desiccated. They're just historical figures now.
Philip Roth—not for the overall effect but for the Dickensian
vignettes, and *great* dialogue. The white hope is Nelson Algren. He
can write a great novel—*The Man with the Golden Arm* was—if he'll
just do it. I liked Salinger's *The Catcher in the Rye*. And Kerouac's
momentum, only he's a little mindless and I'm tired of the people
he's writing about.

For homework I've been reading Cyril Connolly's Enemies of
Promise *because you're "promising" and I wanted to see what your
enemies were going to be. What do you think of journalism-as-
enemy-of-promise?*

(Tom's face is a perfect blank. Question repeated. Same reaction.)

*I mean, don't you find yourself falling into these pitfalls: Immediate
Impact, Necessity to Exaggerate to Make a Point, Writing for Now
Instead of Eternity?*

I'm not bothered at all by the last. And most of the things I've
written have been written under such pressure that I didn't have time
to consider the impact. All I was worried about when I finally handed
them in was whether they were legible, much less readable. But I
don't look at journalism as an enemy of promise.

On the contrary, I think it's really important to stay in journalism. Otherwise you run the danger of getting as completely out of touch as Salinger. What I would have Salinger do is write four pieces of journalism right now because it would force him to get in touch. You can't, by just leading your daily life, really see a goddamn thing. You have to force yourself to get into unfamiliar areas. We're no longer living in a set feudal system.

There have been about twenty parodies of you so far. What do you think of your parodists?

I think I've done a lot for them. Liberated them. I think they all like to kick their heels up a little now and then. Lillian Ross's doing a parody of me in *The New Yorker* was the best thing that could have happened to her. When they all came out at once—along about when my book was being reviewed, I got a little self-conscious when I'd sit down and write. Hesitant about an exclamation point. But since I've been out of New York these past months—to Chicago, San Francisco, Los Angeles, Columbus—and started working again, that's vanished.

What do you feel about your imitators? Cyril Connolly said that Hemingway's tragedy as an artist was that he hadn't the versatility to run away fast enough from his imitators.

Well—I don't know—I think they're great. I'll be told about an article that's supposed to be an imitation of me and I always find I'm reading it right through and enjoying it.

How many times do you see a person you're writing about?

As often as possible and while they're *doing* something. But it varies. Sometimes two hours are enough. Junior Johnson, the stock car racer, took four trips to the South. And a lot of it was boring because I was alone a lot when I wasn't seeing him and his crowd. But I know now that *every* extra bit of effort produces something.

What are your ideal working conditions?

Still to be alert and not tired from eight P.M. to midnight. I've taken more physical punishment while writing than anything else I've *ever* done. My body has been more punished from writing than from any sport I've ever played. I write on unlined paper. I don't type it to begin with. I correct as I go along and I like to think that I'll just type it straight from that, uncorrected. But it never works out that way. I always correct and change as I type, so I'm really doing two drafts.

But I never rewrite after that. With me it seems they either run it the
way it is or refuse it outright.

Who does?

My editors.

You take their word for it?

Sure.

*When you write, have you anyone in particular in mind you are
writing for?*

Malcolm Muggeridge.

*Do you have writer's block, and is there any specific thing you do
to get over it?*

If I can somehow get some organization to my thoughts about
what I'm writing, some concept, I'm O.K. The other thing that
sometimes helps is to go out and have an Arabic meal—some *kibbe*.

What do you feel you have the greatest talent for?

Drawing.

The least talent for?

Creating stable ties with other people.

What economic class do you come from?

A comfortable background. There was never any financial strain.
But then I was never very extravagant when I was growing up. Never
spent any money. I had one good suit, and my family had to force
me to get another one.

*What does your father do? This is going back to C. Connolly
again. According to him, it should be possible to learn as much about
an author from one paragraph of his writings as from his check stubs
and love letters. And my guess—solely from internal evidence, you
understand—is that your father was . . . (dramatic pause) . . . an
undertaker!!*

Why?

*Because you seem absolutely obsessed with anatomical pathology
and you know all the words.*

My father, before he retired, was an agronomist. He edited a farm
journal, was one of the directors of a farmer's cooperative, and he
had two farms. Maybe I'm a frustrated scientist. At Yale I roomed
with two medical students and I picked up a lot of those medical
terms from them.

Oh well. Have you got any old check stubs on you?

(Tom produces check stubs revealing that he spent a week in Columbus, Ohio, at the Holiday Inn motel, while doing a story on motorcycle racing; upon returning, went to the Ondine, a New York discothèque where he drank a bottle of wine, and is walking around at the moment with roughly seventy bucks in cash.)

Do you feel that you had an important childhood—i.e., very disturbed, or unhappy, or ecstatic—in short, one that you find you keep constantly referring back to in your mind?

I was lucky, I guess, in my family in that they had a very firm idea of roles: Father, Mother, Child. Nothing was ever allowed to bog down into those morass-like personal hangups. And there was no rebellion. The main thing about childhood was to get out of it. A child is at a great disadvantage. It's smaller than everyone else. I had a successful school career, I was a day student at St. Christopher's in Richmond, Virginia, and I always liked making good grades—get that extra smile from the teacher.

You've never had a desire to write your autobiography?

No. The first girl I ever fell in love with came from divorced parents. That was her status symbol to me. I was so envious of her because I thought, what dramatic lives they're all having—real material to write about. I guess I always wanted to be a writer. I didn't actually become one until I was thirty-two. I suppose there was a lot of fear involved.

Do you feel having a Southern background has helped you?

Yes, and a semi-rural one especially. I like the way people talk in rural areas—homey phrases, it's a richer speech and phrasing. For instance, there'll be a bunch of men sitting around playing poker all day which, let's face it, is a pretty go-to-hell existence, and one of them will draw a really bad hand and say, '!!!!!@@@@xxxxx!!!!!.'

Every single word of that is unprintable. Any other phrases?

Let's see. I like to slip them in. Sometimes it'll be a thing that probably I'm the only one aware of. Like in one piece I say the way they pass a Saturday in Georgia is to go down to the railroad tracks and watch the Seaboard sleeper barrelling through to New York City. I mean nobody in *New York* calls it New York City. 'Just plain-long tired' is a phrase that's been cut out of *every* piece I've tried to use it in.

After you got your Ph.D. at Yale—what?

I was offered a job teaching history in the Midwest but I turned it down. I'd had enough of academic life. But I stuck around New Haven and decided to become a bohemian. Jack London of all people was my model. I got myself a cloth cap and became a furniture mover for a trucking firm. But I could see that the girls in the offices weren't impressed. They couldn't see that this was a *bohemian* moving all that stuff. The last thing they want is a furniture hauler. Believe me there is *no* insight to be gathered from the life of the working-class milieu.

This guy I worked with thought that all that was wrong with his life was the way his boss made him change the electric light bulbs in all the basements three times a week. Then afterwards sitting in a bar and drinking beer and watching television till it's time to go off to bed. That's all. So after two months of moving office supplies, I quit. I decided I wanted to be a newspaper reporter.

I wrote to one hundred and twenty newspapers and only the *Springfield Union* answered. But I went up there and they gave me the job. At fifty-five dollars a week. All the way back on the train that day I kept singing to myself, I-am-a-member-of-the-working-press! Springfield (Mass.) was a revelation to me. It was the first time I realized that a city could be made up of more than one ethnic group that was politically powerful, that had its own way of life and its own restaurants.

There were the Irish Politicians, and the Italian community, and a Negro Councilman—yes, being from the South, I definitely took notice of that. There were the French Canadians, and the Jewish community and the Orthodox Russians. That was where I first discovered Arab food. I covered all the 'beats' for the paper. The police station. City Hall. The fire department. The railroad station to see who was coming into town. It was very good for a person as lazy as me.

Are you politically Right or Left?

I find Right and Left a totally obsolete idea. I would be tempted to support extremists on both sides simultaneously—you need extremist groups so that no one can get too much power. And I can conceive of joining a civil liberties organization to check a syndrome. The only danger to me as a writer is that any person could get big enough to stop me.

Tell about the lying. For instance, at one point you told me you had eight brothers and sisters and then later retracted it.

That one began in Sunday school when I was about five. The teacher asked each of us in a kind of getting-to-know-one-another way if we had any brothers and sisters, and I said I had eight. She knew I hadn't and spoke to my mother about it, but it still persists. I don't understand it. I've always had a fantasy of lots of brothers and sisters. I have a fantasy brother named Harris who runs a hotel in Cuba and he leads to a fantasy of the F.B.I. being on my trail because of him. I think there must be some symbolic truth underneath the lies.

What makes you angriest?

Humiliation. I never forget. I never forgive. I can wait. I find it very easy to harbour a grudge. I have scores to settle.

What makes you happiest?

A good meal after some kind of victory.

Have you any superstitions?

I *have* to look in the mirror every morning. Immediately. As soon as I get up. And it's not always the pleasantest sight but you have to keep track of how you're going, you know?

What about love or sex? Cyril Connolly says . . . never mind.
Which?
Either.

Love is tremendously important when things are going wrong. This is a part of status because every time I've been tremendously in love it means that my status has been in tremendous trouble. That wonderful love relationship comes when you want to create the second smallest status-sphere—one other person's approval is all that matters. It's comforting—one woman's approval.

And marriage?

Right now I think of marriage as a luxury . . . and as an unnecessary complication . . .

Strange young man. Shy but vain. Alone but not lonely. Self-absorbed yet open to the subtlest nuances of people and places. And promising . . . infinitely promising . . . .

Tom Wolfe on the Search for the Real Me

Lawrence Dietz/1968

From *New York Magazine*, 19 August 1968, 42-43. Copyright ©
1989 by the New York Magazine Company. All rights reserved.
Reprinted with permission.

Two books by New York *contributing editor Wolfe come
out this week:* The Pump House Gang, *a collection of
essays on new status forms, and* The Electric Kool-Aid
Acid Test, *a probe into the LSD-riddled psyche of novelist
Ken Kesey. Both books, published by Farrar, Straus and
Giroux, are based in large part on articles that originally
appeared in* New York. *Following are some of Mr. Wolfe's
thoughts on what's going on today and what it all means.
The questions were asked by Lawrence Dietz.*

**Originally the Kesey story was in three parts which appeared
in *New York*. Your first plan, as I remember, was to rewrite
them and include them as part of the book which had the
Pump House pieces. What happened?**

Well, I didn't intend to do a book on it. Kesey and the Merry
Pranksters started out being a rather limited subject. It was originally
just supposed to be an article on a guy who was a fugitive in Mexico
because of several marijuana arrests. I was really intrigued by that
idea. There were so many "fugitive programs" on television—*The
Fugitive, Haircut of Fugitive, Curl of Haircut of Fugitive*—and I
thought, gee, this guy's a world-wide fugitive and doing a pretty good
job of it. It was only after that that I found out about his whole
involvement with LSD and so forth. And even then it just seemed to
be part of the phenomenon that was beginning to be called the
hippies. Gradually the thing just got bigger and bigger in its scope
because everything that Kesey tried went far beyond the whole
question of drugs, to this whole matter of self-realization and what
you're going to do with yourself on the frontier beyond catastrophe.

After the articles appeared and I started to rewrite them, I thought I
was going to come up with about 60 or 70 pages, as part of a

18

collection. But everything I learned about what Kesey and his group had been doing kept leading to something else, into more involved things. At one point I thought I'd never finish—I was reading books on brain physiology, on religions, on sociology, books on psychology, cognitive psychology, all sorts of things. I was gradually coming to the realization that this was in a way a curious, very bizarre, advance guard of this whole push towards self-realization, and all these things that people are trying to avoid facing up to as the main concern. I think it's very comforting to be able to say that we've got the same old problems: we've got war, we've got poverty. That way we don't have to see that the main problem—if you want to call it that—is that people are free all of a sudden; they're rich and they're fat and they're free.

There's a kind of curious atmosphere developing in which I think people are, in some weird way, beginning to realize that they really aren't needed in the work force in the old way. When you read the diaries of early settlers, at the end of every winter there'd be this big count of how many men were left. "Forty-three men left after a hard winter." Everybody was needed, everybody had to have his shoulder to the wheel. This is obviously not true today. I think that people are sort of beginning to ask themselves, "Well, if it's not true, why should we act like it is, if we can still get money, enough money to get by on, and have time to do something else?" Everybody's beginning to try and discover what I call The Real Me. It's sort of saying, "This job I have, at the telephone company or the whatever they work for, that's not The Real Me. The Real Me is not the hubby or the mommy. The Real Me can come out in some way."

In California I ran into a highway patrolman who got to talking and he showed me a little clock he had, a tiny little clock. He said, "What do you think of this? I collect clocks." He had about a hundred clocks, and he repairs them and he makes them, and that's what he's really interested in. Being a highway patrolman is *just a job.* He said, "My job is scraping up bodies. I do it, I scrape up bodies every day, it's a job. But what I'm really interested in are these clocks." In that guy's case The Real Me was not even the chase down the highway in a car—I guess you have to chase a few people before you can scrape them up—not even that was The Real Me. The Real Me was clocks. If you just expand this idea further, people getting more time, higher incomes, let's say, they're going to be thinking of all sorts of ways to bring out The Real Me. I think there's going to be a tremendous boom in self-realization . . .

It will take many different guises. There'll be what I've heard called "psychological gymnasiums" which may turn into religions of one sort or another. In fact, if you want to invest in a stock today that would be the equivalent of what IBM was back in—when was it . . . that everyone said if you had bought eight shares of IBM in well, 1903, today you'd be worth $27 million; you'd also be pretty old— but naturally no one has the foresight except the people who have the stock. Well, the thing to buy at this point in history would be a good self-realization company. Now I don't *know* of any, but there may be some around. Arthur Murray's dance studio and Fred Astaire studios: they're a very crude type of self-realization business. Now, I don't know how they do financially, but they're not selling dancing lessons so much as telling people they're going to bring them out in some way. Dale Carnegie courses do the same thing. In the future, though, they'll just come right out and deal with the psyche.

How do you think politics will adapt to this? The sort of introspection you've been talking about is pretty alien to most politicians—they tend to deal with action rather than that sort of abstraction.

When Humphrey first came out with his slogan, "Politics of Joy," I snapped bolt upright because I had been predicting this thing I call the politics of pleasure. That is what comes after it becomes absolutely useless for politicians to promise you relief from hunger, all the conventional things, or to protect you from foreign enemies.

Orwell, by the way, in *1984*, predicted that there would always be these little wars, all over the globe, in little places that no one had ever heard of, if for no other reason than for the politicians in each country to seem indispensable to their subjects. Actually, they all knew they couldn't wage war in the old sense any more, so they had to keep these little charades going. Of course, they had to kill to keep it real. Well, when the Korean war broke out people didn't know where it was; some people still called it Chosen. And Malaysia, where's this Malaysia, and Indochina, which became Vietnam . . . Where the hell was it?

Well, after all these things have run out, if it's no longer possible to

keep scaring people by talking about poverty and war, gradually
politics will be forced to another turn. It's going to be the politics of
joy. Everything's going to be directed toward the use of freedom.
Actually, that's very scary. It's very intimidating to be told that you
have all this freedom.

**Hubert Humphrey in a Nehru jacket and beads? I can't see
it.**

Well, the successful politician will be the one to promise you *more*
pleasure, greater freedom. And I don't think that they will worry
about self-realization for themselves, because a good politician has
the kind of job where he feels whole. As soon as you see people
jump when you raise your finger . . . well, there's a great feeling of
wholeness about that, apparently.

Some of these Jobs Corps programs failed because there were so
many kids who—rather than have job training so that they could get
some job paying $75 or $80 in an office, at a low level, some routine
repetitive work—would rather live the street life. They get a little less,
but they get to express themselves. That's why I wonder why people
keep trying to find pathological explanations for why kids become
hippies, to take a case. Usually they try to find a pattern—"Do they
come from broken homes? Has society done this to them? Is there
something wrong with their schools?"—when actually all it is is that
these kids have found a new option.

The old option when you were 19 or 20 used to be either you had
a job, or you went to school, or you lived at home, or you were in
the Army. All of those things had severe drawbacks: the job was dull,
and you were at the bottom of the ladder and nobody wanted to
hear what you had to say about anything. Living at home had a lot of
natural drawbacks: school was a bore, and so forth. But suddenly the
idea of there being enough money around somewhere, somehow, or
being able to live life on your own terms with a lot of other people
like yourself—it is very appealing. The hippies are just part of that
phenomenon. It's what the surfers were doing, and a lot of older
people in terms of various things—the cat life, even Leisure World.
That's why you can't go through these groups and find a lot of bad
backgrounds. They are people who have had a choice. I think it also
explains a lot of the New Left, the Students for Democratic Society
and so forth. With those kids it's not just a set of beliefs and

occasional meetings, it's a whole life-style. You live that, practically
around the clock. You live the New Left life and it's much more
exciting, a much more interesting option, than going to work, starting
a career, or just going to college.

**What you've just been talking about is the thrust of the
collection of pieces in *The Pump House Gang,* and it appears
that this new direction is taking place, for the most part,
outside New York.**

It seems that a lot of people made a great discovery in other parts
of the country, which was that you could take all this money that had
been coming after the war, and the free time that people suddenly
had, and do something else instead of trying to compete in the old
way for status in a community system. The old community idea was
that everybody had his rank in the community and people would act
this out in various ways, by what clubs one belonged to, what stores
one shopped in, who says hello to whom, who wears what. This had
always been the way people achieved status. Well, a lot of the people
outside New York found out that they could form their own little
status groups, set their own rules, like surfers, kids who were living by
themselves for much of the summer, in garages and things like that.
They just sort of live in terms of rules that *they* set up.

It gradually began to occur to me that we were all primitives here in
New York, really, we were back in another century in the way we live.
For example, I remember going into Walter Cronkite's townhouse to
do a story, he has a whole townhouse on East 80-something, I think,
and by New York standards this was a hell of a layout, a *whole*
house, well decorated. This was the real posh existence in New York,
even a sports car parked in a garage three or four blocks away. Then
when I got out to California it dawned on me that nobody making
over $7200 a year would tolerate an existence in a townhouse like
Walter Cronkite's; it was too narrow, it was too dark, the kitchen's
old-fashioned, you have to walk up a lot of stairs, a lot of corners,
twists and turns. And the idea of parking your car four blocks away in
a garage is pretty silly.

**Once you've renounced the idea of traditional status, once
you've decided on the one hand to buy a lot of mechanical
gimcrackery, and on the other to turn inward, then what
Kesey did doesn't seem so totally alien.**

Kesey was really trying to go all the way without being exactly sure what that was. He was trying, through the use of LSD and other means, to get everyone in his group completely out of all of the drags and drawbacks of their own past. Free yourself of that and you could head off in some incredible new direction. And finally he began to feel that once people had used LSD or other drugs as a way of getting onto this new level, they would have to find a way to do it without having continually to go to the drug. The side of Kesey which wasn't duplicated by any other psychedelic group was his attempt to harness all the totally California things—gadgets, TV, movies, the cars, the bus—harness all of these things and take them beyond their immediate, rather limited use, out to some wild edge.

The family car, for instance, is already a fantasy creation—327 horsepower, 18 feet long—and I think Kesey saw a lot of this. Rather than doing what Leary did, which was to say that we're going to get rid of all this gadgetry that's corrupting our lives, the idea was to sort of swing with it, roll with it, let it follow its own course, pull out all the stops, put the pedal to the floor and see what happens.

When you put that metaphysical pedal to the floor, where do you go?

As the Pranksters said on the destination sign of their bus: "Further."

Pop Writer of the Period—Tom Wolfe Talks to Michael Dean

Michael Dean/1970

From *The Listener,* 83 (19 February 1970), 250-51. Reprinted by permission of *The Listener.*

I found myself in the early Sixties living in a kind of bizarre period with some half-insane things going on around me and I started writing about them. Then one day I woke up and looked in the newspapers and I had been dubbed pop writer of the period. Andy Warhol was the pop painter, I guess Merce Cunningham was the pop dancer, there were pop musicians everywhere you turned a corner, and suddenly I was the person carrying the ball for writing. At first this was a little beguiling: I started to fall for a kind of incarnation fallacy like General de Gaulle. This lasted for three or four days, until I picked up *Time* Magazine and I saw myself described as 'America's foremost pop journalist.' Since then I've found this word 'pop' to be as much a curse as anything else. To me pop culture never really existed as pop culture. There's a high culture, in which you keep the opera going because you believe in it. The people who were producing what later came to be known as pop art never had this belief, until somebody from high culture singled them out. They were just doing it for commercial reasons. Also the word 'pop' was used to mean trivial, and to be called a pop writer meant that you weren't coming to grips with serious things: serious things to intellectuals really mean catastrophes. Instead of using the approach of the man dissecting rather tawdry little specimens down there on a plate—like Orwell, whom I admire very much, looking down on the art of Donald McGill and his seaside postcards—I tried the opposite approach, a kind of Method acting, trying to get inside of some of these manifestations: discothèque life in New York, or the stock-car racing in the moonshine foothills of North Carolina, or London debutantes. It's a life I'm not really familiar with, but I tried to make people feel the weird kind of euphoria that people started feeling in the Sixties, in the age that came to be known as the era of pop.

To convey these impressions, you write in a non-stop barrage of exclamation points, comic-strip images and expletives, all tied up with classical references. Was the style consciously contrived, or an accident?

I had to write a piece about custom cars in California once—my first magazine article—and I found myself completely stymied as to how to do it. Finally Byron Dobell, the managing editor of *Esquire* at that time, said: 'Look, we can't wait any longer for this piece, you just write your notes down, and we'll get a competent writer to put it in some kind of shape for you.' I was naturally crushed by this idea, but I started doing it in the form of a memo to Byron Dobell, and it worked: the memo was run as an article. You can't con yourself into thinking that every time you sit down to write you're writing a letter to somebody, or a memo, but I did find some things that worked, such as using the random remark that is running through your mind, and if you feel like putting an exclamation-point after it, put an exclamation-point, because people may not speak very often in exclamations, but they think in them—they think in dashes, they think in dots. I started feeling that you had to get inside other people and get their stream of consciousness. This often involved interviewing them about their thoughts and saying: 'What were you thinking at such and such a time?' Some people say this is ridiculous, that people can't even remember what they were thinking 15 seconds ago, but it's the only way I know of that non-fiction writing is going to get close to the sort of subjective reality that people go to novels for, and that's why I think non-fiction writing right now is the most exciting writing, certainly in the United States. You can find worn-out novelists like Norman Mailer turning to non-fiction to revive their reputations, or Truman Capote.

When you first arrived on the scene there was a curious reaction from the intellectual mandarins in America. The editor of the New Yorker *shook with fury when you described his magazine as a museum.*

A magazine for which I was writing, *New York* Magazine, decided to celebrate the 40th anniversary of the *New Yorker* with an explanation of why it had faded so far. At first we were going to do a parody, but we decided on an anti-parody. In other words, instead of having a typical *New Yorker* title which might be 'Mr. Barnett heads for home,'

it was entitled 'Tiny Mummies! The true story of 43rd Street's House
of the Walking Dead,' which is right out of the *Police Gazette* or
something like that. And hyperbole upon hyperbole started bubbling
up in my brain as I wrote this thing. There was a dividing line as to
what was going to happen in non-fiction, whether it was going to
take on this new excitement that I think that some of us were starting
in magazines like *New York* Magazine and *Esquire,* or whether it was
going to continue in the traditional British essay form. One day
Joseph Alsop, who had a nationally syndicated column about politics
at that time, attacked me as an agent of Ho Chi Minh. On the other
hand, Murray Kempton, who is really a frustrated British essayist,
identified me with Joseph McCarthy. After this started happening I
remember saying: 'The only person that hasn't weighed in with an
opinion yet is Walter Lippmann.' I was joking, but three days later in
the *Village Voice* a letter from Walter Lippmann was printed which
said: 'Tom Wolfe is an ass.' It was the only nice piece of brevity that
Walter Lippmann ever came up with after 40 years of dropping the
early morning drop of mush on your forehead like a Chinese torture.

Were you rebellious as a child?

Not at all, I had a very happy childhood. I was supposed to go into
teaching, but I couldn't face the academic life any more, because I'd
been in it too long. I'd pushed it to its furthest boundaries. So I
decided to become a proletarian. At that time—about 1956—there
weren't very many models for being a bohemian: I was one year
short of the beatnik era, when I would have been shown how to do
the whole thing, but I could only look back to the proletarian novels
of the Thirties in which the thing to do was to get a job, in my case
working as a truck-loader, and somehow let the great intuitions and
insights of what was then known as proletarian life sweep through
you. I did that for about six months until I really found that my store
of insights wasn't being vastly enriched. Today it's much better: when
you're swept with nostalgia for the mud there are so many models to
choose from. You can open *Queen,* you can open *Vogue,* you can
open *Harper's Bazaar.* You can get an Indian bohemian dress, you
can get American hippy dress, cowboy dress, and it doesn't involve
working. The whole point is not to work, you see. The thing that
really intrigues me about what has come to be known as pop culture,
despite my attempts to shake off the adjective, is that there are so

many people, particularly in America, at what used to be known as a
proletarian class level, who suddenly have extra money, the free time
and the personal freedom to do the things that the great utopian
thinkers of the 19th century foresaw that industrialism would allow
them to do. So then you get to the question that intrigues me: after
you've met all the great threats, and found that the great catastrophes
of world history are not bearing down on you, what do you do with
your life? I don't think politicians are ready for this question, I don't
think intellectuals are ready for it. But there are a lot of people, very
common people by occupation, in the United States particularly, who
are instinctively ready to cross over into a really weird frontier in
which more and more of life is dedicated simply to extending your
own ego. I thought Hubert Humphrey in the last election was onto
this, when he started talking about the politics of joy.

*It has always been there, though. The pursuit of happiness, after
all, is one of the first articles of American faith.*

It was never talked about, it's not talked about now. As soon as
they could the Democratic Party in 1962—and the Republicans
would have done the same thing—discovered poverty, on the basis of
a book by Michael Harrington which pointed out that 25 per cent of
the population was under the poverty level. Now just think of that, to
discover poverty. Think of going to India, for example, and telling the
Indians: we're going to discover your poverty for you. In the US this
was a great discovery, because politicians, if they don't have a
catastrophe to deal with, they're going to try to find one. They are
afraid of this frontier beyond catastrophe, because they can't deal
with it, they can't promise people more pleasure. For one thing,
they're such draggy-looking people themselves.

In your book The Electric Kool-Aid Acid Test *the psychedelic set
creates this strange kind of commune, whose object is the frantic,
almost desperate pursuit of joy. Now nearly all these subcultures you
describe, notably the ones in Southern California, seem to be
essentially religious.*

I used to read about ecstasies in the Bible, and I used to think that
these were figures of speech, that you just loved the Lord so much
that you were ecstatic about it, but that's not it at all. Zoroastrianism,
for example, started with heavy infusions of something called homo
water which was apparently a narcotic. The same thing happened

among these early psychedelic communes: the experience under LSD created this kind of ecstasy and then they started forth on a religious mission. I wouldn't be at all surprised to see in the United States a third great awakening, as more and more of what now would be called para-religious groups get started.

How involved are you with any of the people you write about?

What I really try to do is keep some kind of distance. Some people I'm obviously going to like more than others, some I can identify with more. But then when I'm writing I try to go into a kind of controlled trance. I've often got letters from people asking me if I took drugs while I write—well, I don't, but I can remember actually closing my eyes and trying to imagine myself back into a scene that I witnessed three or four days before. It's not like Wordsworth recollecting in tranquillity: I'm not very tranquil at that time.

You criticise Dwight Macdonald for bringing his values with him as a kind of extra payload.

I really feel that the urge to bring morality into writing at this phase of history has become the greatest cop-out among writers. It's so much easier to come to a subject wth your mind made up, or to make a political point on behalf of some cause, than it is actually to go on a voyage of discovery. All the anti-war manifestos about Vietnam, of which there's one every two days in the United States— I've read a lot of them and I admire the passion, but I never in any of them see anyone say: 'Go to Vietnam, write about it, discover, bring back some information about what's going on.' It's easy to get there.

Would it be possible to write about death camps without making a moral statement?

I don't think there would be any question there. In fact, that would be one of the classic places where understatement is going to serve your case, if you wanted to make a case, better than taking the conscious moral position. If, as a newspaperman, I happened to walk into Dachau, I hope I would stick to the kind of approach that I have, which is to get inside of it, get the feel.

Most of the writers I've talked to view the future with at best alarm and at worst absolute despair. You don't seem to me to be a pessimist.

No, I'm not. I see, particularly in my own country, tens of millions of people, who at least have the means of happiness and in many cases actually demonstrate a kind of euphoria. Also the human comedy goes on, and in some cases the more serious it becomes, the funnier it gets, like the New York intellectuals seeking out the Red Indians in the South-West, the Black Panthers in Oakland or the grape workers in Southern California, and then hailing themselves for their new seriousness. You don't see them going into Harlem to do this. The new seriousness has given me as much joy as anything I've seen in years.

PW Interviews: Tom Wolfe

Michael Mok/1973

From *Publishers Weekly*, 203 (18 June 1973), 34-35. Reprinted from the 18 June 1973 issue of *Publishers Weekly*, published by R.R. Bowker Company, a Xerox company. Copyright © 1973 by Xerox Corporation. Reprinted with permission.

The PW interviewer responsible for the following piece about Tom Wolfe is one of the aces mentioned in *The New Journalism,* published this week by Harper & Row. The two paragraphs starring me state only that I am a very strong swimmer. Perhaps Wolfe envisions a time not too far in the future when the shovels will break and all of us will have to dogpaddle for the high ground.

The conversation between Wolfe and *PW* did not actually take place under water. Its murky, submarine quality stems from the fact that Wolfe was not to be found at his miserably appointed bachelor digs in New York's East 60s. Rumors from highly placed publishing sources that he was conducting or undergoing a pancreas transplant in Houston proved unfounded.

Tom surfaced finally in San Francisco, answering the phone himself—a practice not permitted in many luxury hotels, and leading the other party to think that he is probably living under a bridge like a troll.

Despite the static, and periodic interruptions from the operator demanding "$9.65 for the next three minutes, puleez," Wolfe sounded gleeful:

"In this book [*The New Journalism*] I think I have managed to antagonize everybody in the fiction world—plus uncounted members of the nonfiction establishment, who at first I thought would be pleased. But when you pass the fail-safe point in the Alienation Derby, a few more vendettas, dirks in the arras, don't really signify."

Tom did not coin the term "New Journalism" and is by now hyperaware that every time one uses the word *new,* scathing letters will arrive from scores of people, many of them assistant professors at junior colleges too cheap to advertise in the back of the New York Sunday *Times Magazine* ("You send us the boy—we'll send you the

Man"), pointing out that Lafcadio Hearn invented the whole schtick years ago.

"If the book is reviewed—and sometimes in cases of this sort the offending screed is ignored altogether—(no collusion is implied here; it is like when individual members of the Scripps-Howard newspaper chain independently come out on the same day with identically worded editorials supporting one political candidate or another)—IF *The New Journalism* is reviewed at all, it will be a carnival with real blood and flames, like when the old Luna Park burned down. If you accept what we say, the novel is undercut as literature's main event."

The reason that Tom is wandering from the New York island to Houston to the 10-lane superhighways of the Coast is that he went to watch the launching of Apollo 17 and was hooked to the extent that he has promised to do a book about astronauts for Farrar, Straus & Giroux. ("The reigning fantasy is that it will be ready by fall," he says.)

"Everything that I ever read about the astronauts (and I suspect *Life* had a lot to do with this) suggested that they were either Boy Scouts or robots. I finished each yarn with the thought, 'Yes, but what are they *really* like?' so my book—the title will probably be *The Right Stuff*—will assume that nothing is known about these people at all.

"Everybody—or everybody I talked to about it—was waiting for some oddball or Promethean character, or at least an eccentric to emerge, but it never seemed to happen. Then there was the Knox Gelatin school of thought: 'Why don't we send a poet to the moon??!!!' Imagine what Spender or Auden would file!"

Wolfe, who sleeps in pajamas with lapels and piping, says his preliminary research has convinced him of two things:

(1) That when the candidate-astronauts took the psychological tests designed to screen out characters of vivid imagination, hypersensitivity, and even a deplorable tendency *not* to slap American flag stickers on the windshields of their cars, they were sophisticated enough to give the "right" answers. Shown a blank sheet of paper by some horn-rimmed, double-knit Ph.D. with a nagging sense of inferiority about never having attended medical school, those good ole boys didn't answer: "I see a snow field, the blank wastes, the white nights, the aurora borealis." The astronauts, wisely, figuratively

rubbed their great toes in the sand and gulped, "Wal, Doc, that just looks like a blank piece of paper to me."

(2) Wolfe's second premise is that there is a vast subterranean competition toward astronaut-dom, which starts with the kid in the scuffed sneakers and tattered T-shirt on a scratch airfield who finally gets to solo by doing odd jobs. Thence the pyramid goes from student pilot to civilian pilot, fighter pilot (no actual combat experience), combat pilot, test pilot, and finally, at the very apex, the Astronauts themselves.

"Millions, literally millions, are involved in and aware of this competition, even though nobody talks about it. Hell, the counter-man at Nedick's is hip; haven't you noticed the way the drivers on Trailways and the Grey Dog sound more like moonmen every day?"

Wolfe claims that out on the West Coast the classic drive-ins, where underage hopefuls in mini-jupes used to screw on the tray, loaded down with Double-Bubber Burgers, are gone, but he is instinctively sure that fragile little buds in platform wedgies and Capezios are disgorging from buses somewhere. "I've been too busy to discover where the scene is, but I believe, I believe, it somewhere exists."

The best part of working in California, Tom maintains, is renting some huge car, like a Pontiac Honey Badger or Manatee, and tooling down those super-highways, five lanes in each direction. "Your car has a three-foot overhang front and back, and when you hit one of those cloverleaves, you don't feel a thing. *Mushiness* is what I like in an automobile. It's like driving a Chris-Craft with a souped-up Evinrude engine. A troubled person like myself spends 14 hours behind the wheel (the daily minimum necessary on the Coast) and it either cools him out or drives him into fibrillation.

"But the beauty part," Tom went on, "is watching the other cars float by; their windows are rolled up, of course, but you can tell they're listening to the radio because the drivers are pounding on the steering wheels.

"Occasionally, when I notice another driver hammer to a different tempo, I flip my radio dial like a maniac, so I can pound to his number."

Wolfe Tells Why Novel Is Outmoded

Frank S. Swertlow/1973

From *Los Angeles Times*, 18 July 1973, sec. 4, 14-15. Reprinted with permission of United Press International, © 1973.

NEW YORK—Tom Wolfe, the Beau Brummell of "new journalism," sat in the Oak Room of the St. Regis, dressed in vanilla.

"Hello," he said in a gracious Virginian accent, muted by years at Yale. He speaks slowly and precisely. There is no hi-how-are-ya-buddy, quite a surprise from a writer who uses!!!!!!'s, and O-O-O-O-O-H's the way others use periods and commas.

His white silk suit and his sandy hair are as custom cut as his books and articles in the more sophisticated national magazines.

As he breakfasted, he conversed about subjects ranging from weird clothes to Watergate. And, of course, his brand of journalism, a personalized reporting that has sent eye-shaded, cigar-chomping newsmen shrieking through newsrooms in protest.

And perhaps made the novel as outmoded as the Homeric epic.

"There are really two reasons why the novel has faded. One is simply that people who wanted to write stories began to go into film, either in a theater or on television. The one thing that hurts the whole general interest has gone out of it.

"But the other thing, perhaps more important, is that young fiction writers, the serious writers, began to operate from a totally different point of view. Their idols were no longer the realistic writers of the past. Their heroes weren't Hemingway, Fitzgerald or Faulkner, much less writers of the 19th century like Dickens. But because they came out of a university atmosphere, the people they began to look at were Beckett, Pinter, Kafka and others and these were all fable tellers.

"And so this atmosphere meant the new fiction should have a mythic quality, which is very strong now, and you have all these young writers who all believe they should write myths because realism has been taken up by film and journalism. It's as if they are trying to write a perfect enough myth, like the Greeks, which can be retold and retold.

33

"It's ruining certain careers," he said. "Now a novelist who I admire most in this country is Philip Roth. He's a fabulous writer. The guy's terrific. He's the closest thing we have to a Dickens.

"But he is now affected by this idea of the myth. So what does he start doing? He starts writing *The Breast* and now *The Great American Novel,* which are attempts to set up a mythic frame work.

"And he's just got to cut it out. It's terrible stuff. Just two terrible books. And you find this everywhere. And there are talented people writing stories where the hero has no social background or social context. He's just a hero and people don't speak in any language that would betray a social background.

"For instance nobody would have a Bronx accent or they would never have an Italian accent or anything that would have to do with a social class. The action takes place in some very elemental terrain: The sea, the swamp, the forest. The characters are always being pushed by unnamed dreads. And the reader doesn't know what is happening exactly, except the characters are being propelled by unseen forces and for some reason the author uses some sort of archaic diction.

"And it amazes me. How could a generation of novelists turn their back on the most incredible scenes in the history of the country? In the 1930s and 1940s the novelists would have plunged into this. But now they are headed off to Myth City."

But while others have left realism, Tom Wolfe has not.

His heroes became stock car drivers, doormen, go-go dancers. Their clothes, their walk, their talk were painted on his typewriter, just as lavishly as the custom cars builders sweated over *The Kandy-Kolored Tangerine-Flake Streamline Baby,* the automobile that inspired the title of his first book. His latest book, *The New Journalism,* zeroes in on others in his field.

The 42-year-old Wolfe was not always a "new journalist."

Thomas Kennerly Wolfe Jr. was born in Richmond, Va., graduated from Washington and Lee University and spent six years at Yale, earning a Ph.D. in American studies.

His next stops were the *Springfield* (Mass.) *Union,* the *Washington Post,* the *New York Herald Tribune* and the *World Journal Tribune.*

And along the way, Wolfe picked up his wardrobe of custom-tailored suits, the most striking of which were the white ice cream suits, which became his calling card.

"Clothes are a personal vice of mine and I found I could have a lot of fun with them.

"And I found these clothes would begin to outrage people. It is very annoying to see someone, even just in slightly different clothes. That was in the late 50s and early 60s when just to have a suit that was tightly fitted in the waist made you an extremely suspect person. Today these clothes wouldn't even rate a second look. Nobody gives a damn about a white suit.

"But there is one avenue I can still go—pretentiousness is still shocking and I am considering getting some winged-collared shirts for every day wear. That would still annoy people."

Wolfe says he would dearly love to write a book about the Watergate hearings.

"Sen. Ervin is interesting, he's really riding the hambone for all it's worth, and he's winging so fast and furious he doesn't know what he's doing.

"I really think Ervin is going back home and digging out quotes for the next day. And I am sure this will become an obsession with him— the interval in his life between quotes is going to get small and smaller. And he'll become a compendium of Scripture and the bards.

"What this thing lacks is a witness like Ervin. Ervin has this terrific regionalism. We don't think of it as ethnic humor, but that's what it is. And that is a very potent thing. Lyndon Johnson could have saved his whole career if he had let himself be a Texan, which I think he was capable of doing, but he tried to keep this under rein."

Tom Wolfe

Joe David Bellamy/1974

From *The New Fiction: Interviews with Innovative American Writers* (Urbana: University of Illinois Press, 1974), 75-96. Copyright © 1974 by the Board of Trustees of the University of Illinois. Reprinted with permission of the University of Illinois Press and Joe David Bellamy.

"Well, hello there, Senator," quips the over-rouged lady in the air-terminal lobby. Obviously, she is referring to my friend in the Big Lunch tie, the slightly yellowing white suit, the blue suede shoes, the blue-and-white checkered shirt and socks, the one day's growth of light beard on his face, the copy of *Sporting News* rolled up under his arm, the nicely chiseled nose, and the Stetson. . . . Obviously, she has no idea who she is addressing. "Jesus, lady," I say to myself.

Hardly a mere senator, the man in the white suit is, in fact, Tom Wolfe. It is March in New York's "North Country," and that evening at 9:00 Tom Wolfe is presenting another lecture on "The New Journalism"—this time at St. Lawrence University. . . . If he takes any note of the offensive, over-rouged lady, his reaction is skillfully suppressed.

Later, out on the road, we discuss Balzac. "My great discovery of the last eighteen months," Wolfe says, "has been Balzac. I never read anything by him before that. . . . " He goes on to advocate a return to Balzacian principles as a solution to the problems of contemporary fiction writers. Why is it, I wonder, that "the most famous pop writer in America" worries about such problems? Why does he *really* go around lecturing on the "new journalism" and writing articles called "Why They Aren't Writing the Great American Novel Anymore?" What sort of phenomenon am I dealing with here, Jim?

Well, one little-known fact about Tom Wolfe helps put this in perspective: he is really Dr. Wolfe. That's right, Jim. Sorry to disillusion you. Terrible Tom, Tom the Wolfe-Man, *New York's* clean-up hitter, *Esquire's* boy; *Rolling Stone's* latest head; Ken Kesey's buddy—he is really a Yale Ph.D. in disguise. Holy——!

Another thing, Jim. Beneath the elegant flamboyance of his

36

clothes, he is a sort of quiet, easygoing gent. Not a bit of your extroverted, loud-mouthed, aggressive reporter stereotype.

How does he *do* it, Jim??? *The Kandy-Kolored Tangerine-Flake Streamline Baby* (1965)? *The Pump House Gang* (1968)? *The Electric Kool-Aid Acid Test* (1968)? *Radical Chic & Mau-Mauing the Flak Catchers* (1970)? And his newest—out-mailering Mailer on NASA and the astronauts—to be called *The Right Stuff* (1974)? Here's how, Jim.

It is later that night at St. Lawrence. Everyone is just standing around the ol' Fireside Lounge in the UC—drinking coffee, eating cookies, waiting to see Tom Wolfe IN THE FLESH. Then we stroll in, Jim. Tom has on his deep-sea navy-blue suit now with lapels to the shoulders and four-button sleeves. He has his white linen shirt with a matched knit tie and the matched blue side-striped socks, and, to top it all off, Jim, the campiest of gold crescent Man-in-the-Moon tie studs as big as a Florida cockroach. Tom and I stand there in the middle of the room, and the students start to sidle over and crowd around.

Then it starts, Jim. Tom is just sort of standing there in the middle of the crowd, see, relaxed—why, he might as well have been humming the Budweiser beer song to himself—Hum hum humm hummm hummmm. . . . And everybody is suddenly telling him their life stories: childhood experiences, acid trips, boring, funny, in-coherent—a whole crowd suffering from information compulsion, just pouring it all out; and Tom is just standing there, quietly smiling, listening, listening, nodding, taking it all in—clickity-click-click-click-click—with that mind of his. That's it, Jim. That's the magic.

Later yet, we get to talking about the novel again. I wonder, Jim. In spite of all this stuff about the new journalism, does Tom really secretly burn to write a novel himself? It's *true*, he *is* writing a novel. Tooooooooo freaking much! And, Jim, you know what he's calling it? *Vanity Fair!!!!!!*

Joe David Bellamy: Your position of advocating a revival of more or less Balzacian sensibilities and social concerns for fiction writers seems diametrically opposed to most of the credible theoreti-cians and practitioners. John Barth, for instance, predicts that "irrealism" rather than any sort of documentary realism is apt to be one of the more fertile areas of exploration.

Tom Wolfe: Well, I think Barth is a very good example of someone

APPOMATTOX REGIONAL LIBRARY
HOPEWELL, VIRGINIA 23860
07/90

who is so excessively conscious of the history of the novel. In fact, I
read a piece by him not too long ago in an anthology called *The
Novel since World War II* in which he's painfully conscious of the idea
of "avant-gardism" and of keeping it out on a frontier. I'm all for that,
but I think the idea of a frontier today has become restricted to a
sheerly formal frontier. In other words, it's true in every branch of the
arts that the only frontier artists *believe* exists is the frontier of
manipulating form. That's why painting, for example, has gone
through such convulsions until now. Of course, it's no longer painting
but "concept art" and "earth art," etc. Each of these has a life of
about eighteen months—this frantic, hassling, speeded-up search for
the new form. I think people are unconsciously selling themselves
short when they want to make the form do the work. . . .

   The fact that there might be something new in content, or new in
comment, is not anything that impresses people once they get into this
frame of mind that the avant-garde is on the frontier sheerly of form.

   Bellamy: It's interesting that most of these same writers *would*
agree with you that the novel is dead. But the novel they're talking
about is the realistic novel. Whereas I suspect that when you say that
the novel is dead, you would be saying that the fiction they're trying
to write, which embodies a kind of diverse onslaught *against* the
realistic novel, is what's dead.

   Wolfe: It *is* dead, and it is very unfortunate that they should be
spending so much energy on it. Because they've tricked themselves.
They've gone through the history of aesthetics, and so forth, and
they've said, "Because Proust did this much, and Henry James did
this much, and James Joyce did this much, I can't do *those* things.
They're not available to me. So what is there left?" So you really
have to assume a very esoteric frame of mind in order to find out
what's left.

   That's one reason that the fact that journalism has no traditions is
important to me. There are really no traditions in journalism worth
observing. It's a low-rent form—always has been a low-rent form—
and there's always been room for a lot of brawling about and a lot of
mistakes. That's why, in a way, I shouldn't even go around giving
talks about the new journalism; because if enough good writing
comes out of the genre, people are eventually going to start
becoming very self-conscious, just as novelists are now. They're going

to be like Barth, who really does think acutely about what has already been done with the form of the novel. But if you think that way, obviously you're going to paint yourself into a corner. I would imagine that John Hawkes is in the same frame of mind, and a lot of younger writers certainly are in that frame of mind. I mean, I don't know Brautigan, but I'm sure he's proably thinking that way—just this tremendous fascination with Hermann Hesse, for example.

Bellamy: Of course, the way you are going, the skills you're practicing and the forms that you're using aren't really disassociated from all of this. You call journalism a low-rent form, but you're obviously a very high-rent writer at this point and figure *into* this in my estimation of things. It occurs to me, for example, that your formulation about Balzac, even mentioning Balzac—I mean aside from his coffee and his writing habits—but actually mentioning Balzac as a figure to reflect upon seriously, is either, it seems, extremely prosaic or extremely avant-garde.

Wolfe: Well, I call this second-convolution avant-gardism. I think the novel is. . . . The novel is not dead. It's only the novelists who are strangling themselves on what is now a very orthodox, conventional aesthetics based on form. And there are no novelists today who are considered "talented" who would want to do what Balzac did, or what Thackeray or Dickens did. Their reason being: *they* did it. Why should we do it again? But the fact is that Balzac, Dickens, and Thackeray were not living in such an incredible period! Every period, I suppose, is incredible if you really get to the heart of it. But certainly *this* period—still—has so many undiscovered corners. There's so much *terra incognita* that novelists should be getting into that they could easily be wholly concerned with the social fabric, the social tableau. Forget the *ersatz* psychology that they get into.

Bellamy: Of course, that's what you *are* getting into, sketching out of subcultures. . . .

Wolfe: Well, I've done what I can so far, and, well, I've done what I've done. I've completely relished this *terra incognita*, these sub-cultures, these areas of life that nobody wanted to write about—because they thought either they didn't know about them or they were beneath serious consideration. I imagine the most serious subject now is changes in the way people live, not politics, not wars. I think it's just the changes in the way people live, the changes in the

way they look at the world. Perhaps that's always been the most
serious subject.

Bellamy: It comes down to the form-content distinction again,
doesn't it? You're arguing that the content is always changing, so the
same form is viable forever. Because the times are always changing,
the content is always important. It's not just the form that is so
crucially important.

Wolfe: I think this is absolutely true. You do have two new
elements always available. You've got your own priceless, unique
way of looking at things. Emerson said everybody has a great
autobiography if he can only separate what is uniquely his experience
from everybody else's. You've got *that* that's new anyway because
you're born with it. It's just a question of whether you can put it down
on paper. You're not looking at the world the same way as any other
person, unless you've let yourself be so totally conditioned that
you're some kind of automaton. But also—the second element—the
conditions *around* you have changed. I think it's only the artist who is
willing to face up to both forms of newness who is going to do major
work, particularly at this point in history when the novelists have all
crowded into one phone booth. They're just all in there. It's like some
kind of a stunt. It's a shame.

Actually I say it's a shame, but I don't care because it makes things
much easier for me. Really, I've had just a wide-open field; and it's
just been marvelous. There's been no competition. All the people
who would have been writing about the changes in "the way we live
now"—that's Trollope's term originally—have just been off doing
these poor, frantic, little exercises in form. I really have had so little
competition—not just me, but other journalists who have concerned
themselves with the way we live now.

You see, the irony is that despite all the aesthetic arguments, in the
course of time the novelists—we'll just talk about novelists and forget
the journalists—the *novelists* who are great, who are considered the
great figures from their particular era, tend to be people who are
performing this sort of news-bearing function. In 1970, which was the
hundredth anniversary of Dickens' death, I believe, a great round of
books, reviews, articles went on in England during which it was pretty
conclusively decided that Dickens was *the* great figure in the English
novel. The number two figure after Shakespeare. That's really sort of

how this particular competition came out. Now this is a hundred years later, so this may be the final standings—since they start listing them in October after the baseball season is over. Dickens was hardly even reviewed by the serious journals in his own time. He was constantly downgraded as a topical writer. The same thing was true of Balzac. Balzac, for example, was never inducted into the French academy. Also, he generally got bad reviews. In Russia, well, Tolstoy probably outranks Dostoyevsky. There may be a little controversy there. And Tolstoy, again, was the news-bearing novelist. Gogol ranks very high, also a man giving the social tableau of his times. Gogol, Dostoyevsky, and Tolstoy finish in the money in that country.

Bellamy: And Chekhov . . . who also . . . brought the news.

Wolfe: You're right. Chekhov . . . of course, he did, too.

Bellamy: Of course, the argument that certain critics would make, you know, in conjunction with the death of realism, or at least of the nineteenth-century novel is that the form of the community as it existed in the nineteenth century doesn't exist anymore—the dissolution of the organic community. So we have a fragmented society on our hands. There is no way you *could* get it in some kind of comprehensive picture. You have to go around doing sub-cultures, and isn't that a fragmented thing to do or something . . . ? You can't do all of America.

Wolfe: This is an argument that Trilling presented, and it's also an argument that a lot of novelists believe. Mailer believes this. He wrote a piece called "Some Children of the Goddess" in which he said that the novelist had to make a choice today whether he was going to follow the route of Dostoyevsky or Tolstoy, the idea being that Tolstoy presented the tableau of society in his time and Dostoyevsky turned you inward and toward the psychological dimension. I don't think it can be broken down that way, because Dostoyevsky, for example, dealt with an awful lot of social fabric of his time. But nevertheless, novelists believe this now, and they think you have to choose—and that since you don't have a coherent class structure, you can't write a novel that's going to be illustrative or symbolic of something larger, because it's all so fragmented. You write about this fragment, and all you can capture is just this fragment rather than the whole society.

I think all this is just an elaborate way of saying that the novelists don't understand the society, so they've abdicated looking at it.

They've abdicated from the task of looking at it, I should say. And this impels a turn towards fantasy, the psychological novel, the "my first wife" novel. They've all turned towards Dostoyevsky—or Joyce, particularly. We're all, in one way or another, sons of James Joyce. This has just left us all a whole other area for nonfiction writers to make sense out of. But the idea of saying you can't make sense out of it or you can't present it in a way that gives people a larger picture of themselves is just inventing an excuse for avoiding a very difficult task. Sure, it's more difficult now. When you don't have a coherent class structure, it's more difficult to present a picture of the society. It's also more of a challenge, I think. That's why I think: here is a great frontier. It awaits, you know, somebody. All these novelists always talk about changing the consciousness of their times, but they're not even going to come close to it in the kinds of novels they're writing now. You know, there is no novelist in this country, no one who is still writing, who has had an original thought, an original insight into the society, because they insist on being romantic novelists who have a romantic view of their role. . . .

Bellamy: It occurs to me that for future historians if one wanted to get a picture of the twenties one might read Fitzgerald; if one wanted to get a picture of the sixties, let's say, one might read Wolfe. . . .

Wolfe: [Spoken in jest with a British accent] I would certainly go along with that myself. . . .

Bellamy: I mean, I wonder why it is that in the twenties you have the novel form predominating as a historical vehicle, whereas in the sixties you have the nonfiction form—what you might *call* the nonfiction form. Can you visualize what a form of the seventies might be, if it were still Wolfean? Would it be, *could* it be a novel? What kind of novel would it really be?

Wolfe: It could still be done *in* the novel. I think that the only future for the novel is reporting, which means there's not going to be *much* difference between the best novels and the best nonfiction. It's going to get down to a matter of technique. In fact, I'm having this battle with myself right now on this *Vanity Fair* book I told you about. I want to do a book that performs something of the same function of Thackeray's *Vanity Fair,* and I'm weighing whether this should be fiction or nonfiction, because everything in it is going to be based on a journalistic reality. Now, the question is to me a completely technical one. Once I reach that decision, the rest is purely technical.

The novel as a form no longer has any fascination for me as something that is a superior literary form. It's just a way of dealing with reality. And it has certain advantages. You can be more compact in a novel, in the sense that you can have one character express the roles or reality of two or three people in real life, because if they're similar people you can combine characteristics. You have much more liberty in dealing with the psychology of persons other than yourself. You know, you can do it in nonfiction; you have to interview people . . . you have to gain their confidence, interviewing at tremendous length before you can start getting them to tell you about their thoughts and to really level with you about their emotions. It can be done. It can be done much more economically in fiction.

Nonfiction has the advantage of the reader knowing that it's real. Now this is a tremendous thing—it sounds like nothing—but it's a tremendous thing to know that you're reading something that actually happened. That's why memoirs have always been so popular. You get all the advantages of a novel, and yet you know, or you assume, that it's true.

So, with this book I'm working on now it's a great technical problem. I call it a technical problem because it's sheerly, as far as I'm concerned, a matter of what is going to make the thing most real, what is going to give it the force, the richest presentation of the sort of life in our times. I'm not ashamed to be attempting to show the world "life in our times." We were talking about Balzac earlier: he was proud to be known as, and in fact referred to himself as, "the secretary of French society." It was the kind of term that no serious novelist today would be caught dead being stuck with. I mean, anything but that. Because the novel now has the status that poetry had in the nineteenth century. It's the medium of the holy beast.

Bellamy: Could you say some more about *Vanity Fair?*

Wolfe: Well, what Thackeray did was to try in one book to present the picture of ambition and status strife as he saw it in the London of his time. London, at that time, was really at its highest tide, because the British Empire was going strong and the money was pouring into England. He was presenting a picture of the great world capital of its time. And *nobody* has tried to do this for New York in our own time, despite the fact that New York has certainly been one of the most bizarre world capitals that has ever been. I mean, it's an extraordinary period we have lived through and are still living through—in everything from styles of behavior to fundamentals of behavior—the disruption and breakdown of whole class structures and everything else. I think novelists have been very afraid of New York as a subject. It's too big, too complicated. You really can't grasp it.

Bellamy: Do you think that the subject of status, which is implied by the title *Vanity Fair* and has also been a recurring subject for you, is your main territory or interest?

Wolfe: I consider that as such a fundamental subject. It's really more of an analytical tool than a subject per se. It's just so fundamental to everything that people do that it's going to come up. That's the first thing I always look for.

The subject really irritates a lot of people. Some people basically think that to approach things with the idea of status in mind is in itself a rather snobbish way to look at things. People can also get very tired of the term very quickly, I've noticed.

Bellamy: It tends to force them to face their own status, for one thing.

Wolfe: Well it's just *the* fundamental taboo, more so than sexuality and everything of that sort. It's much easier for people to talk about their sex lives in this day and age than it is to talk about their status. I mean, just ask someone once to rank themselves socially, and you see someone squirm. It would certainly make me squirm. I wouldn't want to sit there and do it. I wouldn't want to do it in an honest way. I think my reaction would be to make a joke and avoid doing it.

Bellamy: Getting back to the discussion of realism vs. fantasy, isn't the real crux of the issue the question of the nature of reality itself? It seems to me that one argument that's been given in favor of the new journalism is that so-called outside reality doesn't really exist, that all you really have is subjective reality. So the reporter, instead of using the old rigid forms and formulas, which were supposedly a way of capturing outside reality, assumes now that he's being more honest by giving his subjective experience, which he sees as truer to reality. And isn't that really the argument that the new novelists are giving too—that there is no "outside reality"? So that leaves you open to go into fantasy—because that's part of what really is, after all, because fantasy is part of reality. We're *always* having fantasies.

Wolfe: I disagree with that totally. Because, for my money, the only thing new in this new journalism I'm talking about is the new techniques that nonfiction writers have discovered they can use. The subjectivity that I value in the good examples of the new journalism is the use of techniques to enable the writer to get inside the subjective reality—*not* his own, but of the characters he's writing about. In other words, to use stream of consciousness so that I can present the mind of Ken Kesey—as I try to do in a number of chapters of *The Electric Kool-Aid Acid Test*—to get completely inside Kesey's mind, based on interviews, tapes that he made, or letters that he wrote, diaries, and so on. It's still a controversial thing to use, but I was not at all interested in presenting *my* subjective state when confronted with the Pranksters or whatever they had done. It was rather to try to get Kesey's completely. Same way in *Radical Chic & Mau-Mauing the Flak Catchers*. I do occasionally go inside the minds of other people, as I did with the inside of Leonard Bernstein's mind briefly, here and there.

This is quite different from saying that reality is so elusive that whatever *I* feel is reality. Because—you're not just writing for yourself. I think this attitude becomes a form of taking the easy way out. Honestly, there is *not* just one reality. But there are certain things that are objectively known. For example, I am convinced that everyone sees the color red the same way. There is no proof of this, but I am convinced that it's true. I'm convinced that people sense thickness, lightness, and so on, all in the same way. There *is* this, I think. The externals are the same for everyone. Obviously, people receive this "intracranially," as the brain physiologists say, in different ways. But you can't dismiss the common denominators in the external world and say that there is no reality. Because that's just not true.

Bellamy: I think that some of the writers I've talked to might argue with you that your concept of objective reality is actually the concept of reality that we've gotten from a certain art form, which was the form of the nineteenth-century novel. That is, they might argue, you are seeing reality in terms of the nineteenth-century novel, whereas reality can actually be seen in all sorts of different forms. Of course, you're right that these people are trying to do what Joyce was trying to do in many ways, seeing reality in a different way, as, let's say, made up of fantasy, made up of discontinuity, and that sort of thing. That may not be just "subjective experience," but it actually may be what so-called outside reality consists of.

Wolfe: Well, I mean, I think that concept of theirs is total nonsense. It's egotism, really. It's very flattering to yourself to think that your interior concept of reality is the only one that has any meaning. In a way, Freudianism has conditioned us to think that. Because Freud's great insight was that a person's own concept of reality can be more crucial in his decisions than objective circumstance. As a matter of fact, Freud successfully forestalled advances in brain physiology for fifty years—because people believed that subjective states were that big a part of life. I don't think there's any question but that eventually, scientifically, through research into the central nervous system, they'll find out the actual facts of the matter, or the best there is. Bishop Berkeley was wrong. If you kick a tree, then your foot hurts. Eventually no one will have to argue the fact that there *was* a tree there and your foot did hurt. I think only aesthetes argue about it now. There is a very prosaic, common, external reality, which is filtered through something called your brain. Then you express, you make, your reaction in various ways. Now obviously, as far as we know, there are no two identical brains. There are no two absolutely identical consciousnesses. But this is not to say that the only reality is the internal situation of the individual. I think all great writing somehow knows this. All great writers know this in some way, and they take the external world for what it is. And they also recognize the complexity of internal states.

One Flew Over the Cuckoo's Nest is a good example. I don't know what Kesey's thoughts are on this particular subject, but he tells a tale through the eyes of a schizophrenic Indian. Sometimes the Indian is lucid; sometimes he's crazy. Kesey changes these back and forth to very good advantage, really to illustrate the very point I'm talking about. Sometimes the Indian sees the elements of the outside world very clearly, that is, the world outside of his skull, that affect him in a very rational way: the fact that he is in prison, the fact that he's treated like a secondary form of humanity, and so on. Other times he's completely inside of his cranium. He's imagining that fog has rolled into the hospital unit; he imagines that the pills, the tranquilizers, have a machine inside of them that controls his conduct. He switches off between the external reality and the internal reality, but in a very conscious way—not the way so many novelists do it, which is to hike themselves into the belief that there is only one reality which is that inside of their skulls.

Now to just turn it around, let's look at it through the eyes of the reader for a minute. A reader will put up with a lot, and a reader will try to make sense out of any internal state that the writer has. But eventually he's going to want the guy to "for God's sake, meet me halfway," because we all know that there is a common meeting ground known as external reality. Show me enough of it so I know what terrain we're on.

That's why, in the case of Barthelme, a case of a writer whose work I admire, it's very hard for him to write at length. As long as he's writing in a short space, I think people can enjoy the intracranial exercise he's putting you through. I think he has tried to face up to that. I think the longest thing he's written has been *Snow White,* which was not his most successful work but perhaps his least successful. He's much better in a shorter space.

In a way, this is like the argument about form and content in painting. In painting, there's been a great animus against the literary. In fact, for years people were downgrading the literary elements, which merely meant the pictorial elements. Even when pop art came in, it was not considered pictorial painting. It was considered to be the denaturing of the banal units of the environment! There was a lot of sheer bullshit invented in order to justify pop art. To me, it seems very obvious that in painting you could have in one form, in one canvas, one painting, something that expressed both exciting form, such as shapes, color, use of space—to use one of the real bullshit words of modern aesthetics—*and* literary content. As in the case of Rembrandt. Since Rembrandt existed in the past, he can be ruled out, or El Greco, or Toulouse-Lautrec.

Bellamy: Just because an idea is an old idea doesn't mean it's a bad idea.

Wolfe: Well, you see, *there* you have painters who are combining what is an external reality, which is things that exist, things you can see, things you can sense, *with* their own imaginations. And now, I think, the aesthetic has reached the point where people have been saying for so long: "It's only the intracranial activity that's important." Well, it may be the only thing that's important to the artist, but it's not the only thing important to the audience. The audience desperately wants to be able to make a pattern out of what it really is they're looking at.

That's why, as much as I admire a lot of the things that Burroughs has done, I use his work like a book of wallpaper samples. I like to dip into it to see techniques, and I've stolen a few here and there. I don't enjoy particularly reading anything straight through, because I feel that he's working behind a veil. He's put some kind of a veil up in front of what actually happened to him. Then he gives me a shadow show behind the veil, and he asks me to fill in the missing links and spaces. This can be very exciting up to a point. But if you reach that point after a few pages, after that you want him to level with you and say, you know, "what happened?" You can tell that he is describing what, I imagine, were things that happened to him, but he doesn't want to come out and really tell you. He makes it very cryptic, and he sort of parades symbols in front of you. He makes, in the long run, a rather artistic exercise out of it.

A different approach, although Burroughs probably thinks he's very close to these people, would be Henry Miller in *Tropic of Cancer,* a book I admire very much, or books such as *Journey to the End of Night* or *Death on the Installment Plan,* which is my favorite book title. These guys may be lying through their teeth, but you have the feeling that you're being leveled with—and that the writer is not denying you his picture of the external reality in order just to play these intracranial games. You have a feeling that he's really trying to show you the external reality *plus* the way the show ran inside of his cranium.

Bellamy: Well, what is it then that you *get* with this leveling? That is, isn't it really Celine's perception of the world, which is different from somebody else's, or Miller's perception of the world? And isn't that, in a sense, really the result of his ability to imagine the world better than somebody else does?

Wolfe: Oh, sure, that's a crucial thing. But if he is also not showing you something new in the external world, or giving you a new insight. . . . Let's put it this way: he should also be giving you the thrill of recognition, as Dickens constantly did. I mean, people have been in court. They've been frustrated by their experiences in court. But when they read Dickens, they recognized the scene and then they said, "Oh, so *that's* the way it worked. *That's* why I felt frustrated!" It wasn't a new scene to them, but they got the thrill of recognition and an explanation of what was happening to them. Or, they got a look at a new world completely—the world of the English public school, or a better example would be the world of thieves that he presented in *Oliver Twist.*

Bellamy: How about Zola as a model? Is that the kind of model of the new documentary writer who you say we need? Zola went out and took minute notes about the details of coal mines when he was writing *Germinal.*

Wolfe: Well, there you would have, yeah—the fact that he was bringing you news was a very important thing.

Bellamy: Do you think that's enough? Isn't that Arthur Hailey really?

Wolfe: That's right, it is. The best thing is to have *both*—to have both someone who will bring you bigger and more exciting chunks of the outside world *plus* a unique sensibility, or rather a unique way of looking at the world, a unique fantasy life, even, to use the way Freud explains it, a unique emotional reality of his own that somehow echoes or vibrates with the emotional states of the reader. So that you get both the external reality and the subjective reality.

I'm not denying the existence of a subjective reality. Far from it. I'm just saying that there is also an objective reality that everyone in the world has to deal with. So I think you want to get the fullest experience that you can. That's why I think that the great painting of the future, as of the past, is going to be pictorial—illustration. Illustration done with an exciting use of form, as Rembrandt did it, as Toulouse-Lautrec did it, for that matter, as Dali has done it. . . .

Bellamy: So you don't believe the argument that the camera has made representational painting obsolete, or that, say, movies have made certain kinds of novelistic reality obsolete, the documentary kind of reality that you might get in some novels?

Wolfe: No, I think again this is just an argument that the novelists will tend to use to avoid both hard work and embarrassing work. Reporting is hard, and it's embarrassing.

Bellamy: It's not for introverts?

Wolfe: Well, there are plenty of introverts who force themselves to do it. I mean, it can be done. It's hard, it's time-consuming, but the main resistance is: it doesn't seem artistic. Until people get over the idea that artistic excellence is separate from content, the novel is going to get painted into a smaller and smaller corner.

Bellamy: How about Stephen Crane as an ideal of the way the novelist should behave? You know, a writer who had the sensibility and the equipment, but who also went out after material very much in the way of a reporter. His trip west, for example, on the train. He decides he wants to do western stories, so he hops on a train, takes a ride out west, and does "The Bride Comes to Yellow Sky" and things like that. Would that be your idea of what a novelist, let's say, might do now if he wished to fill in this conspicuous gap in contemporary fiction?

Wolfe: That would certainly be the modus operandi, as they say in the police department. Mark Twain tended to do that.

Bellamy: What do you make of the whole rash of autobiographies that are being written, books which once might have been called first novels except that the people who write them now decide to leave their names in? Or books like *Up* by Ronald Sukenick, for example, which is very much *like* that? I mean, it's very autobiographical, although some of it isn't. Sukenick calls the main character "Ronald Sukenick" and so on, but there's so much fantasy in there, so much stretching of the "truth" that he ends up calling it a novel anyway.

Wolfe: Well, in a way, that's what Henry Miller did. That's what Celine did. Celine would lead you to believe that everything in his novels happened to him. In fact, a lot of it did, but he also gives himself the license to depart from the facts when he wants to.

There's a great confusion now. The novelists are so conscious of literary history, always so self-conscious that they're all reading their literary histories trying to find out what's left. And I guess it's just an age of nonfiction. So you have events like Herbert Gold writing a novel called *Fathers* in which the two fathers in the book are Herbert Gold, Sr. and Jr., and from all the external facts of his life I presume it's his father and himself. He calls this a novel, and I presume this just means that when he got to certain situations if he wanted to change the facts he did so. In Gore Vidal's recent book *Two Sisters* there are two characters in there: one is Gore Vidal, called Gore Vidal; one is his sister, called by her name; and there are some fictional characters, one of whom is apparently based on Jacqueline Kennedy; then there's a straight essay in the middle. Capote's new book, *Answered Prayers*—I don't know exactly what it's going to be, but if in fact it is using real people with their real names in fictional situations, again you have this kind of curious blending. William Styron, writing *The Confessions of Nat Turner,* is an example of this. I think, ten years ago, somebody might have written *The Confessions of Nat Blender* based on the life of Nat Turner.

This is happening because the novel is so confused and novelists very uncertain of what's going on. They still want to be known as novelists. When Capote wrote *In Cold Blood*, for instance, he made sure that everyone knew he considered it a novel. He called it a nonfiction novel. It was very important to him that it would not be called journalism, but a novel, a nonfiction novel. It made me laugh because this is exactly what Fielding had gone through at the very beginnings of the novel in English. It was very important to him that *Joseph Andrews* and *Tom Jones* be called "comic epics in prose." The epic had been the great form prior to Fielding's time, so he was saying, in effect, "I'm not writing one of these novels; I'm writing a comic epic in prose." So people did get hung up on the prestige of a certain form before the novelists. All of them would have been much better off if they had never read a literary history.

Bellamy: What sort of impact do you see the electric media making—if I can ask a McLuhanesque question—on writing forms? Do you think there is a valuable cross-fertilization going on?

Wolfe: No. I used to wonder about this a great deal. There's no question that electric media have had an effect, mostly in effective usurpation. Obviously television and the movies, film of various sorts—when you talk about television you're talking about film, by and large—has usurped a lot of the functions of short stories, novels. One thing, however, that no electric medium can do so far— somebody may find a way to do it—is the interior monologue, or just simply "point of view." You don't have to give it such a name. But the real point of view, in which the audience feels that it is inside the mind, or the central nervous system, of a character—movies have *never* been able to do this. They can do everything else, and they can do it better. They can establish a locale much more economically and in a much more striking way, in a way you'll never forget. They *cannot* get inside of characters. They've tried *every* sort of thing. They've tried voice-overs, they've tried shooting from behind the head of a character, they've tried making the camera like a pair of eyes in which the main character only sees himself in a mirror. That was done in one movie. I forget the name of it.

The closest thing was in the movie *Alfie*, which used the aside. It came closer than anything else. Michael Caine, who was Alfie, would occasionally turn toward the camera and deliver a comment on what he was doing. For some weird reason that I can't figure out psychologically, this worked much better than anything else. You really have much more of a feeling of being inside a character. On stage this is simply an aside. It doesn't work terrifically on the stage either, because obviously the guy's not aside. There are a lot of people around him. But anyway, even that didn't do what a novel can do in terms of making you feel like you're inside somebody's head. Or what nonfiction can do. I did it in a number of chapters in *The Electric Kool-Aid Acid Test.* John Sack did it in his book on Vietnam.

Bellamy: I was going to say that, of course, *you're* doing that all the time. You're always getting *inside* of characters, and you do it without announcing it in any way. You just zip inside of somebody, even sometimes for just a second. I think of the line in "The Put-Together Girl," you know, where you say, "Carmen is very social." For that one line you're getting inside the mother's head. You just drop that, you know, and that's it. You're inside of her head, and then you zap right out again. You're always doing that, like a whirling dervish. It seems to me that, in the form that you use, you get inside and outside of characters quicker and more subtly than most novelists do. That's probably the most characteristic piece of virtuosity one finds in your work.

Wolfe: Well, actually, you're the first person I've run into who seems to have realized what I was doing in that respect. Because it is something I've done again and again. Even in expository sections I often try to adopt the tone of a character. When I write about Junior Johnson's stock car race, often I may be just describing a race course or a carburetor or some damn thing, and I'll try to do it in the language of Junior Johnson to create the feeling that you're still within the person's point of view.

I really learned some valuable lessons in this from reading some of the young Soviet writers—like the brothers Serapion. Most of them are not well known. I guess the most famous would be Eugene Zamyatin, Boris Pilniak, and there's a guy, very seldom remembered, called Andrei Sobol. Alexis Remizov is another one. At any rate, they're all novelists or short story writers. They were writing about the revolution, but they took a panoramic view, so they didn't stick with one character usually. They were always doing very tricky things with point of view. I became very conscious of that sort of technique when I was at Yale. At graduate school I discovered these guys just by roaming through the stacks at the Yale library, all in translation, of course. I found that you can do this in nonfiction to a great advantage. Just carefully manipulate point of view. Your example was quite a good one.

That piece I did on Phil Spector—in the very beginning—it was the first time I ever actually went inside of somebody else's mind. It is one thing to do an interior monologue in your own mind. It's something else to do one in someone else's mind. In fact, it's quite a chance to take because the person may scream bloody murder, and you really don't have any defense except that you feel you're doing it accurately. You really feel you know the person well enough and what their state was in this particular incident or you don't. So I did it with Spector in his own plane. He was having paranoid reactions to the plane starting to take off, so he makes the plane stop. He makes them stop the whole flight and he gets off with a big furor. Afterwards, one of the news magazines—as they occasionally do— got into one of these anti-new-journalism spasms and called up Spector and a number of other people that I had written about and wanted to know if this was *accurate,* you know. Spector hadn't told me about the whole thing, but he said, "Yeah, that's exactly the way I felt at that time." I had never asked him myself, you know, what he thought of that particular thing. They also called up Jane Holzer, from the "Girl of the Year" story I did in my first book, and even went by her apartment to see if I had gotten all the details of the apartment correctly.

Bellamy: I was going to ask you a question about the setup you have in "O Rotten Gotham," where you get up on the balcony with Edward T. Hall, looking down on Grand Central Station. Now, when I read that, it seemed to me that that was suitable license; that is, if you really didn't do that with Edward T. Hall, I would grant you the right to do that. But I wanted to ask you: *did* you actually go with Edward T. Hall up on the balcony?

Wolfe: Oh, yes. Absolutely. Down into the subways with him. If I remember that day, we first went to Grand Central. We did all that, went down in the subways, walked around in the middle of Manhattan a little bit; then *New York* magazine had hired a car. We got in the car. There was a driver so we could both talk and look at things, and we went all through Harlem and all over the place.

Bellamy: If it hadn't happened, would you consider that to be an acceptable license? I mean, it seems to me that piece is utterly defensible for being a beautiful example of a first-rate popularization of important scientific information. By presenting Hall as a figure, a flesh-and-blood person, you've made it more approachable for people who wouldn't ordinarily be able to dig the scientific business, you know. But *would* you consider presenting that particular scene as justifiable license if you hadn't done that *because* it works dramatically?

Wolfe: It would be justifiable, if Hall had done it and I hadn't, to present Hall based on his recollection—without saying this is what Hall remembered, but just have him there.

Bellamy: You would not put yourself next to him?

Wolfe: I would not put myself next to him if I had not been there. No. I'm expecting the reader to allow me a certain leeway *if* it leads towards a better grasp of what actually took place. In other words, I expect the reader to allow me to present what Hall might have done in that particular position without having a preamble that says, "I wasn't with this man at this time; but based on his memory of what took place, this was it." I expect the reader to grant me the right to present that without that preamble. I don't expect him, however, to grant me the right to make up anything. I think it kind of kills the whole thing.

Bellamy: That's fiction, I guess.

Wolfe: Because part of the impact is the fact that you're telling the reader *this happened*. This is not a short story. This is not a novel. This is not fiction.

Sitting Up with Tom Wolfe

Joe David Bellamy/1974

From *Writer's Digest*, 54 (November 1974), 22-29. Copyright ©
1974 by Joe David Bellamy. Reprinted by permission.

Tom Wolfe began a revolution of sorts in the reporting of
American popular culture with *The Kandy-Kolored Tangerine-Flake Steamline Baby* in 1965. At heart a moralist
and social observer and critic, as well as a dazzling stylist,
Wolfe has generated avid attention, both for the originality
of his essays and for his association with the genesis of the
so-called "new journalism," of which he would have to be
described as the leading practitioner. In his more recent
books, *The Pump House Gang* (1968), *The Electric Kool-
Aid Acid Test* (1968), and *Radical Chic & Mau-Mauing the
Flak Catchers* (1970), Wolfe has continued to inspire admiration and controversy by daring to experiment with
techniques previously thought to be solely within the
province of the novelist.

In *The New Journalism* (1973), in fact, he set out to
formulate, define, and illustrate the principles and practice
of the new journalists and paused to take potshots at
contemporary writers of "the new fiction," whom Wolfe
characterized as "busy running backward, skipping and
screaming, into a begonia patch. . . ." Most recently, in his
forthcoming, eagerly awaited book on NASA and the
moon voyages, to be called *The Right Stuff,* Wolfe forges
merrily along the new journalistic path he has worked for
the the last ten years to cultivate.

Now, just past forty, Wolfe seems youthful and chipper
as an athlete, canny and thoughtful as a historian. Two
little-known facts about him: he does, in fact, hold a
doctorate in American studies from Yale and has played
semi-pro baseball. Famous for his flamboyant, especially
his white, suits, Wolfe is dressed to the teeth (in a white
suit), looking every inch what he has come to embody for
many readers: The most famous pop writer in America.

The following interview took place in October in New
York's southern tier, where Tom Wolfe had flown in on
Mohawk's screeching flight 469 from LaGuardia in order

to present a lecture a few miles across the New York-
Pennsylvania border at one of the Pennsylvania state colleges.

Bellamy: What about your writing techniques and habits? I've
noticed from some of your prefaces that you seem to write your
books fairly quickly.

Wolfe: The actual writing I do very fast. I make a very tight outline
of everything I write before I write it. And often, as the case of *The
Electric Kool-Aid Acid Test,* the research, the reporting, is going to
take me much longer than the writing. By writing an outline you
really *are* writing in a way, because you're creating the structure of
what you're going to do. Once I really know what I'm going to write,
I don't find the actual writing takes all that long.

The Electric Kool-Aid Acid Test in manuscript form was about
1,100 pages, triple-spaced, typewritten. That means about 200 words
a page, and, you know, some of that was thrown out or cut eventually; but I wrote all of that in 3 ½ months.

I had never written a full-length book before, and at first I decided I
would treat each chapter as if it were a magazine article—because I
had done that before. So I would set an artificial deadline, and I'd
make myself meet it. And I did that for three chapters. But, as in the
case of most magazine pieces that I've written, I usually ended up
staying up all night one or two nights in the last week that I wrote. It's
horrible.

Bellamy: Oh, that *is* horrible.

Wolfe: And as you get older, it's more horrible. After you finish,
you're wiped out for a week almost, because your system just can't
take it. I know mine can't. But if you're writing an article, as far as
you're concerned that's the only thing you're *ever* going to write.
You're writing *that* article and it absorbs your whole attention, and
you can do that sort of thing and survive.

But after I had done this three times and then I looked ahead and I
saw that there were *twenty-five* more times I was going to have to do
this, I couldn't face it anymore. I said, "I cannot do this, even one
more time, because there's no end to it." So I completely changed
my system, and I set up a quota for myself—of ten typewritten pages

a day. At 200 words a page that's 2,000 words, which is not, you know, an overwhelming amount. It's a good clip, but it's not overwhelming. And I found this worked much better. I had my outline done, and sometimes ten pages would get me hardly an eighth-of-an-inch along the outline. It didn't bother me. Just like working in a factory—end of ten pages I'd close my lunch pail. . . .

Bellamy: How many hours did it take you to write ten pages?

Wolfe: It varied. Sometimes—if I really knew exactly what I was going to say—I could do it in two and a half hours; but it might take me five or six hours. I usually start working in the afternoon around three, and sometimes I wouldn't finish until eleven or twelve at night. It seemed to be psychologically very important to have done at least four pages by suppertime, so that after supper I wouldn't have this horrible task in front of me.

After I finished I would turn on the television and watch late movies and do calisthenics, because I felt a real need to exercise. I remember on many nights doing sit-ups in front of the TV set, and each time as I came up from off the floor during the sit-up I'd catch a bit of the film. I never particularly missed very much by sinking back. All these horror films. All the dinosaur films, you know, and the planet films, the lost planet films. And there was always a pterodactyl and a dinosaur toppling over a cliff in my movie. It's my most vivid memory from that period.

Towards the end of the book, *The Electric Kool-Aid Acid Test,* I found I was able to up the quota. It's all downhill after a certain point. You've got it all worked out. I presume it's the same thing in writing a fiction book. I could go twenty pages many days.

Bellamy: That's a pretty good clip. Were those finished pages?

Wolfe: I was not revising very much. If I still felt fresh at all, I would correct a little bit that night. And before I started writing the next day—both to improve what I'd done the day before and to get myself into thinking about what I was going to do that day—I would go over and edit what I had done. I would type it with carbons, and toward the end I stopped the carbons; the carbons drove me crazy. To make the same corrections twice was too much, so I'd go to the duplicating service down the road—I was writing this in Virginia— and they would run it off for me. And, of course, they could run off the corrections too, done in ballpoint or pencil. And I'd mail it.

See, there was a time problem in writing that book, too. It looked as if the whole psychedelic, hippie phenomenon was disappearing. So there was pressure to just get it done. This was before Woodstock, and, you know, I *believed* people who said, "Well, nobody wants to read about this anymore." And I said, "Well, I'd better crank it out." And I'm glad I felt the pressure because it made me do it quickly.

I remember the first time I knew the book might be successful was when I found out that the girls at the duplicating service were competing to get hold of the thing as it came in, chapter by chapter. They were waiting and were reading parts aloud to each other. Early in the book I used a phrase, "transcending the bullshit." And this one guy, Hassler, in the book, keeps talking about "transcending the bullshit," and they started laughing over this. And there was a guy named George Geer, an Englishman, who was in charge of the duplicating service, and he used to say every time I'd come in the door: "Well, I expect we are gettin' a little bit more of that trans- cendant bullshit now, aren't we?" And I would laugh. I was so encouraged by the response of these girls, you know, because they didn't know that I even knew they were reading it . . . George Geer would tell me they were reading it. They were just waiting for the next installment. It so encouraged me. It really did.

Because, you know, you get in the middle of a book and you don't know what the hell you're doing. You're living off savings, and you're closed into your own mind, and you have this terrible paranoia—at least *I* did—that this could be a colossal failure. "I may have put all this time in, I may have devoted a *year* and it could be a colossal failure. What am I doing?" And you keep plugging on. And writing, unlike painting or drawing, is a process in which you *can't* tell right away whether it's successful or not. Some nights you go to bed thinking you've written some brilliant stuff, and you wake up the next morning and you realize it *is* just pure bullshit. It's terrible.

Finally, when the book came out, I got a copy and cut off the real cover, and I put on another binding myself and I drew a new cover for the book and I put on the title: *Transcendant Bullshit*. Then I sent it off with the rest of the book, the printed book and a note, to George Geer and the CDC Duplicating Service.

Bellamy: (Laughter. . . .) Did you end up using coffee, or any other sorts of stimulants to keep you going?

Wolfe: I tried. I thought this would be good. At this time I did not know about Balzac's coffee habits, but I felt that something might help. And I knew I couldn't take speed. I have no tolerance for Methedrine, for example, or any form of Methedrine, which would include Dexedrine, Benzedrine, all those things. I get so nervous I can't stand it. I just simply cannot stand it. No-Doz I cannot tolerate. I mean, that's pretty weak stuff. But I figured maybe coffee would work. Now coffee, for some reason, makes me feel very logy— except for Turkish coffee—and to start making Turkish coffee was somehow so baroque, or rather it was too much of a process to get into. I mean, you gotta buy a Turkish coffeemaker. At any rate, that didn't seem terribly feasible. I finally concluded, "I've never been able to use anything of that sort, much less anything that would really short-circuit you." Marijuana, alcohol, anything of that sort. I really think that all drugs short-circuit in some way, an interesting way sometimes, but nevertheless. . . .

Bellamy: There has been considerable talk about the changing forms and roles of fiction and nonfiction writing, and especially about the growing relatedness between the two—a change you have been as responsible as anyone for helping to bring about. Could you visualize what the predominate form of the 70s might be like? Could it still be a novel?

Wolfe: It could be, but I think we have to get rid of this idea that the novel, or the fiction form in general, is the realm of the holy beast. The only future for the novel, and a highly neglected function for it at present, is the reporting of "the way we live now," the recording of present social history, which is, after all, different from age to age. I think this function—so characteristic of the 19th century novel—is likely to make a comeback. So, I don't think there's going to be that much difference between the best novels and the best nonfiction.

It's amazing how many successful nonfiction writers still have a yearning to write a novel. I think it's because so many people grew up with that being such an overwhelmingly important form. They just can't get it out of their minds. Gay Talese has always talked about it, and I wouldn't be surprised if he didn't—well, I don't know. He may try it as his next book. I think Mailer is very distressed that he's considered a terrific journalist and a bad novelist. I'm sure it upsets him a great deal.

And it's all part of the whole idea that the novelist now is supposed to be a holy beast. He is a direct conduit from the Godhead, you know. The novelist replaces the prophet; and art replaces God; and taste replaces ethics. This is very much the modern intellectual's frame of mind; and the key link is the holy beast, the prophet, the virtuoso, the religious figure. The new Zoroasters are supposed to be, I guess, typical; and writers are affected by this counter-rational impulse. You know, if you're really hooked in with the Godhead, you're not going to be a rational figure. You're going to be an inspired figure. In fact, your lack of rationality is proof of your divinity.

Bellamy: That's interesting. Kurt Vonnegut was saying—in a symposium he attended with Barth, Fiedler and others at Brown University—that writers now either characterize themselves as thinkers or as shamans, you know, as these magical madmen. And Vonnegut said he was on the madman side, and certainly that is a very good characterization of where he is. . . .

Wolfe: The two adjectives that writers most like to have applied to them today are "brilliant" and "outrageous." All the rest, I mean, forget them. They just don't do the job. But to be brilliant and to be outrageous is to be, in effect, called a mad genius. And that's what the writer wants to be called, just as the artist wants to be.

You see someone like Claes Oldenburg objecting when an interviewer asks him what is the theory behind his work. And he will act as if: "Theory? What are you talking about? You know, don't, I mean, *don't* try to burden me with theory." Of course, the guy is acutely sophisticated, and he's thinking all the time. And I'm sure that practically everything he's done has come out of rational considerations.

This is doubly true for writers, because writing is such an artificial form—just sheer artifice from beginning to end. And for an artist, for a writer, to try to act as if he is a holy man, I think, is absurd. Because you're doing this very artificial thing: translating sounds into visual symbols which are supposed to jog the memory of the reader in various ways. And just the fact that you have to go through such an education to learn to use the medium at all means that you are a rational man by the time you get to the point where you can write. But this is part of the modern sensibility, the modern-world view of artists in all fields.

I think that the new developments are going to come from the people who'd ignore this attitude.

The novel didn't really reach this state of sanctification until the early 20s, by the way. Because before then you run into Henry James still arguing that the novel should be considered as a major form.

Bellamy: Maybe you're a similar sort of precursor. Maybe in twenty years it'll seem absurd that the nonfiction novel, or the new journalism, whatever you want to call it, was once thought to be illegitimate.

Wolfe: And some old nonfiction bellcow will be getting up at the Nobel awards and making some stupid statement, like Faulkner's: "I do not accept this for myself, but for the sweat of the human spirit . . . ," you know, this kind of thing. Well, when you hear that, you know the form is past its prime. It's become religious.

Bellamy: All that business about not accepting the end of man—I always thought that was rather optimistic of him.

Wolfe: Faulkner was an interesting figure in all of this, because he really did a lot more reporting than you would think. He did a lot of wandering around, just to pick up information, accurate details, and that sort of thing.

I think Kesey is a good example of this too. Kesey's first novel, *One Flew Over the Cuckoo's Nest,* was written after he volunteered to work in a mental ward, specifically to get material. Then he went out into logging country, specifically to get material for *Sometimes a Great Notion.* After that he was going to do a novel about a town called Davenport, California, which is down near Santa Cruz. It's a beautiful shore, the Pacific and Route 1, one really nice community after another, until suddenly it turns entirely gray. The leaves are gray, the trucks, cars, houses are gray; and it's all because the only industry in Davenport is a concrete factory. And this huge smokestack belches out this dust, such a quantity that everything is covered in the town. Kesey had been down by the shore camping out with his son. He went to a pile of debris to get some firewood, and he found a crude cross made of a couple planks nailed together, and it said: "This memorial is for all the workers of Davenport, California, who died of silicosis." Apparently, people were just dropping off like flies from breathing in that dust all day long. So he was going to get a job in a factory, or try to, and then write a book about the whole thing. But just about this time he got involved with the whole psychedelic experience [which Wolfe wrote about in *The Electric Kool-Aid Acid Test*—ed.].

Bellamy: Has Kesey wasted himself? I wonder sometimes if he might be so spaced out that he won't ever write again.

Wolfe: I don't think so. You know, I occasionally hear people say that about Kesey. I'm sure he could do whatever he wants. I think he's into very much of a religious frame of mind. In fact, he's written some very amusing things recently. His open letter to Timothy Leary, which was in *Rolling Stone*, is such a witty piece of writing, as well as being so poignant, that obviously if he wants to write, he can write. Because humor, I think, is the one thing that would be the first thing to go if a person didn't have it all going for him. Kesey, I found when I was doing this book, is constantly surrounded by people day and night; I mean, physically surrounded. I don't know how he *could* work if he continues to live that kind of life. There are so many people around him all the time who are either looking for advice, or resolution with problems, or something.

Bellamy: I notice you still seem involved in this book, *The Electric Kool-Aid Acid Test*. Has there been a measurably different response to it? Has it been more popular, for instance, than your other books?

Wolfe: Well, in fact, it has been the most popular book I've written.

Bellamy: Why do you think that is so?

Wolfe: Well, I'm glad it's true because it's the longest thing—it's really the only book-length piece of writing I've done. It's more of a sustained effort, I mean; and it tells a longer, more complicated story than anything else I've done. And also, I think the subject itself is one that's had a great effect on this country, and it continues to have a great effect. We're far from seeing the end of this psychedelic movement. It just takes so many forms.

Bellamy: What novelists interest you the most?

Wolfe: My great discovery of the last eighteen months has been Balzac. I never read anything by him before that, and I happened to read his biography first. I was struck by the fact that for twenty years, from around age thirty to age fifty, he was averaging three books a year, most of them full-length. There are a few collections in there, but most of them are novels. Sixty books—twenty years. . . .

Bellamy: And he slept five hours a night, right? He was writing all the rest of the time, something like that.

Wolfe: Well, he had very erratic hours, according to this biography. I don't remember it saying exactly how long he would sleep, but he would get up at 6 P.M., for example, and he might entertain until midnight—and then start working. And drinking all this coffee that we were talking about earlier.

Bellamy: Right.

Wolfe: And he found that the coffee didn't have its Methedrine effects, its caffeine effects, if he ate too much. So he would make a point of not eating. He would keep a bowl of fruit beside him, just to give himself some sustenance and blood sugar, and then he would have a pot of very thick coffee. Apparently, it was the thickest Turkish coffee. . . .

I really feel writers should produce a lot more than they do. . . . Balzac is an example worth thinking about. That's one trouble with the comparative ease of financial success in writing in this country. The one really successful book like *Catch-22* or *In Cold Blood* is enough to live on for the rest of your life, unless your standard of living is so high that you eat it up. And as a result, it's very easy for writers like Heller or Capote to just put off writing more and more. You start letting five years drift by between books. You don't *live* that long.

Book World—Book Week it used to be—did a very cruel thing once. They decided to do an article on all the novelists who had allowed ten or more years to elapse since their last book. So they interviewed them all; but instead of running the interviews one after another, they would put down the question and then the answers that all of them had given to this specific question. So, one question was: "Do you think that the fact that you haven't written a novel in ten years or more will hurt your literary reputation?" So Ellison says: "Well, it didn't hurt Stendahl's." And Heller says, "Well, it didn't hurt Stendahl's." And Katherine Anne Porter says, "Well, it didn't hurt

Flaubert"—a little switchoff there. The next one was back to
Stendahl again.

Bellamy: What *living* novelists interest you the most?

Wolfe: For my money, the best of the current novelists is Philip
Roth. I think he's terrific. Oddly enough, he's much more of a social
historian than anybody would usually ever think of him. Particularly,
you look at these vignettes, these setpieces, in *Letting Go* or in
Portnoy's Complaint—a picture here of the Bohemian, the aging
Bohemian, a picture of the —oh, the father sitting in the chair in
Portnoy's Complaint. He sits all day in the chair worrying about his
heart trouble and his bowel movements. Those kinds of things are
marvelous. And then the scene with the woman, the girl being
interviewed by the social worker to see if she's fit to adopt a child.
These are marvelous pieces which are real social vignettes rather than
psychological vignettes. I think *Portnoy's Complaint* will grow in
stature as the years go by. Very funny book.

You know, I ran into him on the street the day before he turned in
Portnoy's Complaint; and he told me he had sort of wanted to jog
himself into a new style, because most of his first three novels are
very much influenced by Henry James. So he read a lot of Henry
Miller! And it really worked. You know, it doesn't end up being
something that's written *like* Henry Miller. It just enabled him to break
away from his old style and into something that really has a lot of
drive and energy about it.

I can't make myself read Saul Bellow; I've tried. He leaves me flat.
Actually, I like Kerouac a lot; of course he's dead now. I just liked his
tremendous momentum. I'm a great fan of Calder Willingham's,
though he seems to have dropped out of everybody's memory
somehow. He's excellent on dialogue. Perhaps for that reason he
writes a lot of movies, but I don't think he's ever been happy as a
movie writer. There aren't very many happy movie writers.

Bellamy: Who do you think are the new journalists or nonfiction
writers now who are most worth reading—your competitors, your
colleagues, or however you wish to look at them?

Wolfe: The one who interests me the most would be Hunter
Thompson. He's developed into the greatest humorist in America. He
wrote some things for *Scanlan's*—I laugh just thinking about them,

one on the Kentucky Derby, and one on Jean-Claude Killy selling
Chevrolets. Just marvelous!

Michael Herr is a new writer who I think has written the best thing
written about Vietnam in any genre. There's surprisingly little good
stuff out of Vietnam, in a literary sense. The Herr thing is so much
better than what Mary McCarthy did. Mary McCarthy did this thing
called face-reading, where you look at people's faces and read their
faces. It's somewhat like a phrenologist reading skulls. You see what
you can tell by the vacuity of his eyesockets. This is total demoral-
ization. Every time I read this I want to go up to the writer and say,
"Talk to them, ask them a question, see what they have to say!"
Anyway, Mike Herr.

Gay Talese's work I like very much. Breslin, I think, is awfully
good. I'm afraid Breslin has just turned to the novel for good as his
main interest, which is too bad because he never really settled down
to write what might have been a major piece of nonfiction. He's done
terrific shorter things, and I hope he'll do it some day. Let's see . . .
Capote's *In Cold Blood* I liked very much. I'll be very interested in his
new book, *Answered Prayers*.

Bellamy: I'm thinking of Mailer.

Wolfe: I liked *Armies of the Night*. I thought that was a very
entertaining book. Nothing else that he has written in this form do I
find any good. I think of *Of a Fire on the Moon* as a real skull-
cracker. I can't read that book. It's so boring. You see, Mailer, for one
thing, I think, is very embarrassed. He's too embarrassed to do
reporting . . . I think he finds it awkward. You see, when you're in
the center of the action, as in a conventional memoir, his approach of
writing through his own experience works. Because there *was,* in fact,
no celebrity there in that march in *Armies of the Night* who was of
any greater magnitude than he was. This put him at the center of the
action, and so it worked. It did not work in *Of a Fire on the Moon.*

I didn't like *Miami and the Siege of Chicago* because he did not
come up with anything that anybody with a press card wouldn't have
seen. There are those who apparently thought his intracranial activity
when he looked at Humphrey or when he looked at these other
people was very interesting. It was somewhat less interesting to me
because I could envision the way such an event might be covered. I

mean, he didn't get, as I can remember, any piece of information in
the entire thing that you couldn't have gotten from the newspapers. I
don't know even one bit of information that you couldn't have gotten
if you had had a press card and been able to sit in the convention
gallery. Maybe there was an occasional interlude in a restaurant or
something. But not even much of that. So, unless he is willing to
become a reporter of some sort, I don't see that he can expand the
form.

Bellamy: I understand that you are working on a novel yourself—
called *Vanity Fair.* I gather it's an effort to do for New York in the 70s
what Thackeray did for London in the 19th century?

Wolfe: Well, I'm weighing whether this should be fiction or nonfiction, because everything in it *is* going to be based on a journalistic
reality. The question is to me a completely technical one. I think
novelists have been very much afraid of New York as a subject. You
really can't grasp it. And it's just amazing how few New York novels
there have been. You get the work of Louis Auchincloss, who deals
with a very small segment of New York. His work has been very
much like Marquand's. Of course, Marquand was dealing with
Boston. I have dealt with New York to a certain extent in nonfiction,
in articles. So now I am trying to decide how to do this book,
whether it's going to be technically better to do it as nonfiction or as
fiction.

Bellamy: You seem to be consistently interested in social
hierarchies and status strife. I would assume from the title *Vanity Fair*
that this subject is likely to continue for you.

Wolfe: I consider it such a fundamental analytical tool, really. It's
one of the first things I always look for. It's also an amazingly taboo
subject.

If I were going to stay here a little longer, I'd love to have someone
make me a social map of this town. I've done this many times. What
you do is you get an actual map of the town. The first thing you do is
shade in the area where the wealthiest, young, middle-aged doctors
live—let's say, the doctors in their early forties, maybe early fifties.
Usually this will be the most prestigious new area in town. Often
you'll find there's a prestigious old area which is made up of these
large houses left over from families who made their money before

World War I. This old section will tend to be towards the center of
town. And it may often be very close to what is now a very bad
section. I don't know—that's just an example. Then you shade in
with another colored crayon the worst section. This is usually the
black slum. Then you shade in the old, white working-class
neighborhood. Sometimes it's literally across a set of railroad tracks; it
might not be. By this time you've got sort of the high and low ends of
the hierarchy. Then you start figuring in the rest. . . .

Bellamy: Then you decide where you want to live on the map,
right?

Wolfe: No. You may fill it all in and then decide to get the hell out
of there (laughter).

Once you start getting these variations, there are all sorts of story
ideas or possible subjects if you're writing. Or if you're just looking
for magazine pieces, they'll start suggesting themselves. It's also
instructive to look for the location of the hospital or hospitals which
the rich patronize, and also the schools. Hospitals are very funny
because wealthy people tend to value their skins very highly, and
they really believe that their skins are far superior to others. In a small
town you'll often find the rich sending their sick out of town to the big
city for anything much above the level of a tonsillectomy, maybe
even for a tonsillectomy. So that's kind of nice to get a line on too. Of
course, the schools, I guess, are pretty obvious. Anyway, this
approach of looking at things through this perspective of status has its
advantages. At the very worst it can make you see the relations
between a lot of things that might otherwise not seem to be related.

Bellamy: Do you have any ideas on what you'll be doing next
after *Vanity Fair?*

Wolfe: There are a couple of long-range things that I'd eventually
like to do. One is to write a book on status, which would be to try to
make a very fundamental book expressing everything I think. It
wouldn't necessarily even fall underneath the umbrella of the new
journalism. I'd just have to start from square one, explaining it,
because I think eventually, in this brain research, they are actually
going to find a status mechanism. My prediction—and remember
you heard it here first—is that it's going to be found in a reticular
formation, which seems to be a part of the brain that is like a main
crossroads. It's all sorts of channels and a kind of funnel, a funnel

through the crossroads. The brain seems to be a great yes-no mechanism. And it's in this particular area that such a question as, "Am I hungry or not?" is decided. This center seems to process the information coming in on everything from, "Am I hungry or not?" to things such as, "Am I successful or not?"—which is much more complicated.

Brain physiology really fascinates me. There is some great stuff coming out of the current interest in brain physiology. The idea that people's minds can be controlled through this kind of research—such as these transistorized units that can be imbedded in your skull to control certain things, or a pill that can control certain things—this doesn't interest me at all. This is scare stuff. What does interest me is the horrible possibility that people might actually understand their own minds, the workings of their own minds.

Bellamy: Why would that be bad?

Wolfe: Well, I say horrible somewhat facetiously, but right now I think it's only a matter of years before people understand how, chemically, neurologically, such matters as success in a career are registered in the body. Because it all has to be registered in the body one way or another. They will understand what the libido is, you know. The libidio—you might as well call it "shocktee," or you might as well call it Thor or Wotan—because it's a completely elusive thing. The libido is just a pseudo-scientific name that Freud thought up for something. But eventually people will be able to pin all of this down, the soul for instance. All of these things that really, in a way, now feed our imaginations, keep us going, will all be pinned down. That's going to be a really, really horrifying boundary to cross. It really will be. It'll so shake people when these things are understood. Can you imagine? When the whole chess game is figured out? We know all the genetics, we know exactly what love is, we can trace it through the dendrites and the synapses and to the brainstem, and to the lateral-genicular, and so on.

Bellamy: But does physiology ever explain human behavior really? We know a lot of physiology now.

Wolfe: Well, so far it doesn't; but if it gets down to that point, it may. At that point I think that what might happen is that a certain caste of people will have exclusive rights to this knowledge, and others will be barred from it. It would be like certain taboos.

Everyone knows there is a taboo about incest, for example, but nobody ever likes to think *why* there is one, or how it might have started. They would rather not think about it at all and just accept it.

Bellamy: What was the episode that I heard occurred on Bill Buckley's *Firing Line?*

Wolfe: Well, the funny thing was, Buckley was really trying to get on a particular point, which I didn't tumble to until the end of the show. I'd have been glad to talk about it. He was saying, in effect, that there was a small clique of intellectuals in New York who determine literary reputations. And if you go against the political opinions of these people, you're in serious trouble. Well, after a while, towards the end of the show, it dawned on me what he was talking about. He was talking about the *New York Review of Books* and its constellation. But the premise simply isn't true. I mean, that clique exists, and they are very rigid, very orthodox in their thinking. But they don't have that kind of power. They're not that kind of threat to anyone's reputation. In fact, I wish he would have just come out and brought up the subject, which I would have been happy to talk about.

Because this country is very different from France, Italy, or England in terms of literary reputation. In each of those countries it's true that there are really just about a thousand people, the same thousand over and over again, who make or break literary reputations, particularly in France. Well, Italy's just as bad, and England's not much better. It's just not so in America. In America the number of people who read, who read serious books, is so much greater than in any of those countries and so much more widespread. You probably get more literate people, in the sense of people who are interested in books and read serious books, in the city of Los Angeles than you do in any of those three countries that I mentioned if you add them all together. So it's not that small a world.

Of course, Buckley was very delighted with *Radical Chic,* and with *Mau-Mauing the Flak Catchers* for that matter. So I think he wanted me to come out and say: "Yes, there is a cabal of evil intellectuals who do this and that thing," which I just wasn't prepared to say.

Bellamy: How do you like living in New York? Being from the provinces, I suppose you could be called a non-native. . . .

Wolfe: I still find New York exciting, to tell the truth. It's not the greatest way to live in the world, but I still get a terrific kick out of riding down Park Avenue in a cab at 2:30 in the morning and seeing the glass buildings all around. I have a real cornball attitude towards it, I suppose, which I think only somebody born far away from there would still have. It's still the ambition capital; it has that going for it. Also, if you're writing for a magazine, such as I have done, or for that matter if you're in publishing of almost any sort, it's kind of a company town, too.

Bellamy: Do you think those sorts of connections are essential for a writer? Do you have to live in New York to be a writer, do you think?

Wolfe: No, I don't think that has much to do with it. The best thing it can do for you is just simply fire up your ambition, or keep you working. Because there are so many people around you all the time, hustling to make it in their careers; and they're so intolerant of the lack of success. It does sort of keep you working in a way, but there's certainly no reason why anybody should have to be there to write—unless you're working exclusively for certain magazines. That's a different story, because they tend to give assignments to people they can call up on the telephone. There's no reason why they should do that, because they can call up people in another city; but it's just a state of mind they get into.

Bellamy: Do you think it necessary—as a nonfiction writer—to have an agent?

Wolfe: I don't think you need an agent until you have a book contract to deal with. An agent's not going to help you much—in nonfiction—in getting a piece published. An agent can help you in fiction, because the magazines tend not to pay as much attention to fiction that comes in over the transom, as they say. They'll read it. Oh, somebody will read it. It won't go unnoticed. But if a well-known agent says they have a terrific new writer of short stories they'd like for you to look at, they'll really pay attention to it. It's not true in nonfiction.

Bellamy: One last question: Why *do* you travel around giving lectures?

Wolfe: Well, I don't really do it that much. I give about twelve a year. I will not discount the economic factor. That's certainly a part of it. I also find, though, that the questions that you're asked at a college—and most of the talks I give are at colleges—do a great deal more for you than the questions that you get anywhere else. A student will tend to ask very wide open questions, very basic questions; whereas sometimes older people, whether they're in New York or wherever, tend to be more polite, or they're afraid to ask a question that might seem naive.

For example, once I was asked the question: "Why do you write?"—which really spun me around; because I didn't have any ready answer for it. It really made me think. And the answer I came up with after standing mute at the podium for about thirty seconds, which seemed like an eternity—suddenly, it just popped into my mind—was something from the Presbyterian catechism, which I hadn't looked at since I was seven or eight, I guess. The first question was, "Who created the heaven and the earth?" And the answer was "God." The next question was, "Why did he do it?" And then there was this marvelous answer, which was "For His own glory." You know, that's really something. I don't know—it just jumped into my head. And suddenly I realized that that's probably the only honest answer for "Why do you write?" And after I started thinking about that I also saw that the only possible source of objectivity in writing is that you would be so much more concerned with how you handle the materials than you would with the issues involved, the subjects that you're writing about, that you could end up with a kind of egotistic objectivity. I guess there isn't much other kind.

I see this happening when I read particularly Dostoyevsky, who always started a book with some moral stance that he wanted to demonstrate. He would start in with this in mind, but then he'd get so involved with his characters; he'd be so anxious to make them come alive, that this would take over his entire imagination; and after a while it would be rather irrelevant, this moralistic idea that he was talking about. The same thing happened in Balzac. Balzac was a conservative who was to write conservative pamphlets, but his work ended up doing more to bring on the revolution of 1848 than that of any other writer because he gave such a devastating picture of the decadence of the French bourgeoisie.

Tom Wolfe and the Painted Word
William F. Buckley, Jr./1975

This is the transcript of an interview taped for *Firing Line* in New York City on 9 July 1975, and originally telecast on PBS on 19 July 1975. Used with permission of Southern Educational Communications Association.

Buckley: Tom Wolfe has written another book and mocked another icon. This book, called *The Painted Word,* is a moustache painted in broad daylight on the *Mona Lisa,* and some people are not going to forgive him ever. To go after Leonard Bernstein and modern art in one lifetime is to stretch the bounds of the First Amendment beyond the point intended. Mr. Wolfe has shouted fire in a crowded theater. Most of the people are laughing about it because one cannot read Wolfe without laughing. But although his book has been called a masterpiece by the *Washington Post,* for instance, some of the critics have sworn an eternal hostility to him. In their criticisms they would appear to score on one point. I say they would appear to score because it is true that there is no internal evidence in *The Painted Word* that Tom Wolfe is himself a connoisseur of art or that he has read deeply into art history, though he may have done so and decided for editorial reasons not to encumber his thesis with that knowledge. He is speaking, after all, about a social phenomenon, the hold of a few art critics on art fashion and the grotesqueries to which a middle class is willing to submit in order to distinguish itself from the philistia whence it came.

Tom Wolfe is actually himself a Ph.D. in American studies from Yale University. Before that he went to Washington and Lee. Before that he was a schoolboy in Richmond, Virginia. After college he went into journalism, here and there hitting the big scene as an innovator of the new journalism in 1965, when he published an essay on what they do out in California to cars the owners want to customize. That essay was the lead in his first collection, *The Kandy-Kolored Tangerine-Flake Streamline Baby.* Then came *The Pump House Gang, Radical Chic & Mau-Mauing the Flak Catchers,* and now *The Painted Word.*

I should like to begin by asking Mr. Wolfe, why did you choose to devote so little time to the work of the artists mentioned in your book?

Wolfe: The book is really a social comedy—to me the comic process by which fashion can enter into the world of art just the way it can enter into the world of hem lengths—and to me it really wasn't necessary to like or dislike a single work of art or a single artist in order to point this out. And I think in a way this is what has gotten under the skin of more critics and art historians than anything else. The one thing they're not prepared to deal with is the process by which art becomes serious, the process by which it becomes praised, and so on.

Buckley: Well, but it is true that in making sport of the people who made certain of these painters famous you in effect suggested to the reader that charlatanry was at work. Now, if you have a charlatan, let's say a blind man who is actually arguing the qualities of Da Vinci, you somewhere along the line, normally speaking, drop a footnote to that effect, don't you, that although they are primarily flax and although they are playing on certain weaknesses in the buying public, nevertheless they're talking about genius? Did you feel that they were, or did you feel that for obstinate disciplinary reasons you were going to require the reader to be ignorant of your own opinion of the artists that they encouraged?

Wolfe: Well, you see, I don't really even call them charlatans, and, you know, they're really quite ready to deal with the idea that you say that there's a conspiracy or that there's fraud and they're fakes and that there're people who get together in a room somewhere who are deciding to put over Jackson Pollock or de Kooning or whoever. This isn't what I'm saying. I'm saying something really much more devastating, I think, which is that they believe in what happened. I think it's a much more catastrophic thing to have happen to you—to believe in what happens to you when your head is in the sand—than to be accused of having conspired. At least if you were accused of conspiring there's a certain dignity implying that you're the master of the situation and that you're in control of what has gone on. I'm not even saying that that happened. I'm saying that it's really a religious thing.

One thing I didn't say in *The Painted Word* that I should have said

is that art today is the religion of the educated classes. And I don't
mean that by analogy, that it's like being a Baptist in 1870. It is being
a Baptist in 1870.

Buckley: You said that in 1965 in the *Saturday Evening Post,* and
I think you're right, though you used the word "culture."

Wolfe: I didn't say it in *The Painted Word,* unfortunately. I wish I
had.

Buckley: You used the word "culture."

Wolfe: Yes.

Buckley: Well, actually, let's focus for a moment, if we may, on
sort of three categories here. One is the critics. Specifically in your
book are Clement Rosenberg and Harold Rosenberg—

Wolfe: Clement Greenberg.

Buckley: Clement Greenberg, sure.

Wolfe: Yes, that's right.

Buckley: And Harold—

Wolfe: Rosenberg.

Buckley: —Rosenberg and Leo— Now you've got me all mixed
up.

Wolfe: Steinberg.

Buckley: Steinberg, yes. Now, the second is the artists whose
eminence is associated with their patronage. And the third is the
people who bought. Now, for the third you have, I take it, nothing
but contempt because you feel that by and large you are discussing a
class of people whose gullibility here is yet one more attempt to atone
for their quick wealth, and that under the circumstances they
distinguish themselves from the philistine class by following the lead
of somebody like Clement Greenberg. Now, am I correct so far?

Wolfe: In fact, it isn't an attack on any of the three. It describes
what they have done. They've all chosen to find it an attack except
for the critics, which I think illustrates something, and it is that the
critics are really, in effect, flattered by all of this. You don't hear
Clement Greenberg shouting out, "This is a lie!" you know, "What
this man has said is terrible!" because he's been, in a way, established as the Samuel Johnson of his time. There are very few critics
who dominate their age in any field of art. Samuel Johnson is really
one of the few exceptions. Clement Greenberg is another exception.
Although Clement Greenberg doesn't like to have his theories made

sport of as I have done, I'm sure that he's also extremely happy that
he's been placed in this particular position. I mean, what more could
a critic ask for?

Buckley: Well—

Wolfe: All right. With that exception, go ahead with what you were
saying a moment ago.

Buckley: Well, I asked you several years ago in connection with
your book about the Black Panthers and the party given for them at
Leonard Bernstein's house whether you felt any obligation in that
book to reveal where your own attachments were—to the dissenters
or to the establishment class or to the pseudo-establishment class—
and what you said in answer to that question was, "I really don't
care. I mean, it's not a way I'm able to approach a subject like this. I
know it's a very typical way of approaching a subject like this and
many writers today either approach a subject out of compassion or
out of some kind of moral or political motivation. To me, it's really
beside the point." I take it that it's beside the point whether you
happen personally to admire the art of the principal beneficiaries of
the muscle of these identified and identifiable critics, right? In other
words, is it fair to say that nobody, on reading *The Painted Word*,
could himself with any authority say Wolfe does or does not enjoy
the work of de Kooning?

Wolfe: It really shouldn't matter. And this is the one thing that art
historians and art critics are not used to dealing with. Art history is
very much an amateur sport which has not developed since the 17th
century. And, you know, this could be very easily demonstrated
because the key thing in art history as opposed to political history or
most other types of histories is that values are always uppermost.
Whether a certain painter or sculptor is good or bad is the key
question. And this is also true of literary history by and large.
Whether someone is good or bad is the key thing; all else sort of trails
off from that. And once you establish the fact that Melville is a good
writer, then you can go into Melville's life and the times that Melville
lived in and so on. And the same is true in painting. Once you
establish that so and so is a good painter—that Pollock is a good
painter or for that matter that El Greco who was established as a
good painter very late in his posterity, not even in his lifetime—then
you can go into the rest of it. The idea of going into art history

without waving your standard of good and bad is something that nobody in the field wants to deal with because this makes it a field much like any other. A historian, after all, a political historian, doesn't have to like or dislike Napoleon in order to study Napoleon or the Napoleonic Era or even Napoleon III.

Buckley: No, but a historian of Napoleon has to convey to the reader something of Napoleon's vision, not necessarily compassionately but at least informatively. Now, it is the position of many of the critics of your book that you don't convey their theories about what these artists tried to do, less because you are being petulant than because you don't know. Now, you either don't know—I'm reading here between the lines—because you have no appetite to know, no curiosity, or because you have a tin eye. And this is something that a lot of people try to understand about you because you do in fact withhold any communication about Napoleon's vision.

Wolfe: Well, first of all, just to start with Napoleon as you did—

Buckley: As you did.

(laughter)

Wolfe: Very few historians that I'm acquainted with, and perhaps you are acquainted with those, really cared anything about Napoleon's vision other than the fact that he had a vision of a communications system in a battle situation. Now, that's a vision, but I don't know how much of a vision it is.

Buckley: Well, he changed the law in the whole continent—

Wolfe: Which?

Buckley: —in the 19th century, codified it. And lawyers are still living off his legal vision even in New Orleans.

Wolfe: Well, I'm not acquainted with historians who approach this as a vision. I've seen those who say, "This is an extension of Napoleon's ego," saying that his idea of law should— Well, to get into the— You've, I think, elided two subjects when you get into art: one, what I like or don't like, which I'm perfectly willing to go into.

Buckley: But not to theorize on?

Wolfe: And you also mentioned the theories of the artists involved, which I think raises more questions than it answers, and the idea of what I know about the particular artist. Now, I think that at the very least you should separate what anybody knows about a particular artist and his career, and what he thinks.

Buckley: I'm not trying to be bad mannered about this, you understand.

Wolfe: No, I understand. But I think these are all things that have to kind of be separated out because within the world of art itself—Cultureburg, as I call it, the *beau* hamlet—these are things that nobody wants to separate. Nobody wants to sort these questions out because this really makes you look at the process. You know, nobody wants to look at the process.

Buckley: Well, when you say nobody wants to look at the process you're talking now about people on the bandwagon, I think, aren't you? They would much rather buy and admire and invoke the authority of Clement Greenberg for admiring a particular piece of art than understand it, right? They don't desire to examine either the aesthetic process or the social process which you analyzed. However, I find people like Kramer—who is the *corpus vile* in your book, at least one of his statements—pretty convincing in his final answer to you, which is a little bit wordy but maybe I better read the whole of it. It's only three sentences. "In Tom Wolfe's world it is comical even to entertain a theory of art, comical perhaps even to create a work of art that attempts to modify consciousness and alter our views of experience. It is this fundamental incomprehension of the role of criticism in the life of art, this enmity to the function of theory in the creation of culture, that identifies *The Painted Word*, despite its knowingness and fun, as a philistine utterance, an act of revenge against a quality of mind it cannot begin to encompass and must therefore treat as a preposterous joke."

Wolfe: Oh, well, actually the first sentence of that is a very good example of what I'm talking about. In other words, to criticize theory—that's what my book does—to criticize theory since 1943— I really start with '43. That's really when the Jackson Pollock Consummation took place. To criticize theory since 1943—or to make sport of it, is really more like it because in fact I even say it's beautiful because it's amazing and, you know, wonderful to behold and so forth—becomes equivalent in Kramer's language to disliking theory *in toto* and to looking down on theory *in toto*. And I've seen this crop up again and again in the furor that's arisen over this book: To be against this segment of theory is to be against all theory. Nothing can be further from the truth.

What delights me— And I do actually use the somewhat ironic expression, I will admit, "beautiful" for Greenberg's theories. I think they are beautiful! And the reason they are beautiful is that they turned art into a game of Jeopardy. I think the game of Jeopardy is played by giving someone the answer to a question and then they have to give you the question. And this is what art became after 1945. The paintings became the answer—it's a puzzle picture—to the question. Start with Abstract Expressionism; Pop Art was the same thing; Minimal Art, Op Art, Conceptual Art and so on. And then you had to know the question to complete the game. Now, this is something, despite the demurs of many, many people within the field of art— It's absolutely a new situation. There's never been a situation before in which you have to say, "Yes, but what's the theory?" when you look at a painting or a piece of sculpture. This has *never* happened before in the history of art.

Buckley: No. I understand, but I also understand the critics not to be saying—unless you read Hilton Kramer's original provocation for saying this—that artists can't arrive on the scene simply as a result of an exuberant serendipity which people can then go on successfully or unsuccessfully to assimilate into a fashionable theory of art. They understand you to disdain any effort at constructing a theory that explains, for instance, the inclinations of a generation of artists—

Wolfe: Oh, not at all.

Buckley: —but you simply deny it. You just flatly deny it.

Wolfe: That isn't what I say at all. I mean, the theory really should come after. And theory should be welcome—or it doesn't really matter when it takes place. But for an artist— You see, the implied criticism in all this is really on the artists. It's saying that artists willingly—and believe me, I've known so many examples personally since I've lived in New York of artists who quite willingly gave up their own vision, their own best techniques, their own uniqueness of any sort, in order—

Buckley: To kiss critical ass.

Wolfe: Yes. I didn't condense it in quite that way in the book, but that's— Although with—

Buckley: Just a form of careerism.

Wolfe: No. This is what I— Kissing ass indicates absolute careerism of the worst sort.

Buckley: Yes.

Wolfe: It isn't that at all. It is that partially, and I shouldn't say that it's all. It's what I call double-tracking in which you hold your finger up into the wind; you see which way the wind is blowing; you appraise your own work; you do not then say, "I'm going to deliberately go the way the wind is blowing"—

Buckley: But you're not going to go in the opposite direction.

Wolfe: —you say, "I'm going to look at my work again."

Buckley: I see.

Wolfe: And then you take down your finger and you begin looking at your work. And it may take you a couple of years, but suddenly, however it's done, your work is going in that direction. And really sometimes there's more pathos than I've indicated. I've had artists who I thought were really quite talented tell me, you know, "It is impossible for me to show this kind of work anymore or try to show this kind of work anymore." And I say, "Well, why is it impossible?" "Well, it just is an impossible thing." They can't get off of this word "impossible" which absolves them of any responsibility in the thing.

Buckley: Well, would you think that there was a musical analogy there? The great musicians of the 18th and 19th centuries were many of them criticized by prominent critics and went unrecognized but nevertheless continued to write—you and I are busy thinking of the same people—the way they wanted to write, and were not in fact influenced to crawl back into the mold because that's what the local prince wanted to hear. Now, what is it that is the distinctive catalyst of the current preposterous situation? The wealthy class and its insecurity?

Wolfe: It's the fact that in art as opposed to most of music, most of literature—

Buckley: It's easy to con.

Wolfe: —the situation hasn't changed since the era you were describing. There was a time when all the arts existed in the courts, and serious art was inseparable from court art in every field. Now, this began to change in the 19th century, most strikingly in literature when the novel became so popular and at the same time such a spectacular form of art. This absolutely broke literature wide open, and then you had suddenly the thing called the reading public—that phrase was an invention of the 19th century—in which you had millions of people buying books.

Buckley: It's own arbiters.

Wolfe: And having this huge—as they say in economics— undifferentiated mass of consumers began to change critical standards even in literature. In music it took place through records. In drama it took place through popular stage and movies. Movies have changed drama drastically. This has never happened in art. In art to this day, there is probably no— The art world is very little bigger— I'd say maybe perhaps by 1500 people larger than it was in 1720.

Buckley: Well, how do you handle Malraux's thesis that because of the high state of reproduction in art it in fact has become like music and literature and that all museums are now without walls?

Wolfe: This is obviously not true. There is a marvelous essay by Arthur Koestler on snobbery. One of his great examples of snobbery is the young couple who as a wedding present were given what they thought was a reproduction of a Picasso lithograph. You know, this is number one of 720,000 published in Akron. They put this underneath the staircase. A famous art dealer happened to come to dinner. He looked. He said, "My god! You've got one of the original five taken off the stone!" It then went over the fireplace in the living room. Well now, everyone knows in even their own lives examples of why this simply isn't true in art. I think if you had a copy of a book by Edmund Wilson and in a fit of pique were so furious with this book—

Buckley: I can think of the one.

(laughter)

Wolfe: —that you threw it into the fire, some people might say, "Bookburner," but most people would say, "For chrissake, he bought the book, and if he wants to destroy it he can." That's because it's a mass-produced item. I have often wondered— In art, if some collector bought, let's say, a Frank Stella and then discovered that the pattern was exactly the same on the wallpaper in his mistress's house in East Hampton, and in a fit of pique he destroyed the painting, I think there would be a howl such as you wouldn't believe for this sort of destruction because it is so important to have the original. There's so much magic still existing in art to have the original by the artists.

Buckley: Oh, you mean this is even if the painting you speak of has been reproduced.

Wolfe: Right.

Buckley: Yes. Well, I don't think that's really all that odd. Suppose somebody destroyed the original of the Declaration of Independence. God knows there are enough copies of it lying around. But there is something about the holographic copy that—

Wolfe: Right. We're again talking about religion.

Buckley: But you're talking about a museum instinct.

Wolfe: But we're talking about religion.

Buckley: I'm glad you brought the subject up because it seems to me that some of your critics succeed when they say that what you're doing is drawing a caricature of a situation which is easy to caricature without paying attention—

Wolfe: But which they had not bothered to caricature.

Buckley: Oh, yes, yes, yes. That is a very nice point. It's easy except nobody's ever succeeded—but which is intrinsically comic if you deprive it of its inherent sacredness. It seems to me plain, for instance, that the wedding ceremony, the coronation, the Christian funeral service, the bar mitzvah, or whatever are terribly, terribly easy—I say terribly easy. You've got to assume that somebody has the skills—to parody unless you accept certain axioms about it. If in fact the Host is the Incarnation or if in fact there is a sacramental union between the man and the woman, if in fact the corpse is being dispatched in some formal way to another existence, then you treat the funeral and the wedding and the ordination in a slightly different way. Now, they're really saying about you that you're so carried away by the ease with which you, given your skills—very few of them deny your skills—can caricature the situation that you don't pause to examine what it is that a Clement Greenberg has accomplished or what it is that he may have done for a Jackson Pollock that might otherwise have been undone.

Wolfe: Well, the fact that even in devil's advocacy that you can equate these various rituals that have existed—well, for 3000 years that we know about and probably more than that—with art, with Clement Greenberg and Jackson Pollock is in itself a marvelous form of evidence of what I'm talking about.

Buckley: Well, why? Becase you consider it profane or because you consider it unbalanced?

Wolfe: Well, I'm again just—

Buckley: Because I—

Wolfe: —a lowly social historian. Forty years ago it would have been inconceivable that devotion to art would be equated with devotion to the Upland Baptist Church.

Buckley: Well, no.

Wolfe: Well, not inconceivable, but it would not be a usual thing. When Mrs. E. Parmallee Prentice died—she lived on East 53rd Street and had two adjoining town houses—she left these two town houses to the Museum of Modern Art. The Museum of Modern Art then built the new wing of the Museum of Modern Art, which was one of the great social events in New York of 1964. It seemed absolutely appropriate when she died—I think it was about 1959—that she should leave this parcel of real estate—which was worth about $1.5 million at that time; God knows what it's worth now—to the Museum of Modern Art.

Buckley: To Cultureburg. Yes.

Wolfe: Fifty years ago it would have been inconceivable that she would have left it to anyone except the church down the corner where she went, at 53rd and Fifth Avenue, because there was, even in New York, once an institution known as tithing in which people of great social esteem gave 10 percent of their incomes to the church. Well, this has all shifted into the arena of art today, so that it really becomes absolutely plausible to equate a funeral service or a bar mitzvah or a wedding or any of these things with—

Buckley: I think you're skirting on dangerous ground here because part of your book insists that the enthusiasm for art is synthetic. The real people go to rock and roll stuff. You say—

Wolfe: Oh, no, no, no. Not—

Buckley: Not the real people but the quantity of people. You say that in your last closing parts of your book.

Wolfe: No, not even a line. Not even so much as a phrase.

Buckley: Well, I'm sorry. I'm sorry. You said that in your *Saturday Evening Post* piece.

Wolfe: No, I doubt that I even said it there.

Buckley: Well—

Wolfe: Your memory of my *Saturday Evening Post* piece is much better than mine.

Buckley: Well, it's three hours old. (laughter) But the—

Wolfe: Mine goes through the century.

Buckley: —fact of the matter is that the free marketplace took into account in 1964 that there were bulging museums and empty churches and under the circumstances—

Wolfe: You're absolutely right.

Buckley: —you quite legitimately take into account if you are, you know, inclined to philanthropy what it is that most needs philanthropizing. Is that right? What most needs help?

Wolfe: Well, it's what most puts your foot in the door of heaven, and—

Buckley: Well, that's another consideration, I agree.

Wolfe: —today, what most puts your foot in the door of heaven is giving to art.

Buckley: Yes.

Wolfe: And in fact art today fulfills the two historical functions of religion apart from matters of theology. One is for the rich the legitimation of wealth. Just as tithing used to put your foot in the door of heaven, giving to art will do today. And for people without money, it's the established form of religious abnegation of the world. Now, I'm one of the few people that I know who rides the subway often. And it's marvelous any morning, particularly on the West Side—

Buckley: Line.

Wolfe: —IRT, to get on there and, when the meat spigot is turned on full tilt and everyone is elbow to rib and shank to flank and haunch to paunch and all the rest of it, and you think you can't survive another second, to look over at a seat and see a young lady or a young man who seems to be enveloped in an absolute pink shell, absolutely apart from all of this, absolutely unaffected by it. You always see in his or her lap a book by Herman Hesse or Kierkegaard or Martin Buber or someone of that stature, and you get the picture immediately. And this individual is saying, "I may be in this rat race, I may be headed for my job as file clerk or bank clerk or stenographer, but I'm not *of* it. I am *of* the world of culture and cultivation." You can even see their room at this point. You can see the monk's cloth and you see the—

Buckley: But when you say it, even in the manner in which you say it—is that a vacuum word?—it's not plain whether you mean to say that it's genuine or not.

Wolfe: Oh, I think it is.

Buckley: For instance, in the case of John F. Kennedy, you say that when he had to sit down and listen to Pablo Casals he was in physical torture, and I think the probability is that you are correct. Still, he was doing the right thing in the same sense that the Queen of England, when she goes to the museum every ten years, is doing the right thing. But you did say, "This is all great, i.e., the hegemony of the new religion, except that the American people have always had a great talent for not giving a damn about what their spiritual leaders expect them to do. They have taken their money and their free time and started expressing themselves in highly visible ways that are having much more impact than anything that is going on in culture. Their music has been rock and roll. Their dance has been the twist. Their theater has been the movies. Their sculpture has been California custom cars. Their kinetic art has been the electric signs of Las Vegas." You sound like Nabokov, by the way.

Wolfe: Oh, I don't mind that company. I don't endorse it wholeheartedly. There I was specifically talking about the culture centers such as Lincoln Center, the ones in Los Angeles and all over the country in which public land has actually been appropriated in the name of high culture. In fact the last segment of the masses of the people that actually attends a concert at Lincoln Center, let's say, is the night that the wives, children, and members of the Brotherhood of Operating Engineers are invited to the dress rehearsal. It's the last time that they show up. Nevertheless millions are actually expended in the name of the public. Now, that is somewhat different from what is going on in art except that within the world of art it's always important to have as devil figure these millions of people in the country who are denouncing, causing to whither away, or otherwise assaulting the artists and keeping them from having their just desserts as—

Buckley: What would be the musical analogy in that?

Wolfe: I'm really much less well acquainted with music. Now, there is the field of serious music still. The tone was set really by 12-tone music, dodecaphonic music, of Schoenberg and others.

Buckley: That's experimental music, not serious. It could be both but—

Wolfe: I think you're right.

Buckley: —it's primarily experimental.

Wolfe: I think it was considered serious when it was done.

Buckley: Yes.

Wolfe: There is a corner of modern music to which the same things might apply, but I think it's only a corner. I'm sure you could find the same thing in drama. You'd have to look awfully hard in the field of drama to find it and perhaps in literature, if we get into what I call the neo-fabulism in the novel in which finally you have to set up a fiction collective in order to get your works published. And some of these things exist in a small way in other fields, but in art—

Buckley: A drama's regulated by the expense in its production, right? I.e., it has to attempt to be more appealing because you can buy a canvas for $10 but you've got to put up $100,000 to stage a play.

Wolfe: Well, it's even gone beyond that into movies. It's the technology more than anything. The technology has changed it. Mass production of books was a technology. Now, the technology of reproduction in art never went over despite Malraux's statement. It just simply never went over.

Buckley: By which you mean what? That it was not popular?

Wolfe: It wasn't popular. It was not accepted as a true reproduction. Now, a book can be accepted as a true reproduction of a manuscript. You could make a very esoteric argument that the manuscript has something more in it, as many libraries do. But the book is usually accepted as a pretty fair copy. This is not true in art, and actually if you look at reproductions you can see that the reproductions don't have certain qualities of the original. You can't see the paint. You can't see certain colors. And this has kept the magical quality of art alive. But attached to all of this is the mythology that critics and art historians have wanted to keep alive. I think that's why so few art critics today know any art history. They seem to have taken a survey course, probably the one that the Museum of Modern Art sends out and John Russell wrote. I was absolutely astounded to read in— I think quite apart from whether it redounds to my glory or not, I think one of the nice things that's come out of this whole furor over this book is the way it has smoked out certain unbelievable assumptions and beliefs on the part of people who really should know a great deal and who know very little. I mention Franz Kline in the book. So the art critic of *Time* magazine takes my reference to— I mention, you know, that Franz Kline once did pictures of social realism, of unemployed Negroes, ex-servicemen—

Buckley: And he says that you were thinking of somebody else.

Wolfe: —and he says, "In fact, Franz Kline never painted such pictures." The first thing I was taught on the *Springfield Union* when I started in journalism was never to use the word "never." It always leads you into serious trouble.

Buckley: It's unsafe, yes.

Wolfe: You shouldn't use the word "always" either. That was another word you couldn't use. Well, I have sent off to *Time* magazine a copy of— I fortunately was able to find both in it, an unemployed Negro and a crippled ex-serviceman (laughter) which I hope they will print. But for a critic of *Time* magazine not to know that Franz Kline, who was famous as an Abstract Expressionist, went through a realistic period including a period of social realism, seems to me unbelievable because I'm not an art critic or an art historian— although I did get into this field somewhat in graduate school—but this seems to me to be just one of the things that along the way you just simply notice. It is incredible to me that a man who's the art critic of *Time* magazine—that's one of the leading magazines in the country—doesn't know something like this. Or John Russell, who is the second-string art critic of the *New York Times,* began a piece in which he said, "Art and ideas are one." Now, I must give him credit for this. If you ever have a preposterous statement to make, and I offer this as a suggestion to anyone who has something they know to be preposterous they have to get off, say it in five words or less, because we're always used to five-word sentences as being the gospel truth. Usually it's in a novel and someone says, "His pants leg was torn." Well, you accept that. His pants leg was torn, for God's sake. I mean, you know, you don't dwell on it. And usually short sentences give you a statement that you can accept and pass. But, "Art and ideas are one"! This encapsulates the argument of my book about modern criticism.

Buckley: Yes.

Wolfe: Even on the most physical level, art and ideas are not one.

Art is made up of objects. Ideas are in the realm of philosophy. But on a higher plane, art wouldn't exist if it were not supra-rational, if it were not above the rational, above the realm of ideas.

Buckley: Extra, anyway.

Wolfe: Or extras, and I'm avoiding the word "irrational," because that's not the point.

Buckley: Yes, yes. Extra-rational.

Wolfe: It goes straight to your memory bank; and it affects it in a way that ideas don't, just as music does if it's good. We're assuming talent here. And so to say that art and ideas are one is preposterous on the face of it. Even Russell seems to realize this, because he then says, "Of course it's possible to enjoy," although he puts "enjoy" in quotes, which I rather like, "a painting without knowing the theory behind it, just as it is possible to 'enjoy' a kabuki play without knowing Japanese." Already you're getting into language where—

Buckley: (laughing) He just repealed his dictum.

Wolfe: Yes.

Buckley: Yes.

Wolfe: And then he's realized that something has gone badly astray in this whole thing and so he then says, "The history of art is a subdivision of the history of ideas." Already we're into the history of art rather than—

Buckley: Art.

Wolfe: —art. Well, I think it's important that this has been smoked out, that someone can say that art and ideas are one, because that is really what the book says in a nutshell, that they have become one and it's an unnatural alliance.

Buckley: Miss Frances Barth is an artist who has exhibited in New York, continues to do so, and is teaching now at Princeton. Miss Barth.

Barth: I don't think I know where to begin. I think that when you said earlier today that practically all of the response or all of the response that you know about against this essay, book, is the uncomfortableness of everyone dealing with theory, or art criticism, or whatever— The outrage that I personally have heard among the people that I know is not at all about that. It has nothing to do with criticism. I think that in the book there are lots of worthwhile avenues to investigate. I think one of the problems is that they're not investigated, and I think that the book isn't just about theory or art criticism. It's really about painting, and your disparagement of all the artists that you mentioned, in terms of their sincerity, their honesty, their goals, why they paint, is incredibly irresponsible.

Wolfe: Well, I don't think you can give me a single example of criticism either of the paintings themselves or the motives of a single artist.

Barth: I think when you say that all the artists from 1943 and through the Fifties, the people who happen to be the Abstract Expressionists or second-generation Abstract Expressionists, were painting according to theory, which you state, that the idea comes first and they're illustrators of the theory is not a true statement. I mean, I think that we can sit here and sort of argue about that, but I don't think it will get anywhere.

Wolfe: Oh, I think it might get quite a mess— I'll give you an example of Franz Kline whom we mentioned earlier. In 1949, Franz Kline was with a friend who had some slides of drawings that Franz Kline had done. And he was a realist up to that point. It was shown up on a screen, which made it very large, and the friend said, "You know, if you'd just put a square around this part, you'd have a marvelous Abstract Expressionist painting." And this was the beginning of Abstract Expressionism for Franz Kline. Now, this is not to say that this was a conspiracy and the two said, "Let's get together and have you make it, Franz," this sort of thing. But he was responding to a critical climate. I think that's unquestionable.

Barth: Well, I think that we all respond somewhat to a critical climate, but an anecdote does not make a truth, and —

Wolfe: Well, you suggested illustrations, but go ahead.

Barth: —well, one case— I mean, like, I think that the whole book is a characterization. And it's very humorous. It's very funny. It's very witty. It's very clever. But it seems that perhaps the cleverness of the article is doing for literature what the theories you imply were doing for painting.

Buckley: Well—

Wolfe: Well, I think— Go ahead.

Buckley: Let's rest with that which I think is more of a judgment than a question, and move on to Mr. Tony Robbin, also an artist, who teaches art history and is a writer for *Art News*. Mr. Robbin.

Robbin: I have a passage here where you do criticize artists' motives. You say, "The artist's payoff in this ritual is obvious enough. He stands to gain precisely what Freud says are the goals of the artist: fame, money, and beautiful lovers." I agree with Frances that this book is filled with half-truths. You accuse us all of having the worst possible motives. You support it by illogical arguments and inaccurate reporting. The half-truths are supposed motives. The illogical arguments, Mr. Buckley referred to. You prove all this by saying that some critics write nonsense about art. Saying that proves nothing. And I think what's worse is the inaccurate reporting. You accuse us of following the critical stance of the critics. But Abstract Expressionism was well set, completely defined, long before the "Action Painting" article by Rosenberg, which was in September of '52. I noticed the dates are missing from your book, and that's important. And the same is true of Pop Art, that Johns and Oldenberg and Rauschenberg, you know, had completely developed the idea of Pop Art long before flatness or any other critical support of it. And Minimal Art was, you know, first worked out by Held and Kelly and Bladen in the early Fifties. This is 15 years before Greenberg's statement of flatness in any definitive form. And it is not true on the basis of the facts that artists are following the lead of critics.

Wolfe: Well, if you're formerly editor of *Art News* I hesitate to accuse you of poor reporting, but I think you— Well, first of all in my own book I start with the year 1943 with Peggy Guggenheim and Pollock and Greenberg. And no one said anything that affected this thing 15 years before Clement Greenberg, believe me or believe anyone you care to go to on that score. Greenberg was talking about flatness long before the 1950s. Greenberg set the tone that then Rosenberg picked up in 1952. Nothing would have happened with Johns and Rauschenberg without critical support in 1959, and I can go on and on. I have the uncanny feeling that I can cite chapter and verse better than the people in the field. This is one of the things that bothers me about art reporting in this period.

Robbin: The art came first in every case. And, you know, after it was published, perhaps then the money came. But the art came first. It's not true that artists are following critical stances.

Wolfe: Well, why did Clement Greenberg go around lower Manhattan saying "Rothco has joined; Kline has joined," and so on if people were not following standards that were being set up? What I'm saying is I really think you are mistaken on that. I think you're loyal, but I think you're mistaken.

Buckley: Mr. David Hickey is an art dealer and a critic and a former editor of *Art in America*. Mr. Hickey.

Hickey: Well, first, I don't really see the historical point, I don't see the difference in the social exclusive convention, say, in contemporary art. I don't see how that differs, say, from the elaborate iconography of a Joshua Reynolds which served the same sort of social purpose. You had to have a classical education in order to perceive the art. That is, this particular aspect of beaux-arts I don't see as particularly new. That kind of function of an exclusive, finite commodity market is not unusual.

But I would like to ask you. I mean, like you're a reader and like— I mean you've met some of these artists—Johns, Rauschenberg, and these people. Do you really think that men of this intelligence and sophistication could actually be seduced by Greenberg's sort of primitive discourse? I mean, do you actually believe that they believed it? I mean, that's just an opinion.

Wolfe: Well, now, the people you mentioned were Johns, Rauschenberg, and—

Hickey: Yes. I exclude the innocence of the Abstract Expressionists. That is, do you really think that most artists are so unsophisticated as to be drawn in by the sort of things that are written in art magazines?

Wolfe: Most, yes.

Hickey: Do you?

Wolfe: I don't think, though, that again it's a careerist sort of thing. I don't think it's a situation in which they sit down and say, "Tonight I'm going to sit down and do such and such in order to gain critical acclaim."

Hickey: But that would be all right, wouldn't it? I mean, you don't have to be nice to be good.

Wolfe: Well, whether it's right— Whether it's all right or not all right doesn't bother me, but—

Hickey: I mean, what I'm saying is not implying that there's something wrong with careerism. Right.

Wolfe: —again I'm trying to describe what happened. And I doubt that there are many artists who are immune to this whole process that we are talking about, as most people in the world are not immune to this sort of thing in their own fields. It is the rare individual who I think decides to go in the opposite direction of the Freight Train of History, to use the metaphor that I used in the book. And it would seem to me that this would be the sort of individual that people within the world of art would have a special eye for. In fact they don't.

Hickey: Well, would you think then that there are Rembrandts tucked away at the University of Wisconsin?

Wolfe: If they are, we'll never know about it—

Hickey: Well, I've looked at a lot of them.

Wolfe: —because they never appear in the pages of *Art News, Art in America,* or *Art Forum.*

Hickey: No, but would you say this is really possible?

Wolfe: Of course it's—

Hickey: That is, you know—

Wolfe: Well, you know, at Yale Art School there are very small studios tucked away on the third and fourth floors of buildings; God knows what goes on up there. It may be true. And I think that if one thing could come out of all this, it might be that there would be critical chaos. It would be the best possible thing that could happen for all of these artists that you mentioned who are tucked away here and there, so that standards will fricassee, so that all of the people who have any sort of a vision of their own could come forth and let it be seen and possibly noticed.

Hickey: Well, in essence isn't that the situation today? I mean, certainly if Greenberg were not so vulnerable— I mean, you know, that is, you're a professional amateur. I mean, if that discourse is that vulnerable, then it's pretty obvious that he's not autocratic.

Wolfe: Well, I hope it is. I don't think that Clement Greenberg, for example, any longer has a hold. He's somewhat retired from the battle. I hope you're right. I hope it has reached that particular point. I hope the art world itself has weakened so that it is not a little hamlet as I described it and might be a broad plane that all sorts of people can walk out upon.

Hickey: Well, it's all right, though. People don't have to like it though, do they?

Wolfe: (laughing) I've never said that for a second.

Hickey: No. That is, you seemed as if you felt deprived if you didn't like it.

Wolfe: Oh, not at all. Not at all.

Hickey: I mean, that's one of the great privileges, you know, that you don't have to like it at all.

Wolfe: We finally agree 100 percent.

Buckley: Miss Barth.

Barth: My questions have more to do with caricatures than— Well, there's one sentence that you said that—I can't remember which artist it was who is leaning down over the painting and looking up and, you know, trying to see that the paint was into the canvas and stuff like that reminds me of a very bad biography of Monet where Monet turns to Clemenseau and says, "It's like you were there." And I suppose it's a valid part of satire, but it seems to me that people who read this, people who read it in *Harper's,* who buy magazines—which is a broader base according to you than people who go to museums—tend to believe everything they read in this. I mean, if one needs knowledge or theory to look at a painting, don't you think that one also needs knowledge to be able to read through this book and determine where you're wrong, what's satire, what's truth, you know, what the balance is in this?

Wolfe: You're talking about Morris Louis lying down and painting—

Barth: Yes.

Wolfe: —and looking across the surface. Well, now you happen to have picked an instance in which I was there. I worked in Washington on the *Washington Post* at the time, just after Morris Louis began what was known as the Washington School. And Morris Louis did—

Barth: Okay. I mean—

Wolfe: —used to do this. So I purposely chose something that I did know about.

Barth: But, I mean, can you honestly say that throughout this, you know, this business of— I mean, it's rampant with illustrations like that. I mean, we could go through it page by page and—

Wolfe: Well, I wish you would because I can honestly vouch for every single one of them.

Barth: Okay. Clement Greenberg says to Pollock, "You're

terrific." I mean, were you there? Were you witnessing the conversation between Pollock and Greenberg?

Buckley: Well, he said it in print.

Barth: But there's a whole atmosphere of he says to him, this person says to this person, then, oh, yes, the flash, the balloon goes up in the comic strip, I'm going to go out and I'm going to lay up this paint, and I'm going to do this and—

Wolfe: Well, the second example you've cited, the relationship between Greenberg and Pollock, all appears in great detail in B. H. Friedman's book about Jackson Pollock.

Barth: Yes. I know. I know.

Wolfe: And Friedman was a friend of both men. He seems to be an honorable man, and I assume that he didn't make these things up. I would love, I mean, if we had the time that you or anyone else would go instance by instance by instance through the piece.

Barth: Okay.

Wolfe: I really welcome that.

Buckley: We have only a minute and a half. Maybe Mr. Robbin has an instance he wants to challenge you on.

Robbin: No, I don't have an instance, but I would like to say that I think the critical world is starting to self-destruct in the ways that you and Dave were describing. And, you know, we're cleaning our own house. The only trouble with your doing it is that you're from the literary world, and as Dore Ashton and Irv Sandler make clear in their book, there has been since 1900 a prejudice against painting and painters on the part of literary people. And this is something that we suffer from and I think it's something that you suffer from, too. This wasn't the case in France where the best novelists and the best literary critics were also art critics, were also active participants in it. And I think that your book, coming from where it does, will further enhance that prejudice rather than break it down.

Buckley: You have 15 seconds.

Wolfe: I really think that artists could benefit a great deal from what I have written because I do not tell them what they should do and I do not pass judgment on any single artist. It describes a process that I really think artists should know about and be able to deal with because it talks about the relationship between art and fashion.

Buckley: Thank you very much, Mr. Wolfe, and thank you, ladies and gentlemen of the panel. Thank you all.

Wolfe Foresees a Religious "Great Awakening"
Philip Nobile/1975

From *Richmond Times-Dispatch,* 17 August 1975, sec. F, 1.
Reprinted with permission of United Press International, Copyright 1975, and with permission of Philip Nobile.

Tom Wolfe is called America's most famous journalist. And well he should be since he founded the popular school of New Journalism. This ex-semipro first baseman with a penchant for white suits also invented a lively prose style of his own that seemed perfectly consonant with the roaring Sixties.

But despite three best-sellers to his credit, Wolfe is not everyone's taste. There are more than a few critics who rue the day he wrote his first sentence. The highbrows dislike this courtly native son of Richmond for his parody of the *New Yorker,* his lampoon of leftist celebrities in *Radical Chic,* and lately for his satire of the New York art crowd in *The Painted Word.*

Wolfe laughs it off. You can't really hurt a guy who dresses like a Good Humor man all year 'round.

Q. First I must ask you: why do you affect those crazy white suits?

A: In 1962 I was in a tailor shop and had a conventional summer suit made from some white silk tweed that impressed me. But the suit was too hot for the summer. Then I began wearing it in December.

People became annoyed by the sight of a white suit in winter. (Those were innocent times in 1962.) Soon I discovered I had this marvelous, harmless form of aggression going for me. So I branched out into white suits with double-vested weskits and rows of white-covered buttons. Getting dressed in the morning was suddenly fun.

Q: Why do your critics despise you so? What have you done to merit such contempt?

A: Intellectuals aren't used to being written about. When they aren't taken seriously and become part of the human comedy, they have a tendency to squeal like weenies over an open fire. I knew what I was in for, but it was irresistible.

95

Q: What quality, what quirk, what flaw in your subjects brings out your uncharitable instincts?

A: The blindness of people who think they see all. That's what makes it funny and, if written accurately, what makes it hurt.

For example, it never occurred to Leonard Bernstein that there could be anything humorous about the spectacle of the Black Panthers outlining their ten-point revolutionary program in his 13-room duplex on Park Avenue.

Q: Have you ever been involved in an incident with gentlemen you have savaged in print? In the small world of Manhattan litterateurs, you must bump into your enemies frequently.

A: I ran into a "New Yorker" writer once at a party. He said to me, "I promised myself if I ever met you, I'd punch you in the nose." "And?" I replied, after sizing him up. "Well," he said, "I guess I'm just not the type."

I may be tempting fate by saying this, but nobody in New York has ever gotten hurt in a literary fist fight, including Ernest Hemingway.

Q: Where did you find your style—the dots, the exclamation points, the onomatopoeia, the internal dialogues with yourself?

A: It happened one night as I typed up notes for an *Esquire* piece on stock car racing which became *Kandy-Colored Tangerine–Flake Streamline Baby*. I realized what I had done was what many people often do in letters. By the way, many people are excellent letter writers. But the same persons tend to freeze when writing for publication. We censor out our emotions and best phrases so as not to reveal too much of ourselves. I simply learned not to censor out the things that run through my mind as I write.

Q: One of your detractors told me that he pitied you because you weren't "serious" about serious matters like the state of the nation.

A: In many ways, since I don't mind putting myself in good company, I feel like Balzac. He was a great supporter of the old order in France. Yet there's probably not a single French writer who did more to bring on the French Revolution of 1848. That's because he was totally engrossed in his characters.

As a result, Balzac's portraits of the decaying nobility and upper bourgeoisie were absolutely devastating. The polemicists of his day, in contrast, are forgotten.

Q: You mean if you had it to do all over again, you'd still devote yourself to the marginalia of American society?

A: The subjects I wrote about were the major history of the Sixties. Changes in the way people lived will turn out to be more significant than Vietnam and the assassinations. As a newspaper man, I was over and over again drawn to this part of life.

For instance, in 1961 I was a Latin American correspondent for the *Washington Post,* but always preferred doing stories on items like escaped apes. To me this was really more fascinating than taking Rafael Trujillo's latest press release down to the cable office in Santo Domingo.

Q: If you were in the same pop frame of mind nowadays, what would you write about? Have people's lives changed in the Seventies?

A: Not very much. Plenty of things have become part of the landscape and aren't news anymore. For example, the extraordinary ways of dressing in the Sixties are now standard.

If you walk down the street in New York, you may see a couple emerging from a co-op wearing tie-dyed pre-faded bell-bottomed Levis with aluminum studs up the outseam who happen to be the owners of a $175,000 apartment upstairs. The legacy of the hippie movement has blended into the scenery.

Q: There's nothing new in the Seventies?

A: Yes, there are, and maybe I'm the one who should write about them. There's a religious movement in the country that I call the Third Great Awakening. The First Great Awakening occurred during the American revolution, according to historians. The Second Great Awakening produced Mormonism and many evangelical sects that accompanied the settlement of the West.

The current awakening consists of psychedelic communes, Synanon, encounter groups, the oriental religions, the Jesus people, the charismatic branches of the Catholic and Protestant churches; plus the ESP phenomenon and even the UFO believers are essentially religious. It might be worth discovering where all this is headed.

Q: You don't seem given to self-celebrity like many best-selling authors. What do you do to keep yourself out of the columns?

A: I get questionnaires for various reference books. But I can never figure out what to put down under "hobbies and recreation." I've always wanted to write "hunting and fishing," or maybe "catamaraning."

Finally, I decided to be honest and put down "window-shopping." When I got the proof back, the editors had stricken the line. They thought I was joking. In fact, window-shopping is my hobby. To me, New York is still the state fair.

Tom Wolfe: In Big League as a Writer

Peter Gorner/1976

From *Chicago Tribune,* 7 December 1976, Sec. 2, 1-2. Copyrighted, Chicago Tribune Company, all rights reserved, used with permission.

If he'd only had a decent fast ball, Tom Wolfe would have missed the 1960s.

No "Wowie!" style New Journalism guru "Poet Laureate of Pop" Edwardian suits big byline-big bucks for him. No decade of brilliant journalistic performances ranging from *The Kandy-Kolored Tangerine-Flake Streamline Baby* to his recent *The Me Decade and the Third Great Awakening.* America would have lost one of its wittiest and most controversial social commentators to some remote farm club outpost of the National League.

It may already be forgotten that Wolfe founded an eccentric style which a whole generation of journalists has tried to emulate. His immortal story about California's custom car cult sang of a new journalism—"There Goes (Varoom! Varoom!) That Kandy-Kolored (Thphhhhhh!) Tangerine-Flake Streamline Baby (Rahghh!) Around the Bend (Brummmmmmmmmmmmmmmm)"—which tried to take the reader *there.*

And Wolfe, himself, still is there. His latest fascination is the wave of religious fundamentalism that has swept the land, "and this one has the mightiest, holiest roll of all, the beat that goes . . . ME . . . ME . . . ME . . . ME . . . " But this time, let's talk about him.

At 45, Thomas Kennerly Wolfe, Jr., is a bachelor, tall and slim, soft-spoken and nice. "I was very serious about baseball," he says. "This country really is made up of half failed athletes and half women. That's what America is. I went to Washington and Lee University and played semipro ball around Virginia. When I was 22, I headed for the New York Giants training camp. After two days, I was cut. I couldn't believe it. I had a great assortment of junk screwballs, sliders, and even a fork ball. I lacked a fast ball, though. It was my tragic flaw."

Shattered, he proceeded to Yale, traded five bleak years for a doctorate in American studies, and decided to become a bohemian.

"To be a bohemian in those days, you took a low-rent job, and I became a truck loader in an office equipment warehouse. I always wore a turtleneck sweater with a striped shirt over it, and rolled my sleeves up so the sweater sleeves showed down below. But those great insights you're supposed to get from proletarian life escaped me.

"Mainly, I'd end up each day sitting in a bar cheating the company by drinking Utica beer and watching the record hop on television. In those days, the girls wore pleated skirts and their dancing was hypnotic. It was like a stroboscopic effect, sitting drinking Utica beer and watching the pleats. . . ."

So until he could get a teaching job, he got a newspaper job. As he described it, "Chicago, 1928, was the general idea . . . drunken reporters standing on a ledge of the *Daily News* building urinating into the Chicago River at dawn . . . nights down at the saloon listening to 'Back of the Yards' being sung by a baritone who was only a lonely blind bulldyke with lumps of milk for eyes. . . ."

Stints at the Springfield (Mass.) *Union* and *Washington Post* finally led him to the *New York Herald-Tribune,* which was just like his dreams ("wreckage and exhaustion everywhere"). You had to be brave in those halcyon days at the *Herald-Tribune.* With the likes of Clay Felker and Jimmy Breslin and Dick Schaap battling Michael Mok at the *Daily News* and Gay Talese at the *Times,* you had to fight to be noticed. And Wolfe, more than anything else, wanted to be noticed.

As a heavyweight writer on the Sunday magazine, he got noticed fast. "The supplements in those days were like brain candy," he says. "If a story didn't grab the reader right away, he threw it away. So I'd wait to see how a story would be laid out, and I'd count the space on the front page. Then I'd begin my story by repeating the word 'HERNIA' over and over (to mimic the sound of a Las Vegas roulette wheel). If it took me 58 repetitions to get past the front page, I'd do it. I figured anyone whom I could get to turn the page probably would finish the piece. Looking back, I probably did far too much overstating because I thought journalism was too understated. But I got noticed."

To Wolfe, New York was like a state fair, and still is. His favorite hobby, which he says nobody believes, is window-shopping. He couldn't understand why no big-time novelist came to *do* society in

the 1960s—"the social tableau, manners, and morals, the whole
business of 'The Way We Live Now.' Manners and morals were the
history of the '60s." New York, he found, was "pandemonium with a
big grin on."

"It was," he wrote, "a universe of creamy 45-year-old fashionable
fatties with walnut-shell eyes out on the giblet slab wearing the hip-
huggers and the minis and the Little Egypt eyes and the sideburns
and the boots and the bells and the love beads, doing the Watusi and
the Funky Broadway and jiggling and grinning and sweating and
sweating and grinning and jiggling until the onset of dawn or saline
depletion, whichever came first . . . it was a hulking carnival!"

But no novelist ever came to challenge Wolfe, and he wrote like
crazy. People said he was brilliant. Urbane. Suave. Trenchant.
Objective. Empathetic. He became a court favorite at *Esquire* and
New York magazines. Along, too, came a stable of enemies who said
Wolfe was snotty, and racist, and made up quotes. He was (*gork!*) a
chameleon who instantly adopted the coloration of whomever he was
writing about.

"Exactly! Perfect! You've got it!" he trumpeted back. "Do it. Do
IT!" And countless journalists did it, often badly, but the tools are on
the table now; the narrative techniques, detailed interviewing, heavy
use of color, scene, and dialog, everybody knows them now. The
New Journalism is no longer new. Wolfe doesn't like to talk about it
any more.

"But compare the stories Woodward and Bernstein wrote for the
Washington Post with *All the President's Men.* They covered the same
ground, but one is written in the very rigid, investigative journalistic
style. Today, it's practically unreadable. The same material then is
converted in the form of the New Journalism and becomes a
compelling narrative. So it is almost a perfect demonstration of my
main point: It is not the subject matter, but the techniques, that were
really at issue."

As he moved into the 1970s, each major Wolfe piece became an
event. His style, though, has settled down considerably, perhaps as a
reflection of the times. "Nothing's new any more," he says. "The
word 'pop' became the curse of my life. I was a pop journalist, a pop
sociologist, all of which was fine until I realized that what was really
meant by a pop is trivial.

"When I came along, Warhol was a pop painter, Merce Cunningham the pop dancer; there were pop singers galore, and they needed a pop writer to fill out the set. So that was me. I've been trying to get rid of that adjective ever since, but it probably will dog me the rest of my days."

Wolfe's latest book is *Mauve Gloves & Madmen, Clutter & Vine* (Farrar, Straus and Giroux, $8.95) and it reflects his remorseless ear, X-ray vision, panache, and wit in a variety of stories, sketches, and essays.

His next major project is a massive biography of the astronauts. Each day he dons suit and vest and sits at his typewriter ("I dress formally, I guess, so that I can feel what I'm doing is important") to do his stint for the day. He also does a lot of hopping around with his Royal Canadian Air Force exercises.

"Then at night, I go out and see somebody," he says. "I like to keep up on what's going on."

The Earthling and the Astronauts

Adrianne Blue/1979

From *Washington Post Book World*, 9 September 1979, p. 9.
Reprinted with permission. © The Washington Post.

There has never ever been anything cosmic in Tom Wolfe's assessments of humankind. "If I would do a story on the president, I'd just be interested to know what the daily life of the plain man from Georgia is like. What the kicks are," Wolfe says in the Virginia-gentleman voice that matches his antebellum-beau apparel so perfectly.

"I have a feeling that the reason presidents always run again has nothing to do with a sense of destiny or devotion to party or love of country. It has to do with limousines," Wolfe says. "With being treated like a baby—or a king, depending on how you look at it. With having private elevators. And breakfast is always waiting for the president. Even for a senator it's marvelous. But for a president—you could be the worst president who ever came along, and people will still jump all day for you."

So, in 1972, when Tom Wolfe began his down-to-earth chronicle of the nativity of NASA's Project Mercury, he was not hampered by awe of the voyage into the Unknown, nor was he seeking any Great Abstractions. "I was interested in who do you get to sit on top of these enormous rockets, on top of really enormous amounts of liquid oxygen. Highly volatile stuff. The Saturn 5, as I remember, was 36 stories high. You just light a match and varoom! it goes up. My god, I wondered, how do they sit there?"

Rolling Stone had sent Wolfe to report on the launch of the last moon shot, and in three frenetic weeks, he wrote the four magazine articles which three other books and seven years later became the basis of *The Right Stuff.* "I was going to convert that series into a book very quickly—so I decided to make it a study of what goes into the making of an astronaut. I very quickly found out that there's nothing really very unique about the background of astronauts," Wolfe says.

Twenty of the first 23 astronauts happened to be first sons. But Wolfe, a first son himself, didn't put much stock in that factor. Like most of the astronauts, Wolfe was also a WASP whose early obsessions included baseball batting averages. Of course, going intellectual—he had gotten himself a PhD in American Studies at Yale—was a fairly serious deviation from the flying-jock pattern. But Wolfe never deluded himself—he was no candidate for the top of any rocket.

Nearly all of the astronauts were test pilots. "So there you go," Wolfe says. "The way to approach it was to find out what test pilots were like—and this led to the whole theory of 'the right stuff.' "

Wolfe crisscrossed the continent to talk to test pilots and ex-test pilots, former astronauts and failed astronauts—to the whole conscientious and highly conservative brotherhood. The right stuff, he discovered, was an amalgam of stamina, guts, fast neural synapses and old-fashioned hellraising—military macho which had been emboldened by the exigencies of the cold war.

But it wasn't until late 1977 that he was able to sit down and begin a draft of *The Right Stuff*. "Originally the book was going to go through the whole space program up to Skylab, but I finally got up to 450 pages and I said that's it, I think I've got a book."

Wolfe also had a hunch about the nature of bravery. "I'm now convinced that physical bravery only happens in a social context. There has to be a sphere of people, a fraternity which sets standards and whose approval is all-important to you—and there has to be no honorable alternative to bravery," he says. "Otherwise you're just not going to have brave people."

That finding, of course, contrasts sharply with the shape of Wolfe's own career—and the dissonance just may be the reason for Wolfe's writer's block toward *The Right Stuff*. Fame—figuratively an upgrading from cerebral corporal to captain—came when he decided to break away from the conventions of the newspaper fraternity. It was then that he joined (some say led) the rebellion of the new journalists and began substituting exclamation points and utterly un-homeric catalogues (all the pimples, blackheads and festering sores of everyday life) for the standard, bland lead paragraphs full of manly who-what-wheres.

After a three-year stint at *The Washington Post*—"a typical story would be nine inches, about 360 words. Writing to that length was really bad for you, for your mind"—Wolfe emigrated to Manhattan. There *Esquire* let him run on to 10,000 words for "There Goes (Varoom! Varoom!) That Kandy-Kolored, Tangerine-Flake Baby." On his first assignment as a feature writer for the now-defunct *Herald Tribune* Wolfe asked the city editor how long he wanted the story to be. "The city editor looked at me like I was crazy and said, 'What do you mean how long do I want it?' I said, 'Do you want six graphs? 10 graphs?' and he said, 'Just stop when it gets boring.' "

That was 1962. Now at 48, Tom Wolfe frequently looks back. But he'll never go back. "New York is still the company town for writers," he says. "If you want to be in the towel business, you should go to Kannapolis, North Carolina. If you want to write, you should join the other cottage weavers in New York."

New York is, after all, the most pockmarked and populated city in America, and Wolfe is at his barbed best when he is writing the real stuff about Manhattanites. That, clearly, is more natural to him than speculating on the aspects of eternity. "Space exploration really doesn't excite me in the slightest," Wolfe says. And he means it. "In science-fiction books, wherever a spaceship lands, there's always some superior civilization. If they're not superior morally and mentally, they have some extraordinary physical powers that earthlings can't deal with. Well, I have a feeling that the opposite is true—that there's really not much out there."

Down to Earth with Tom Wolfe
William Overend/1979

From *Los Angeles Times*, 19 October 1979, sec. 4, 1, 14–15.
Reprinted with permission.

There's this enormously important decision you have to make at
some point while you're talking to Tom Wolfe. It's in the back of your
mind all the time you sit there scribbling notes about his latest book
and trying to get some kind of feel for him. *Are you going to ask him
about his wardrobe or not?* The whole rundown, the way Wolfe has
done himself so many times? What kind of suit? What color socks?
Underwear?

After all, this isn't just another interview with somebody on the
book circuit. This is some kind of weird journalistic ritual where, as
often as not, the interviewer feels this unspoken pressure to . . .
what's the best way to put it, copy the guy? Try for the hundredth
time to do another Wolfe parody. Squeeze in every microscopic
detail, just the way HE does?

There's a built-in danger to that, of course. To put it simply,
nobody can do it quite the way Wolfe does, although half the feature
writers around have tried at some time. For some reason, certain
Wolfe tricks . . . those VARROOM! VAARRROOOOMMS! for example . . . just don't fit in somebody else's stories. Maybe the imitation
becomes too blatant . . .

But no point dwelling on all that. Here he is now, sitting in the
patio outside his room at the Beverly Hills Hotel, the man who
introduced a generation of journalists to long paragraphs, the heavy
use of italics and the joy of exclamation points. He's wearing shoes,
socks, a shirt and tie and a suit. They all look pretty expensive . . .

Varroom.

His new book is called *The Right Stuff.* It's about the beginnings of
the U.S. space program, from the test pilots who flew the first
supersonic planes to the seven original astronauts selected for Project
Mercury in the early '60s. Once again Wolfe is trying to do what he

always does with a subject—turn it around and get a fresh angle on it.

Wolfe, however, had some problems this time, not only with some of the critics who have suggested the subject is boring no matter who is writing about it, but also in actually finishing the manuscript. He originally planned to take the book through the Gemini and Apollo programs, but found the whole thing was more than he'd bargained for.

"I really learned the meaning of writer's block on this thing," he says. "It's fear . . . How can I bring this subject alive? As it was I spent six years on it. I would do almost anything at times to avoid working on it . . . which may be the reason I published three other books during that period."

Almost everything Wolfe has written, the very way he writes, has been controversial. But in conversation, he comes across as soft-spoken, slightly remote without rubbing that Yale background in, and possibly just a little bit on guard, having played the game himself so many times from the other side.

There's also a tone of modesty.

"If you're bored, you're bored," he responds to one critic's comment that he had a hard time finishing the book. "I can only say I'm sorry."

He adds he's rather happy with the book, although his own Wolfe favorites were Radical Chic & Mau-Mauing the Flak Catchers, published in 1970. This time around he "worked harder on structure" than before and "worried less" about style.

Wolfe has the look of a scholar about him as he sits there in his fancy duds. But he comes across as friendly, sometimes even a little bit shy. Book tours put the observer in the position of being the observed, and he seems to have mixed feelings about it all.

"It's rather good for your vanity . . . but it's exhausting in a strange way," he says. "Your mind slowly turns to jelly . . . It's the sound of your own voice. At first it's intoxicating. But let's say there's a day where you have a lot of radio interviews . . . Your voice begins to sound a bit eerie, and sometimes you tend to drift off . . .

"In many ways I'm the incurable Southern gentleman," he says, referring to his Virginia boyhood, when asked to describe himself. "That doesn't put you on any special plane because the South

produces gentlemen a mile a minute . . . This can tend to soften
things, though . . . I'm sure my ego is as big as any other writer's, but
a real Southern gentleman isn't supposed to reveal his arrogance or
his ambitions."

It's been 14 years since the publication of Wolfe's first book, *The
Kandy-Kolored Tangerine-Flake Streamline Baby.* He's 49, married
for the first time just this May. He and his wife, Sheila, the art director
for *Harper's,* lead a quiet life, as Wolfe tells it. They live on the East
Side in New York, and they work a lot.

"I've had people who want to do stories about a day in the life of a
writer," he says. "I don't think it would be very interesting . . . I stay
at home all day, and walk around the typewriter from time to time.
As a diversion, I'll go window-shopping. That's really my only hobby.
I'm like a kid looking at store windows."

Most of his friends are journalists, he says. But maybe he's too
much the observer to be part of any special New York clique.

"I'd like to have a crowd," he says. "I'd feel better . . . It's
reassuring to have a crowd . . . I'm not a misogynist, but I guess I am
a loner."

A basic theme of Wolfe's new book is that "the right stuff" in the
exclusive world of the test pilot and astronaut involved a willingness
to face death for a worthy cause and not make a big deal about it.

Some critics have expressed disappointment that Wolfe's writing
isn't as uniformly flamboyant as in past works, but he responds that
he felt it was best to try to capture the tone of the people he was
writing about.

Not that there aren't all kinds of examples to show that the dean of
New Journalism is alive and well . . . One is his description of Muroc
Field, later to become Edwards Air Force Base, in the late '40s and
early '50s, during the earliest days of supersonic tests . . .

"Muroc was up in the high elevations of the Mojave Desert," he
writes. "It looked like some fossil landscape that had long since been
left behind by the rest of terrestrial evolution . . . Other than
sagebrush the only vegetation was Joshua trees, twisted freaks of the
plant world that looked like a cross between cactus and Japanese
bonsai. They had a dark petrified green color and horribly crippled
branches. At dusk the Joshua trees stood out in silhouette on the
fossil wasteland like some arthritic nightmare . . ."

It was deadly business testing supersonic aircraft, and Wolfe records how the test pilots looked down on the first astronauts. They wouldn't even be flying the space capsules, as the test pilots saw it. They'd just be riding in them, like the chimpanzee named Ham who was, if you want to be technical about it, the first U.S. astronaut of all.

But to the surprise of the test pilots, there wasn't the least bit of interest in whether the seven men chosen for the Mercury program were the best fliers around. All the public and the press seemed to care about, Wolfe says, was whether the astronauts were afraid of getting killed up there on top of those rockets blowing them out into space to salvage the country's reputation in the post-Sputnik years.

Nobody anticipated the media interest in the astronauts, which made them instant heroes. Not even NASA officials. Wolfe describes the first news conference at which Alan Shepard, John Glenn and the others were introduced. Photographers were converging on them even before their names had been read, he says. Of course, he spices it up a bit:

". . . all these grim little crawling beggar figures began advancing toward them, elbowing and hipping one another out of the way, growling and muttering, but never looking at each other, since they had their cameras screwed into their eye sockets . . . like a swarm of root weevils which, no matter how much energy they might expend in all directions trying to muscle one another out of the way, keep their craving beaks homed in on the juicy stuff that the whole swarm has sensed—until they were all over them within inches of their faces in some cases, poking their mechanical beaks into everything but their belly buttons."

Wolfe concludes that the astronauts, like the test pilots before them, were made of "the right stuff." In researching the book, he interviewed 35 to 40 of them, and he says he basically liked a lot of them. In general, he is much more impressed with the way the astronauts handled fame and hero status than the way it was thrust on them by the media.

Which brings the subject around to just how well the New Journalism is faring these days . . .

"I keep hearing things about it, but I never saw many newspapers do it," he says. "I really worry about newspapers, I really do . . ."

His own debut was something of a fluke, Wolfe concedes. He was doing "fairly conventional" stuff for the *New York Herald-Tribune* when he received an assignment for *Esquire* to do a piece about California car customizers. But as deadline approached, he was having problems writing it, at which point an editor decided to publish his *notes* and the Wolfe style—VARROOM! VAAR-ROOMM!—came roaring into view . . .

For a few years, things got out of hand. Everything Wolfe wrote—even the typographical errors—was dutifully set in type. Nobody could really tell what was a mistake and what was intentional. Needless to say, any writer who could bamboozle editors in such a fashion became an immediate hero himself to other writers who weren't quite so lucky.

"At the risk of being immodest, I suppose I'm probably the most parodied writer in the last 15 years," Wolfe says. "But I don't see that much of it anymore. It's flattering in a way. Of course, other people can use your style and debase the currency . . . "

Actually, he took a vow in 1973 never to discuss the New Journalism again, Wolfe adds. Conceding the less frenzied tone of his latest effort, he admits that maybe he's "shifting gears" himself.

So far he's only published one attempt at fiction—a short story called "The Commercial." But his next major project may be a "Vanity Fair sort of novel about New York," he says. But he also has a book of drawings coming out, will be finishing a piece on architecture soon, and is also tempted to try his hand at books on U.S. high schools and "the new religions."

"I've been thinking about the novel for some time now," he says.

"Of course, there are a few people who have suggested I've been doing fiction all along."

Tom Wolfe Examines Why "The New Left Disappeared"

U.S. News & World Report/1979

From *U.S. News & World Report*, 5 November 1979, 68–69.
Copyright, 5 November 1979, U.S. News & World Report. Reprinted with permission.

An accomplished artist as well as writer, Wolfe is the author of eight books on subjects ranging from race-car drivers to New York society's flirtation with radical causes. His most recent work, *The Right Stuff,* explores the lives of America's first astronauts. In this conversation, he discusses the rise of the "Bourbon Louis period" in this country.

We don't have any universal heroes

We still have heroes in America, although not in the sense of national heroes. We only have national heroes when there is a real external threat to the country.

In the case of the astronauts, who certainly were heroes, the threat was the cold war. It's hard to remember now how much of a threat the cold war seemed. That was why the first seven astronauts were instant heroes and why the astronauts selected later, when the cold war had faded, were not.

Ethnic and racial heroes exist today. All you have to do is go to a closed-circuit-television showing of a Muhammad Ali fight and you will quickly find out that he is a real hero to colored peoples of all sorts.

We don't seem to have any universal heroes. I don't think of show-business and sports figures as heroic, except in the case of Ali, who actually represents a great deal more than just sports. But I think there would be a great flood of heroes coming up if we really thought the country was in danger.

It seems easy to go backwards in the arts

I look upon the arts as one of the chief areas that disproves our assumption about constant progress. We're so used to progress in the scientific and technical side of things, we often think there's going to be progress in every area. In fact, it seems to be very easy to go backwards in the arts.

I'll just mention two areas that I'm personally interested in:

One is caricature. I do a page of caricature every month in *Harper's* magazine, and I'm acutely aware that caricature has reached its lowest ebb in the last hundred years. The reason is that most artists today are no longer trained in many fields, as they once were—in anatomy, architecture and landscapes, just to mention three.

Those who couldn't make a go of it in the higher forms of painting would make a living doing illustrations and caricatures. They tended to be awfully good at it because you cannot do caricature well unless you can deal with human form, human raiment and the trappings of rooms and buildings. Now many art schools do not emphasize such broad studies, and the result is that we have a very sad lot of caricaturists, over all.

The last little obedient colony of Europe

In literature, something similar has happened. Realism in fiction was mainly an invention of the 18th century, when writers began to portray the everyday life of all types of people with detailed attention to dialogue and natural surroundings. It turned out to have a power that no other written literature had ever had. The most sophisticated British critic of his day, Lord Jeffrey, confessed to having broken down and cried upon reading of the death of Little Nell in *The Old Curiosity Shop* by Charles Dickens.

Now, you don't have to like Dickens or *The Old Curiosity Shop* to see the power of a form using realism that can actually move people to tears. But many writers have given up realism in the novel. That is like an engineer saying: "We've been using electricity for a hundred years. We're going to do something else from now on."

Since the second World War, there's been a fashion reigning in the universities, where most writers come from, that has turned away from realism and has begun what I think of as the "new fabulism." In that form, you tell modern fables, usually nihilistic in tone. There are many talented writers operating in this area—people like John Gardner, John Barth and Thomas Pynchon. I think they've put themselves in a corner. They're using a tenth of the wattage that is available with realism.

I'm just getting ready to write a sequel to *The Painted Word,* which will deal with architecture and serious music, and a little with dance and philosophy. In all of these areas, as with painting, I think, for the past 40 to 60 years artists have been devoting all of their talents not to some vision that they themselves have had but to theoretical concepts that usually came from Europe. When it comes to the arts, we're the last little obedient colony of Europe. In architecture, for example, we have often looked toward Europe for the lead, ignoring even great American architects like Frank Lloyd Wright and Louis Sullivan.

The European intellectuals who fled to the United States in the '30s were bowed down to—like white gods in jungle movies of that period. This country, which seemed so maverick and self-confident in almost every other area, was intellectually timid in the arts.

Black Panthers, the Weatherman and radical chic

There is no more radical-chic society.

The people who were involved in what I call radical chic were always much more interested in the chic part than the radical part. They were not anxious to endure the heat if it became unpleasant. So they were quite ready to jettison the Black Panthers or the Weatherman or any of those groups when it became known that they were supporting those causes.

Unnoticed: A "most important" dropout

In 1970, the New Left disappeared within six months. The New Left had reached a kind of second great peak of power in 1970 after the shootings at Kent State and the invasion of Cambodia. Many leaders of the student movement of that time were saying they were going to take a very active part in the congressional elections in the fall of 1970. But they didn't; they just faded from sight.

Since then, there has really been no left in the United States. The only thing you really find is the antinuclear movement. But even that is very broad based, including many people who 10 years ago were simply referred to as conservationists. It also attracts those with left-wing sympathies. But there really is no left. This is one of the most important things that's happened in the 1970s, and yet very little note has been made of it.

"Fading intellectual antagonism" in the West

One of the reasons for the disappearance of the left is the influence

of Alexander Solzhenitsyn and his *Gulag Archipelago*. I have the
feeling that that book will be seen eventually as one of the most
influential pieces of writing in history.

What Solzhenitsyn did was to establish once and for all that there
were concentration camps in the Soviet Union. Others had said it
before, but he had cultural cachet: He was a respected novelist. And
Nikita Khrushchev gave Solzhenitsyn even more credibility by putting
his arm around the author at the time of the publication of *One Day
in the Life of Ivan Denisovich* and saying: "Yes, this is true. This
happened." So there was no denying after that that socialism can
lead to the concentration camp.

I feel rather optimistic about the 1980s in the West because a lot of
the intellectual antagonism in the United States and the other
Western democracies is fading. There's still a strong left wing in Italy,
but I think it's slowly diminishing and has diminished considerably in
France and England.

It really can be traced to Solzhenitsyn.

Let's celebrate "our season of the rising sap"
We are in America's Elizabethan period and don't know it.

We have been told so often that capitalism and the West are in
their twilight and the best we can hope for is to make the remaining
years as comfortable as possible. In fact, this is our season of the
rising sap.

This is the century in which the United States became the most
powerful country on earth militarily, the wealthiest country on earth,
the country that developed the capacity to exterminate mankind with
the atomic bomb but then went ahead and developed an escape
route to the stars through the space program.

This is the country that started the phenomenon—which Europe is
beginning to catch up with—of wealth at every class level except the
class that doesn't work at all. This is our Bourbon Louis period. It's
been a time of tremendous exuberance, tremendous energy, tremendous growth. Yet people of influence in this country so often act as if
it were the opposite.

Because of these achievements, it's hard for me to be terribly
pessimistic about the rest of this century.

Tom Wolfe Comments on Being a Social Commentator

Roslyn R. Dawson/1979

From *Dallas Magazine*, December 1979, pp. 26-30. Reprinted with permission of *Dallas Magazine*.

Since serious writers, the novelists, aren't tackling the subject of the city—be it Dallas or New York—journalists, the realists, are left to deal with the momentous themes of the city, he says.

Dallas: What is the expected longevity of a social commentator?
Wolfe: About three months.

Well I'll tell you this: there's never any shortage of subject matter. I wrote so many things about the '60s, with which I'm identified. People say, "Aren't you worried that the times change and things get quiet?" The '70s seem quieter than the '60s, and that's never bothered me at all because the social comedy goes on. It's just that different things become fashionable. But there's always the element of comedy about us.

Actually, the '70s haven't been all that quiet. It's like traffic noise. A lot of things that started in the '60s are just accepted now and they are a part of the "Muzak" in the background. For example, the co-educational dorm would have seemed an impossible, shocking, outrageous proposition 15 years ago. Now they're just accepted everywhere. And music which—in 1964 when the Beatles first arrived in the United States—seemed so raucous is now, literally, part of the background noise.

Dallas: Do you think a commentator like yourself can remain appropriate and to the point indefinitely? Does there come a time when you become known as the spokesman of a particular era?

Wolfe: It depends on how much reporting you are willing to do. As writers get older, they like reporting less and less. Not because they're running out of energy, although they tell themselves that. It's because reporting is undignified. It's tedious; you're always on someone else's terrain. You may have a perfectly boring time but you have to put up with it and occasionally it can be kind of pleasant.

Writers like to think that, after all, it's not the material that is responsible for their genius, but their brilliant imagination. And all writers like to think it's 95 per cent their genius that accounts for their success, if any, when in fact it's probably more like 60–40 or 75–25, with the material being the most important part.

So I think if you're willing to continue to do reporting, you're all right. It's when you think that you've done reporting in one period and you stop doing it and you think that you know it all, that's when you're in trouble. For example, a couple of magazines called me up about a year ago to ask me what I thought about the punk phenomenon. At first, I started expounding, then it dawned on me that I knew absolutely nothing about it. I hadn't been to any punk establishments. I didn't know the names of the groups. I hadn't been paying any attention to it. It's just something I had read about. And that's the time when it becomes necessary to stop commenting and start reporting, if you're interested. Frankly, I don't care if punk lives or dies without me. But if you care, you've got to do reporting.

Dallas: You said at one point that the success of the New Journalists was due to the fact that fiction writers of our time were dealing with vague, mythic sorts of subjects, leaving the realm of reality to the journalists. Do you think this still holds, or do you think that fiction writers in the last decade have become more realistic and have recovered some of the ground they previously had relinquished to the journalists?

Wolfe: It hasn't happened yet. I think it will. I think it will in the next five or six years. I can see there is still a vogue in the universities, where almost all writers come from now, for the fable. And the idea is that realism's day is done and that to be a realist, in the novel particularly, is to be old fashioned. It's as simple as that. I think they're making a terrible mistake, although it's good for journalists.

Dallas: Do you think, then, that we'll have a turnaround in the next few years toward a more vital form of the novel?

Wolfe: Well, I think that certain novelists are backing into realism, such as Doctorow, who wrote *Ragtime*. It was a fable, but he decided he would use real figures. He used them in a fictive way, but he has names—Freud, Trotsky—running through the novel. It's a fable using real names. You see young novelists (That's anyone under 52! It's true. It's amazing to see John Gardner called a young novelist when he's a man 46 or 47 years old, but anyway, that's another subject.) beginning to back into realism. For that matter, Irving in *The World According to Garp*; it's still a fable, but it's one of the few successful fabulous novels in a commercial sense.

And I mention a commercial sense, because it is the lack of commercial success that tends to make these writers eventually start backing into realism. And if they start doing it, then the younger novelists will say, "Well, it's OK to write like this." I hope they never get the message because it's made it an absolute field day for journalists. We've had this whole terrain to ourselves. Ask yourself how many serious writers—those that are taken seriously in literary magazines—have tackled the subject of the city. Try to think of the great novel of city life in Dallas, or for that matter New York or Los Angeles. These novels don't exist. And it's journalists who deal with the momentous themes of the city—the collision of the races and all this kind of thing.

Dallas: Do you think the journalistic novel has had its day and is no longer extant as a vital form?

Wolfe: You see them done all the time. A lot of them are crime stories, non-fiction done in a novelistic way, chiefly because that's the easiest real life subject to tackle in a novelistic form. Usually you have dialogue that has been recorded in court proceedings, and the criminals have been convicted so they have no rights when it comes to libel. The victims are dead, so they're not going to sue. So it's easier. A lot of the work has been done for you by investigators.

The Right Stuff is novelistic in treatment, but that term isn't all that important to me. Fielding used to call his novels "comic epics in prose." He called *Joseph Andrews* that and he called *Tom Jones* that. The reason was that the novel had a very low status in the 18th century. It was considered trash, and the great form was epic verse drama. So Fielding said: "I haven't written one of these novels, one of these pieces of trash. It's an epic verse drama, except it doesn't happen to be drama, it's prose." Well, today writers will often say, "This isn't journalism I'm writing; it's a novel," which is another way of saying, "This is not trash, this is the highest literary form."

Dallas: What drew you back to the '50s?

Wolfe: I met some astronauts. And I very quickly saw that we didn't know anything about them, about their families. And that we really didn't know anything about what had gone on in Project Mercury or the space program, except in the abstract or broad sense of "this was accomplished." The experience of these people had really never been recorded. It's extraordinary, considering the millions of words that have been written about it. So it seemed to me like a challenge to bring all of this to the surface and try to bring the whole experience alive in the sense of making it a drama of real people.

And, as I got into it, I found more and more areas that had never been covered. The life of the military is a vacant lot as far as literature is concerned. There's been a bias against the military among writers that dates back to the First World War. So it's been proper to treat in a sympathetic way only dog soldiers. Once you get above the level of sergeant, the fashion has been that you have to be treated as either vicious dolts or bureaucratic idiots. As a consequence, they really haven't been looked at except in an occasional novel. But you don't find that very often. You're more likely to have something like *From Here to Eternity* in which the corporals and privates are the focus.

Dallas: Do you ever play prophet and talk about what you anticipate or expect?

Wolfe: My vanity leads me to do it sometimes although my greatest successes come if I allow myself to wait on it. Like I wrote the piece, "The Me Decade," in 1976, six years into the '70s. That's a safer way to play it. But I have been thinking about the '80s a lot and maybe I'm crazy, but I have a great optimism about the '80s. I think we're in a period where there's this word "crisis" that is used as a substitute for "problem." None of these things are problems any more, everything is a crisis: fuel crisis, a crisis of inflation. In fact, we're still riding an economic boom that has been going on since 1943. And it's now 36 years down the line, isn't that right now? This is a prosperity that reaches into every level of the population, except for people who are unemployed. And this thing is so big, and it's been going on for so long, people don't see it anymore. It's sort of like the Big Dipper. Last time I looked at the Big Dipper, I was seven. But it's still there, and it's really quite large. It's up in the sky every clear night, but it's just not seen.

On top of that, America's prosperity had quite a long run while our main opponents in the world have been thoroughly discredited in the 1970s. And no small part due to Aleksandr Solzhenitsyn who really was the first person to convince the world finally that socialism leads directly to the concentration camp. And it's only now that we are beginning to understand that the Nazi system was socialism. They didn't hide the fact; they called themselves the National Socialist Party. It was socialism of a particular form. Now whenever a socialist—now by socialist, I'm talking about Sweden; I'm not talking about England; I'm talking about real socialism in which there is a state apparatus that controls every facet in a national way—now when a socialist regime arises, everyone in the world says, "Where is the Gulag?" They usually find it. They found it in Cambodia, in Vietnam, and now they have found it in China. This is something they say you cannot argue around. You argue around concentration camps; there is no rationale for dismissing the phenomenon. It's now obvious that it is an absolutely necessary result of a socialist government. What this means is that the alternative of a socialist utopia that has been the counter vision, that is always held up against governments and people of the industrial nations, can no longer be held up as an alternative. This is going to solve a lot of problems for the United States in the next decade. It's not clear yet, because it's a thing that happens slowly and there's still plenty of a strong Marxist force in Europe. There's no Left in this country, incidentally, there is no Left in the United States now. It has vanished. There is only something like the nuclear, anti-nuclear movement, but that's a very broad-based movement, not particularly radical. And that includes all kinds of people who are just simply very seriously concerned about radiation. But that's it, and there is no more Left Wing in America, and this means that a lot of demoralizing voices are no longer around, all of which is going to probably lead to more confidence.

Dallas: Living in Texas these days, there is a lot of attention being focused on this state. I'm curious as to your opinion of regional writings. You've probably been at least exposed to *Best Little Whorehouse* and Larry McMurtry. Do you think that what they are doing is perhaps going to be a precursor of something like the New York or California groups of writers that "happened" at a certain point? Do you think that something may happen here, because wealth and power are coming into this area?

Wolfe: It could happen if writers would be realists and write about

it. There is *North Dallas Forty.* But what's another novel about
Dallas?

Actually people love regionalism. One of the great reasons for the
success of the Beatles was their Liverpool accent. People loved that.
There has been a regional school of New York writers. Most of them
were Jewish, but they weren't thought of as Jewish New York
regional writers because they were in New York, which is perceived as
a cosmopolitan city; they were just American. They were just seen as
American writers. But that is an example of how regionalism can be
attractive to everyone and can thrive.

You know if somebody would just do it, it could all happen all over
again. But so many writers just want to get to New York or like to be
reviewed in New York, and they'll probably go way out of their way
not to be perceived as regional writers. Larry McMurtry once told me
that before he became so well known, students of his at the
University of Houston would keep coming up to him and showing
him survey articles of American fiction in which there would be a
paragraph that would say, among the regional novelists of the
southwest are so-and-so and so-and-so. Larry McMurtry finally got a
sweatshirt made with letters on it, "Minor Regional Novelist." And I
loved that because it really told the story. Of course, now he could
put a sweatshirt on that said "Major American Novelist" without any
fear of being contradicted.

Dallas: If you are a regional writer, do you think the tendency is
to stereotype your region for the benefit of the rest of the country?

Wolfe: I think the real trick you should try to perform is to come
up with new characters, new types who are so striking that they soon
become stereotypes.

Conversation with an Author: Tom Wolfe

Martin L. Gross/1980

From *Book Digest Magazine,* March 1980, 19–29.

This tape-recorded interview with Tom Wolfe was conducted by *Book Digest* editor Martin L. Gross. Mr. Wolfe is also the author of *The Electric Kool-Aid Acid Test, Radical Chic & Mau-Mauing the Flak Catchers, The Painted Word,* and other books.

MLG: How did the reviewers react to your latest work, *The Right Stuff?*

TW: I could hardly ask for a better reception. Just about the time you think the world has it in for you, suddenly you're buried in orchids and things even up.

MLG: When I mention your name, people seem to first think of your book *Radical Chic.* In fact, that phrase has become part of our language. What made it so popular?

TW: It was laughter in church. It's already hard to remember, but there was a strong intellectual fashion in the late '60s to be on the side of the various radical causes. I was a heretic for saying there was something amusing about Mr. and Mrs. Leonard Bernstein giving a party for the Black Panthers in their 13-room duplex on Park Avenue, at which the Black Panthers were invited to rise up and tell all assembled exactly what horrible things would happen to them the day the Black Panthers had their way. And of course the Black Panthers obliged.

MLG: Were you at that historic party?

TW: Yes. I wangled my way in. I wanted to go because I was reminded of a party that Andrew Stein threw for the grape pickers in Southampton in the summer of 1969. It was quite something. One of the grape workers went to the microphone and said, "Close your eyes and imagine that you are a grape worker's wife. You're getting up at 4:30 in the morning in the dark to cook the breakfast of sliced

121

hot dogs, Nabs and Coca-Cola, and then you'll be slaving in the field all day."

Here were all these women in their Pucci clings and Kenneth hairdos and men in their Savile Pseud bell bottom pants. The women had their eyes shut and one hand on their heads, as if in an attitude of meditation. It turned out there was a wind coming off the sea and they were holding their heads because their $85 hairdos were in danger.

MLG: Are you political? If so, what is your basic viewpoint?

TW: I have never been very much interested in politics. I'm much more interested in intellectual fashions. But I've also had something of a contrary streak. I was in college at a time when students tended to be conservative. I remember being a liberal. Then when I got to graduate school where everybody was a liberal, I made a point of being a conservative. I've always been a lot more interested in what people did with the ideas than with the issues themselves.

When I got to New York, I found that there are so many people who totally accept what is the current intellectual fashion and then pat themselves on the back for being nonconformists.

MLG: Is this typically American or typically New York?

TW: It's probably typical anywhere you have an intellectual sphere. Radical chic, for example, is by no means confined to the United States. The Italians always made our local practitioners look like amateurs.

I remember the case of a well-to-do artist, Italian Communist Party, who had his two sons driven to a private school every day by a chauffeur. One day, kidnappers stopped the car. The chauffeur, a man named Carlo, was seriously wounded but managed to speed off and save the two boys. The television interviewers asked the boys what they did. They said they did exactly what daddy told them to do. He told them to hit the floor and let Carlo take it. I doubt that Italians even blinked. They were used to Communist culturati with faithful old yassamassa family retainers.

MLG: Is hypocrisy involved?

TW: I can't really call it hypocrisy. It's just double-track thinking. Many of us, and I wouldn't exclude myself, do it. On one track you see the political expediency of accepting a certain set of ideas. And on the other track you work out the reasons why you really believe in them.

MLG: A lot of what you write about seems related to status—or what you call "intellectual fashion." Why?

TW: I think a great deal of what passes for intellect is a pure exercise in what I call the influence of "status spheres." The field of architecture today is a good example. In fact I'm now writing about it for *Harper's* magazine. It' a sequel to *The Painted Word,* my book about painting.

MLG: What have you found?

TW: I learned that in order to achieve a first-rank reputation in architecture, you must enter the academic sphere. It is now more important to have academic architectural concepts and to do architectural drawings of unbuilt buildings than to build buildings. Once you have reached the top within this kind of pantomime world, then the new patron of today—which is almost always an institution, a corporation, or a government—will look around and say, "Who's the hot ticket now in this particular shpere?" And that person is finally tapped to do the building.

MLG: In *The Painted Word,* you pursued a similar theme: that the explanation of the painting is often more important than the painting itself.

TW: Yes. I describe what I call the BoHo Dance, in which the artist feels he must first come to lower Manhattan. He could do the same paintings in Albuquerque but he is not going to be noticed unless he gets involved in the lower Manhattan art world.

MLG: How big is that art world?

TW: The art world in the U.S. is no more than three thousand people, and they practically all live in New York City.

MLG: Why lower Manhattan rather than the Upper East Side?

TW: You must go through this period of being Bohemian, all the while looking over your shoulder to see if people uptown—the Museum of Modern Art, certain painters, certain collectors are watching. And if you do the BoHo Dance well enough and have a knife in your teeth against the corruption of uptown life, you're tapped by uptowners and you get all the things that Freud said that artists want: fame, money and beautiful lovers.

MLG: How does intellectual fashion start and how does it disappear?

TW: Most people put themselves into a status sphere. Whether they're intellectuals or stock car racers, they tend to emphasize values that, if they were absolute, would make them special people. About 1920, for example, we began to hear the phrase "the booboisie." The idea was that Americans were in fact idiots, even if powerful idiots. This one notion—that the United States was dominated by a vast middle class made up of brutes and idiots—stayed with us for 60 years. It's only amended from time to time.

MLG: Who popularized it besides H. L. Mencken?

TW: It happened as a result of the First World War. A large number of American intellectuals and artists went to Europe and ran into that absolutely dazzling figure, the French intellectual—Andre Breton, Louis Aragon, people of that sort. They seemed like art deco ivory figurines laced with silver and gold set against the rubble of European civilization.

So what did these young Americans do when they returned home? They said, "Well, we don't have real rubble, but we have these terrible middle-class people who are so pious and pompous and puritanical on the one hand and absolutely soaked in greed and lust on the other. It's psychological rubble." So they stood in front of that for 60 years.

MLG: Weren't the early novels of Sinclair Lewis based on this general theme?

TW: Sinclair Lewis is an excellent example. It was only the Second World War which brought this fashion to a temporary halt.

MLG: You are given credit for the phrase "the Me decade." Has it become an egalitarian movement in which everyone is able to participate in the new largesse, both psychologically and mentally?

TW: Yes, in the sense that the "me" phenomenon has been the ultimate luxury. It was during the '60s that Americans began to believe that the economic boom was permanent, and they began cutting loose in all kinds of ways. We started having communes of young people that would be impossible without prosperity. I look upon this period as the third "great awakening."

The first was in the colonial days, in the 1730s–60s. Some historicans credit it with creating the mental atmosphere that made possible the Revolution. The second was from about 1825–50. Starting in the mid-1960s, we have the third great awakening. They all came after periods of prosperity.

MLG: You have written a lot about status. Does it relate to your new book on the astronauts, *The Right Stuff?*

TW: Yes. I tried to show that there is a status sphere created specifically by pilots, and I gave it a name, the fraternal order of "the right stuff." To me the major riddle was, what would make a man be willing to sit on top of a 36-story rocket and let someone light the fuse?

MLG: How do you think the astronauts came out in your book?

TW: For a start, I think I was the first person to show that they came from this world of "the right stuff" at all. I found that there was a code of personal conduct, which was that of the fighter jock. It was a much wilder code of conduct than the astronauts were presumed to have observed. Drinking, wild driving, and displaying one's manliness toward the "cookies," as they say, were by no means out of bounds.

MLG: You pointed out that John Glenn was an exception to this.

TW: Yes. We knew so little abut the world of the hot young pilot— the fighter jock—that when John Glenn demonstrated his exceptional personality, his became the profile of all the astronauts.

MLG: Did the fighter jocks laugh that they were being presented as if they were all John Glenns?

TW: I think that they more likely said to themselves, "Gee, how can we keep the lid on this?"

MLG: Did they all cooperate with you?

TW: Neil Armstrong wouldn't. He was in the Apollo program, of course. I spent much more time working on Gemini, Apollo, and Skylab but ended up writing only about the Mercury program. Someday I may do the rest of it.

MLG: You have written about the media, radicalism, the communes, art and astronauts. What other areas do you want to look at?

TW: One of the subjects that interests me very much right now is high schools. Only there—and, it so happens, in the military—do we see all sorts of different types of people actually dealing with one another on a daily basis.

But I think probably the next thing I do will be a novel. Probably a *Vanity Fair* novel in the same sense that Thackeray wrote his.

MLG: You dress like a 19th-century man. If you're not pretentious in relation to social observation, why should you be pretentious in dress?

TW: It's more fun being pretentious in dress. Casual has been taken as far as it can go. I think the ultimate was when Jerry Rubin and Abbie Hoffman appeared on "The Dick Cavett Show" in body paint.

MLG: How does your wife react to your clothes?

TW: Well to some and badly to others. I had a yellow suit made, and she really will not go out on the street with me when I'm wearing it. She walks a block behind.

MLG: In addition to being a popular writer, I understand that you also have academic credentials.

TW: I have a Ph.D. in American Studies from Yale. In fact, my original idea was to teach. But I received my Ph.D. in the summer of 1956, and it was too late to get a teaching job for that fall, so I thought I would spend a year working on a newspaper. I got a job with the *Springfield* (Mass.) *Union* and immediately found it great fun. I never returned to the academic world.

MLG: Since you are a Ph.D., do you feel your criticism is somewhat sociological?

TW: In a way. I have been using a lot of concepts that I've learned from the sociologist Max Weber, particularly concerning status.

MLG: How do you view the American civilization of the 1970s that has just been completed, and how do you see the upcoming '80s?

TW: The 1970s were really a continuation of the 1960s, but in a bigger way. This was true in many fields. For example, the ecstatic religious movement which began with the hippies changed in the 1970s to the Jesus freak or Jesus people movement.

In the 1960s we heard talk about "the sexual revolution," but it was only in the 1970s that it actually spread throughout the country.

MLG: What about promiscuity and pornography? Do we have a new view of them?

TW: I'll say. Even the smallest Baptist crossroads in the South. In addition to the Second Baptist Church and the hot-wax carwash and the Arby's and the general store with the Pepsi-Cola medallions, there is now the village whorehouse at the side of the road—a windowless shack, painted black or maroon, with a big sign: "Totally

All Nude Girl Sauna Massage & Encounter Sessions." They are even advertised in the local newspapers.

Pornography became just part of the landscape in the 1970s. In any town of 100,000 people there would be fourteen movie houses, two showing *Jaws*, one showing *Benji*, and the rest showing porno movies, including two open-air drive-ins, the better to beam all the glistening nodules and stiffened giblets to the surrounding countryside.

One of the most extraordinary developments in the 1970s—and people seem not to notice it at all—is the coed dorm. The idea of nubile girls living together under the same roof with the young men in the season of their rising sap would have been unthinkable in most parts of the country as late as 1968. Today it is accepted without protest.

MLG: Is sexual license going to continue in its present form? Or is it possible that we have already gone too far?

TW: Well, it is possible that the antidote has already been built into the procedure. Ken Kesey said that a lot of people would like to be amoral but very few of us are really up to it. So in my opinion, in the 1980s we may see the antidote to much of this excess of the 1960s and 1970s.

MLG: What about divorce? Can it continue at the present high rate?

TW: I have a feeling that the divorce epidemic can't continue at this rate very long. I don't know how, but I do visualize a change about to take place.

MLG: What about women's liberation? What do you see in the '80s?

TW: It may be the period of Thermidor. Theoretically a woman can treat sex as a game in the same spirit as men do, but the actuality may be quite different, if only because men are often considered sexually attractive to 60 or 65 years of age, and women's sexual attractiveness declines far earlier. No matter what the theory, relations between men and women are in many ways shaped by this social bias. A man can afford more mistakes.

MLG: Despite your very flamboyant writing style, I suspect that you are a serious social critic. Do you think that your style keeps some people from taking your observations seriously?

TW: People are used to receiving serious information in a particular form. In my case, I'm sometimes treated less seriously than I want to be. But I wouldn't want to change my style. I want to keep my material alive. I suppose if I have to be considered less serious by some because of it, I have to accept that.

MLG: In reviewing *The Right Stuff,* did the critics realize you had done some serious thinking about the whole question of bravery?

TW: Yes. I was generally pleased by the reception of the book, both commercially and critically. Many of the reviewers appreciated the concepts that I advanced about the single-combat warrior, the questions of bravery and status that were aspects of the early space program.

MLG: I don't mean for you to starve, but is it possible that you may someday change your extraordinarily successful style and write a serious tome of social criticism?

TW: I do intend—someday—to do a general theoretical book on the question that interests me the most—status. But if I want to be treated seriously, I suppose I will have to present it in a difficult-to-read form.

MLG: What about the politics? How would you describe politics in the '70s, and what do you see ahead in the '80s?

TW: We don't realize it in America, but we are an extremely stable, democratic country. We went through Watergate and there was no junta, no tanks in the streets, not even a drunk Republican out throwing a brick through a boutique window, so far as I know.

We actually enjoyed watching it on television, wanting to see what would happen next. And the resigning President picked a new President for us without a peep of criticism from anybody. And then we went ahead and elected the most off-the-wall candidate we could find, who spent the next three years in office wearing picnic clothes. And we enjoyed it all thoroughly. I don't believe we should get very worked up over whether Carter or Kennedy or Reagan is our next President, because it isn't likely to make any profound difference.

I personally don't see anything gloomy coming up, assuming there isn't some terrific explosion abroad, in the Middle East or wherever. In fact, I see a rather rosy ten years ahead of us in the 1980s here in the United States.

The Rolling Stone Interview: Tom Wolfe

Chet Flippo/1980

From *Rolling Stone,* no. 324 (21 August 1980), 30-37. By Straight Arrow Publishers, Inc. © 1980. All Rights Reserved. Reprinted by permission.

KA-THUNKA-KA-WHOMP! KA-THUNKA-KA-THUNKA-KA-WHOMP-KA-*WHOMP!* KA-THUNKA-KA-THUNKA-KA-THUNKA-KA-WHOMP-KA-WHOMP-KA-*WHOMP!* KA-WHOMP-WHOMP-WHOMPWHOMPKATHUNK-AKAWHOMPAKAWHOMP-A W H O M P A W H O M P a WHOMPaWHOmpaWHompaWhompawho mpa . . . What inna name a Christ we got going on here? This is the famous writer's orderly and even very literary study, I mean, the white bookshelves seem to zoom up about eighteen feet straight and they're just chockablock with, you know, the *heavy* lumber: old Henry Miller and D.H. Lawrence and everybody else up there in gleaming binding, the expensive first editions, none of these half-price reviewer's copies from the Strand Book Store, where every Saturday afternoon you can see every low-rent book reviewer in Manhattan struggling in with these D'Agostino shopping bags full of review copies—*Scruples!*—staggering down the metal stairs into the basement and weaving through the aisles—tachycardia time!—to finally dump these goddamn shopping bags full of books they've heaved and carried all the way down from West Ninety-sixth Street, the goddamn bags ripping and *The Complete Scarsdale Medical Diet* falling out on the goddamn sidewalk there at Twelfth and Broadway, so they scoop it up and finally dump all these goddamn books on the floor there at the back of Strand's basement in front of this rope they have stretched across there, and they avert their eyes and try to look literary—bug-eyes and wheezing and army-navy turtle-necked and Frye-booted, real-Levied literary—while some goddamn pustular NYU lit major behind the rope takes his goddamn sweet time to sift through the bound detritus and hand them this little chit like it had a bad smell, like it had dogshit all over it or something, and this NYU *twit!* calls out "$27.50!" and they take their dogshit chits and heave their way back upstairs to collect $27.50 and buy a seventy-five-cent paperback of E.M. Forster's that they always meant to read but something always came up and they just never got around to it, but *tonight,* this very night, they *will,* after hitting Zabar's with their remaining $26.75 to get the latest goddamn new cheese and some real coffee, this very night they will read the whole goddamn book and feel very self-righteous and very literary.

Nosiree, no goddamn dogshit reviewer's copies of books in *this* here office, this precise, white-on-white office looking right out on one of the . . . *better* treelined Upper East Side streets, where the author can look right out and *see* these perfect East Side priapic buds just undulating their way over to Bloomingdale's for more of those crotch-grabbing Jordache jeans that just deliciously creep and slither into *every* secret fold and fissure.

But—KA-THUNK-KA-WHOMP—the famous writer is not peering out at the undulating buds. He's not even pacing back and forth, stopping to leaf through the fifty-pound *Webster's* dictionary (to see how to spell *hummocky* or some damn thing, for those hummocky shanks, you know) that lies there like the world's supreme authority on its very proper wooden stand. KA-THUNK—the famous writer in his handmade English suede shoes and those transparent socks with the little stripes on them and the handmade suit—*real* buttonholes, nothing off the rack at Barney's for *this* boy—the goddamn writer is standing out there flailing away, just beating the shit—KA-WHOMP—out of this Everlast punching bag—the real thing, just like what they got down at Bobby Gleason's Gym, whamming the bejesus out of this punching bag that he finally decided he needed in his study to combat that goddamn writer's block that just comes sweeping over you like a goddamn migraine and just poleaxes you. KA-WHOMP! Take that, motha! Let me meet my quota. That goddamn *quota!* TWO THOUSAND words a day. Count 'em; onetwothreefour . . . it just never stops. 1999 won't get it: two-fuckinthousand a *day.* When you're in your agent's office and you're signing that fifty-page contract—you practically get a goddamn hernia just lifting the thing—and you look at that due date for The Work—which is the way they refer to your *creativity,* your life's essence, your goddamn blood and vital juice, you figure mentally, oh, I can hit about 2000 a day easy.

Well, Tom, boy, nobody ever said a writer's goddamn life was *easy*.
Exactly!

(*Sorry*, Tom, boy, but you know how impossible it is to avoid . . .
just *kind* of slipping into that Jax-Slax-kind-of-clinging Tom Wolf-ese
just to sample what the air is like at that altitude, and then before you
know it you leave oxygen behind and you find that your respiratory
system is running on soma or some damn thing. If there is a
practicing young American writer alive who denies ever having lifted
anything from your style . . . well, we all know that's impossible:::::::am I . . . *right?* Exactly!)))))((((((((Perfect!)))))))

Thomas K. Wolfe Jr., now forty-nine, was an extremely unlikely
candidate to be the writer who would happen along in the Sixties
and propel American journalism into a new realism that would
become known and worshiped and vilified as the New Journalism.
Wolfe grew up in Richmond, Virginia—he still retains the careful
inflection of aristocratic Southern speech—where his father was
editor of the *Southern Planter*. Tom decided to be a Writer and went
to Washington and Lee University, where he was surprised to find
there was no such thing as a major in writing. He studied English
literature instead, was sports editor of the school newspaper and
distinguished himself by wearing a hat and carrying an umbrella, rain
or shine. A course in American studies led him to pursue a doctorate
in it at Yale. In 1957, as he finished his Ph.D. and still yearned to
write, he took a "prole" job as a truck loader to try to get Insights and
become a Writer. All he got was drunk after work every day.

He decided that a newspaper job would let him write, and he
applied at all the New York City papers. The *Daily News* offered him
a post as copy boy for forty-two dollars a week. He was ready to take
it, until he heard laughter behind him during his job interview: an
editor told him, "We never had a Ph.D. copy boy here before; the
Times has them all the time." Wolfe foresaw a future of fetching
coffee for reporters and decided to rethink things. He bought a job-
hunting book, from which he learned how to prepare a résumé, and
he wrote to 100 newspapers around the country. He got three replies.
The *Buffalo Courier-Express* and the Worcester, Massachusetts,
Telegram said no, but the Springfield, Massachusetts, *Union* invited
him for an interview and hired him as a reporter. He remembers that

his most important assignment was tallying the number of empty stores on Main Street. Wolfe moved to the *Washington Post*. He thinks he got the job because he was totally disinterested in politics: the city editor was amazed that Wolfe preferred cityside to Capitol Hill, the beat every reporter wanted. Wolfe's apartment overlooked the DuPont Theater, which had *Never on Sunday* for an extended run. Every morning he could see the marquee, which read *NEVER ON SUNDAY*—TENTH BIG WEEK or whatever week it was. When the movie reached its forty-fourth big week, that marquee was a big reminder to Wolfe that *he* was having no big weeks, and he saw that marquee as a big clock ticking his life away. Tom still wanted New York City, so he made the rounds of the newspapers again.

He was lucky. Lewis Lapham (now editor of *Harper's*) had just quit the *Herald Tribune* and Tom got his job. It was there that Wolfe and Jimmy Breslin and Pete Hamill and others were encouraged by editor Clay Felker to try new avenues in journalism. *New York* magazine, begun by publisher Jock Whitney as the *Trib's* Sunday magazine, was the birthplace of New Journalism. The *Trib's* ad campaign was, "Who says a good newspaper has to be dull?" and Felker let his writers take the bit and run. They were encouraged to go beyond the "objective" journalism that ruled daily newspapers, and the result was crisp, alive writing that, more than anything else, made its subjects personal the way fiction did. It was like the difference between Jack Webb, cop (just the facts—but only the facts I like), and Frank Serpico, cop (facts don't tell the whole story). Tom went out to Fort Lee, New Jersey, to interview the widow of slain "rackets boss Tony Bender." Tom couldn't understand, if the dailies called Tony a mob chieftain, why Tony didn't seem to have any money or a big house or a big car. The widow showed Tom the modest house, let him see the "rackets boss'" little woodworking shop and described the last bag of garbage that the "rackets boss" himself had neatly tied up with string. All of a sudden—all of a goddamn *quick* sudden, newspaper targets became *people*. This irritated most newspaper editors in America. What would later be called New Journalism was ignored or denounced as biased reporting or even fiction. By now New Journalism has been examined enough so that even William Safire should admit that it's an attempt at honest, personal reporting.

Tom blazed the national trail by accident. He covered a hot-rod

and custom-car show in New York for the *Trib* and treated it as a
sideshow, which was what was expected of him—the sort of coverage
that any respectable newspaper gives to anything the chamber of
commerce wouldn't endorse.

Tom was uncomfortable, though; he sensed these car nuts had
bypassed the system and were operating in a stratosphere they had
created and knew could exist on its own. *Subcultures.* Tom thought
these weird car people were a story.

He talked *Esquire* into an assignment to talk to car geniuses in Los
Angeles but couldn't make a story out of it. Tom is not a fast writer.
He worried and worried over it. *Esquire* already had the piece laid
out, was not patient and directed Tom to type out his notes so a good
rewrite man could get on it. Tom sat down at eight p.m. and started a
memo to his editor, Byron Dobell ("Dear Byron, The first good look I
had at customized cars was at an event called a 'Teen Fair' "); it took
all night and ran to forty-eight pages. *Esquire* x-ed out "Dear Byron"
and ran the piece as it was: presto, chango, New Journalism! Tom
had read history; he knew historical patterns, but he was obsessed by
what he sensed to be a new wrinkle. He had stumbled on the fact
that the United States of America post-World War II had broken all
the rules of history: it no longer took generations for change to take
place—after the war, the sudden injection of money into every level
of American society had canceled all bets and called off all games.
Wolfe was the first to see a major upheaval. The enormous changes
allowed subcultures to create themselves despite the fact that the
media failed to recognize their existence: Vegas high rollers, rock
tycoons, forever-young surfers, Manhattan high-class groupies—
America finally was financing a fantasy island for anyone who would
lift a little finger. Tom began reporting about a movement that
disturbed a great many people, mainly those who controlled the
media. The disturbing message from the heartland—from North
Carolina, where Junior Johnson's racecar fortunes were more
important than Lyndon Johnson's electoral fortunes—was that the
aristocracy was finished; that Americans cared about their neighborhoods and their neighbors but not much else. That chauvinism
narrowed down quickly to the predictable minimum: me and myself.

Everyone credits Tom for naming the Seventies the Me Decade.
What's funny is that he was out of sight for most of the Seventies. He

was a late-Sixties hero, especially for *The Electirc Kool-Aid Acid Test*, about Ken Kesey and his Merry Pranksters, and also for *The Pump House Gang* and *The Kandy-Kolored Tangerine-Flake Streamline Baby.* But once he pegged the Seventies with the Me flag, he took himself off the college-lecture circuit, where his first question from audiences was invariably "What's Ken Kesey doing?" followed by "How many times did you do acid?" He was not rich, but he was tired of being a Kesey travel guide. Tom was, after all, a journalist, he told himself.

He did take an assignment from *Rolling Stone* to cover the space program, and he wrote a series of four articles (for *RS* 125, 126, 128, 129) that he eventually expanded into his recently published book, *The Right Stuff.* It took him six years to report it, he said, but only six months to write. It takes, he said (and he should know), any writer only six months to actually write any book. The rest of the time is . . . *leisure time,* eh, Tom?

Wolfe does guard his time jealously. He postponed *The Right Stuff* for one year just to polish it after it was written. His magazine assignments are like pulled teeth. He is reluctant to talk about New Journalism; he caught flak for it from everyone, especially the writers he anthologized.

Tom and Sheila Wolfe seem to live very quietly in their East Side town house. Tom's only excess seems to be tailor-made clothes. He does not light up the sky at Elaine's. He sits at home in his white-on-white studio and sketches illustrations for *Harper's* and works on outlines of his next book, which will be his first novel and which he hopes will be a sort of *Vanity Fair* of New York City. He feels New York—*any* major city—should be a central part of a book. Dickens and Zola and Balzac and Thackeray did it, Tom said, so why shouldn't he?

Probably the most striking thing about The Right Stuff *is that it has made you very respectable. You're no longer the hit man who literary people fear and hate. Now you're eminently respectable.*

Most of the things I have done have *not* been sendups or zaps, but those things are remembered somehow. People love a little merciless mockery. So they'll tend to remember something like. . . .

'Tiny Mummies,' for example.

Yeah. Or *Radical Chic*, particularly, or *The Painted Word*, since, if you even make *gentle* fun of people who inhabit the world that you and I live in or the world of the arts, or anything having to do with expression, they *scream like murder.* And of course they have the equipment to bite back, so the fight starts. Everyone kind of enjoys it whether they're paying any attention or not. But *The Electric Kool-Aid Acid Test* was not a sendup, was not mockery or satire.

It was not necessarily a subject the literary world understood or endorsed.

Well, the literary world certainly doesn't endorse the subject of astronauts; it hasn't been a very popular subject. As a matter of fact, one of the things that interested me most was not the space program but military life. I could see that the military, particularly the officer corps, had really been a vacant lot in the literary sense. Serious writers stopped looking at the military around 1919—in any sympathetic way or even empathetic way. It's around then that you start finding the fashion of dealing with the military in a way in which the only acceptable protagonist is the GI, the dog soldier, the grunt, the doughboy, who's presented as a *victim,* not as a *warrior,* a victim of the same forces as civilians.

Did Radical Chic *start with you finding an invitation on a desk at the* Trib?

Yeah. It was an invitation for David Halberstam, and he wasn't even there. I just happened to see it on his desk and there was an R.S.V.P. number. Some people had told me about the thing, but I was not invited, so I called up this number, and I said this is Tom Wolfe, I'm with *New York* magazine, I accept. It turned out to be a defense committee for the Panthers. There was just somebody there writing down the accepts and regrets.

Incidentally, I came in very openly, with a National Brand stenographic notebook and a Bic ball point pen. I introduced myself to Mr. and Mrs. Bernstein. At the time, they figured anybody who was there was riding the same wave they were. The idea that there might be anything funny about it, or amusing, was unthinkable.

How accurate were your notes?

It turned out I took very good notes. Leonard Bernstein's sister later wrote me a long letter in which she said I did several terrible things, but apparently the worst was that I brought a hidden tape recorder into her brother's home. And I knew then that I was right on course. Kind of a left-handed compliment. Actually, I knew that if I hadn't been accurate, that would have been the first cry.

I then spent a long time trying to establish the world that they lived in: who they were and why they were interested in this particular cause. It took me an awful long time to work out the *concept*. I had the phrase in my mind already, *radical chic,* 'cause I knew that by then there was a fashionable quality to certain radical causes.

I started writing in the first person, which was a big mistake, telling how I saw this invitation, how I wrangled my way in. I wrote about thirty pages like that, and then it dawned on me that it was useless information and really detracted from the *scene,* which was the important thing. In fact, I find that the use of the first person is one of the trickiest things in journalism, and something that's rarely understood. If you write in the first person, you've turned yourself into a character. And you have to *establish* yourself, you have to make yourself become a character, and you have to have some organic involvement in the action. It's not enough just to be an observer and to use the first-person singular. As the years go by, I've tended to back off from that device more and more.

In his anthology, The Great Shark Hunt, *Hunter Thompson takes a shot at you for always being the observer, never the participant.*

I *must* read that.

I found out that when I wrote this New Journalism book, I managed to waste nine, ten months' writing. I hoped I would antagonize the novelists, 'cause I was touting New Journalism and saying the novel was in disarray. To prove my point, I brought out my aces: Hunter Thompson, Gay Talese, Jimmy Breslin and a few others. Well, the novelists seemed to be able to contain their emotions, if any, quite successfully [*laughs*]; I haven't seen any of them jumping out of windows. Instead, the only people who got angry were *my stars,* who all ended up despising me for saying they were the shining galaxy of New Journalism.

The next thing I knew, Gay Talese was on the same platform with me at a *More* convention—remember *More* [a now-defunct journalism review]? And there was a panel on the New Journalism. Renata Adler was on it, and she later told somebody that she had had a can of tomato soup or paste that she had intended to empty on my white suit as her comment on the New Journalism, but then somehow she lost the nerve. I had a feeling it was because I was in a pale gray flannel suit that night, maybe it just ruined the picture she had.*

At one point Breslin, I think, said, "There's no such thing as New Journalism, there's only *boutique* journalism and *real* journalism." And Hunter said, "I wouldn't touch New Journalism with a ten-foot pole. I'm a gonzo journalist." As soon as I tried to say. "Here's the great champion of the cause," he says "up yours" with the standard "I'm gonzo."

Actually, I kind of understand their feelings. Each one said, who the hell does Wolfe think he is, lumping me into his raggedy battalion?

The battalion that is wrecking the novel?

Well, they didn't care one way or another about the claims I was making for the form or the way I was putting down the novel. It was just the idea that I could put them in a category. I suppose if one of them had written the thing, I would have had the same reaction.

I would think the astronauts weren't eager to talk to you, some weirdo saying, I'm from ROLLING STONE *and I want to investigate your private life. Obviously you didn't say that; how did you go about it?*

They weren't all that tough. By that time, some had left the astronaut corps. They were a lot looser about the whole thing, they were no longer under the *Life* magazine contract. I think many had become rather bored with the way astronauts had been described. They tended to be pretty open if they agreed to talk at all. A few wouldn't be interviewed. Alan Shepard told me that he only cooperated in documentary ventures that had a scientific purpose . . . later on he indicated that he had read the *ROLLING STONE* pieces and didn't particularly like what was there; I don't know why. Neil Armstrong said he had a policy of not giving interviews and didn't see any reason why he should change it. I think he had hopes, and perhaps still does, of writing his own book. All the Mercury astronauts who were still alive—[Gus] Grissom was dead—were willing to talk and were cooperative.

Was John Glenn open?

---

*Renata Adler recalls, "My memory is a bit hazy, but as I remember it, it would have been soup, probably vegetable, poured over his head, not his suit."

Very open. I spent a day with him when he was campaigning for
the Senate in 1974, the year he finally won the primary against
Howard Metzenbaum, who had beaten him just a few years before.
Then I spent an afternoon with Glenn after he won; he was actually
pretty generous with his time, as senators go, and he was very
helpful.

I've been surprised by the number of reviews that found my picture
of John Glenn negative. I wasn't trying to send him valentines, but in
my mind he came off as an exceptional and rather courageous figure.
He did a lot of unpopular things. He told off a lot of people, and he
almost lost his flight by telling the administrator of NASA and everybody else that Lyndon Johnson couldn't go into his house, that he
and his wife didn't want him in there. That took a lot of courage.

*When did the notion first strike you—of course it should have been
obvious to everyone—that the original astronauts were not the Boy
Scouts who were presented to America?*

I guess from the first conversation that I ever had with any of them.
It's not that they bragged about their exploits or talked about things
like driving these wild races on the highway. At the same time I was
starting this thing, in late 1972, there had been reports in the press
indicating trouble in paradise among the astronauts. Buzz Aldrin's
nervous breakdown had been revealed. That was the same year
there was a stamp scandal, which wasn't really much of a scandal,
but nevertheless it made people stop and ask, "What, astronauts took
a cut of some stamp sales?" One of the astronauts had just become
an evangelist. Two or three had been photographed with long hair,
and this was immediately interpreted by newspapers and magazines
as a sign that there were astronauts who were turned into hippies,
which never happened as far as I can tell.

Perhaps because the general white-wash of the astronauts' flaws
had gone to such an extreme at the beginning, the least little crack
was overinterpreted. To this day, so many people think that most of
the astronauts who went to the moon have suffered breakdowns or
become alcoholics. It just isn't true.

For a while there was the assumption that this voyage was
traumatic because it removed them from all familiar environments,
and that this just had devastating effects on these simple men who
weren't prepared for it. The truth was, they had had such sophis-

ticated simulations that there was very little new to see when they reached the moon. By the time Armstrong got there, he had had probably 500 simulated-missions in replicas of the Apollo command module, with moving pictures of the moon, based on films that had been brought back by manned and unmanned vehicles. I think it was false for Armstrong to have delivered some apostrophe to the gods or some statement of poetic awe about what he had seen, 'cause he had already seen it all simulated in such high fidelity, how the hell could he pretend there was something startling about it? So he said it's "a small step for man, a giant leap for mankind." When I asked him about it, he said, "Sure, I worked on it for a couple of weeks."

How did you get the notion to cut this book off where you did? The idea of the end of innocence—I believe you make the point that the astronauts' parade was, in a sense, the peak of American innocence.

I think that was the last great national outpouring of patriotism. There was some of that with Gordon Cooper's flight, but it was much bigger in the case of Glenn. By the time Cooper flew in 1963, there were many signs that the United States and the Soviet Union were reaching some sort of rapprochement, so that there wasn't the tension about the flight. The cold war was still a big thing at the time of Glenn's flight.

I liked your characterization of the press as the proper Victorian gent, that the press was reverent through all this. Did you really review all the clips, or was that a generalization about the way Americans perceived those astronauts?

I noticed things like James Reston's piece on the astronauts. If for any obscure reason anyone wanted to finish off James Reston, all you would have to do is reprint that piece.

Where he wrote, "This is a pretty cynical town, but we were misty-eyed" and so forth, after the astronauts' parade?

Yeah. And reading that stuff also pulled together some thoughts I had had along these lines. I'll never forget working on the *Herald Tribune* the afternoon of John Kennedy's death. I was sent out along with a lot of other people to do man-on-the-street reactions. I started talking to some men who were just hanging out, who turned out to be Italian, and they already had it figured out that Kennedy had been killed by the Tongs, and then I realized that they were feeling hostile

to the Chinese because the Chinese had begun to bust out of China-
town and move into Little Italy. And the Chinese thought the mafia
had done it, and the Ukrainians thought the Puerto Ricans had done
it. And the Puerto Ricans thought the Jews had done it. Everybody
had picked out a scapegoat. I came back to the *Herald Tribune* and I
typed up my stuff and turned it in to the rewrite desk. Late in the day
they assigned me to do the rewrite of the man-on-the-street story. So
I looked through this pile of material, and mine was missing. I figured
there was some kind of mistake. I had my notes, so I typed it back
into the story. The next day I picked up the *Herald Tribune* and it was
gone, all my material was gone. In fact there's nothing in there except
little old ladies collapsing in front of St. Patrick's. Then I realized that,
without anybody establishing a policy, one and all had decided that
this was the proper moral tone for the president's assassination. It
was to be grief, horror, confusion, shock and sadness, but it was not
supposed to be the occasion for any petty bickering. The press
assumed the moral tone of a Victorian gentleman.

I say Victorian gentleman, because it's he who was the constant
hypocrite, who insisted on public manifestations of morality that he
would never insist upon privately in his own life. And I think that one
tends to do that on a newspaper. Less so in a magazine. A newspaper
seems to have such an immediate tie to the public. Television doesn't
have it. Newspapers do. I'm not entirely sure why, but it makes newspapers fun to work for.

It also leads to these funny sorts of reactions. People *never* read
editorials. All newspapers know this. And yet if you would publish a
newspaper without editorials, it would be as if you had sold your soul
to somebody. Everyone would ask, in effect, "Well, where are the
editorials? They must have sold them. They're taking something on
the side." And so newspapers are quite right to run editorials. It all
has to do with this moral assumption.

Hell, to this day you can't get anything in newspapers. I think of
this as the period of incredible shrinking news. I'm really convinced
that there's less news covered in America now than at any time in this
century. Television creates the impression that there's all this news
because the press has become very incestuous and writes stories
about the press, with all these marvelous phony wars about television
and what it does or doesn't do. But television as a news medium has

no reporting at all, really, except for some cosmetic reporting done by
so-called Washington correspondents, who usually stand in front of
some government building with a microphone covered in black
sponge rubber, reading AP of UPI copy. In effect, every shred of
news on television comes from either the wire services or from *non-
events,* to use Daniel Boorstin's phrase—the press conference, the
basketball game and so on. So you then have to ask, "What are the
wire services giving us?" Well, the wire services are totally creatures of
local newspapers. Those big wire services just cannibalize local newspapers. Suddenly you're up against the fact that there's no
competition in most parts of the country *at all.* I doubt if there are five
cities where there is still newspaper competition. There's a little bit left
in Los Angeles, a little bit left in Boston and some in New York, but
not much. Maybe one or two other places. When this happens, the
monopoly newspaper cuts back on its staff—always happens. They
just stop covering local events—too expensive. And they'll hire
children from journalism schools at the lowest possible scale. They'll
let them work for a couple of years, send them to the Statehouse,
'cause at the Statehouse they can pick up four or five stories a day
handed out by public relations people. That's your local coverage—
canned items from the Statehouse. When these people have had
enough experience to begin getting good, getting a feel for reporting,
they manage to get rid of them or ease them out of the job because
they will be wanting more money. They also will be wanting to create
heat; it's very hard for a managing editor—an older man—to resist if
a young reporter says, "Look, I dug up a hot story." There's still
enough pride in the business, so it's hard to say, "Well, forget it, kid,
we're not interested in hot stories here. We just want the wire-service
stuff and a few handouts from the Statehouse and that's it."

So really, what you're seeing on television via the wire services is
just getting smaller and smaller. It's really very sad. I don't know how
much corruption there is at the local level, but there's never been a
better time in the century for there to be corruption in local
government, because the press is not gonna spot it.

*Is this kind of head-in-the-sand policy deliberate on the part of the
publishers?*

I don't think it even gets to that exalted level; it's just that since
there's no competition, why knock yourself out and send a larger

number of reporters to cover, say, the federal courthouse or city court, why beat your brains out by doing it better? And it's only the occasional newspaper that has pride, a kind of lingering, vestigial pride in the business, and tries to do a job right.

Television, which has the money to do the reporting, has gotten away so beautifully *without* doing it that it's not about to start. Within the television news operations there's such a premium put on *not* being a reporter, everyone aspires to the man who *never* has to leave the building: the anchor man, who is a *performer.* The reporters are called researchers and are usually young women, and the correspondent on television is a substar, a supporting actor who prides himself on the fact that he doesn't have to prepare the story. You talk to these guys and they'll say, "Well, they sent me from Beirut to Teheran, and I had forty-five minutes to get briefed on the situation." What they should say is, "I read the AP copy." The idea is that as a performer, you can pull together this news operation anywhere you go, and the whole status structure is set up in such a way that you're *not* going to get good reporters. Just try to think of the last major scoop, to use that old term, that was broken on television. I'm sure there have been some. But what story during Watergate? During Watergate there were new stories coming out every day. None were on television, except when television simply broadcast the hearings. They can do a set event. And that's what television is actually best at. In fact, it'd be a service to the country if television news operations were shut down *totally* and they only broadcast hearings, press conferences and hockey games. *That* would be television news. At least the public would not have the false impression that it's getting news coverage.

Truman Capote talks about the nonfiction short story. What is that about?

It's interesting that it's important to people like Norman Mailer and Capote to call what they do in nonfiction—if they think it has literary value—a novel or short story. It reminds me so much of the impulse that made Fielding call his novels "comic epic poems in prose." In the eighteenth century, when he was writing, the novel was a very low-rent form. The reigning form was epic verse, particularly the epic drama. Actually, Shakespeare wrote in the form of the epic drama, classical verse, classical drama, and many times he chose classical subjects. As I said in *The New Journalism,* Fielding made this claim for both *Joseph Andrews* and *Tom Jones,* which is another way of saying, "You've gotta take me seriously." And the fear is that you won't be taken seriously, if you're considered part of a low-rent form. Mailer called *Armies of the Night* the novel as history; history as a novel.

Throughout the world of letters, a curious thing is going on in which all sorts of fiction writers have been struck by the power of nonfiction, *good* nonfiction, in this era. And they also are instinctively aware of the power of realism. They try various ways of tapping into this current. It was so interesting to see E.L. Doctorow start backing away from the fable in *Ragtime.* It's a typical modern fable in many ways, but Doctorow also started using real names, usually of dead people—of course avoiding problems of libel. And the book would not have been . . . it would hardly have been noticed if he hadn't done that.

Gore Vidal, you may remember, wrote a curious novel called *Two Sisters,* in which he used real people like Jacqueline Kennedy and fictional people. And it was also about that time that William Styron did *Confessions of Nat Turner.* In the old days, such a novel would have been based on Nat Turner, but would have changed the name of Nat Turner to something else. Well, this one again tried to draw on the current of realism, and the reader is led to believe that this *is* the story of Nat Turner, when of course the novelist had to fill in a few gaps. All of this was during the period in which the fable was sort of fashion. But the fable wasn't working. Not only were the writers of fables losing readers, but they were losing publishers. There was a depression in the stock market about 1973, and it had a terrible effect on the publishing industry. A lot of publishers just began lopping the deadwood, as they saw it, off their lists. This meant experimental novels had to go. And that, I think, indirectly began to have a lot to do with this backing into realism. It's sort of like somebody leaving the presence of the king: bowing backward, bowing and walking backward, but getting the hell out of there very rapidly. So I have a feeling that by 1984, well, in a few years, there'll be a whole new vogue with realistic novels. It's so obvious now that that is the direction for the novel to resume.

I believe it was in the New Republic *that Mitch Tuchman wrote that the reason you turned against liberals is that you were rejected by the white-shoe crowd at Yale.*

Wait a minute! Is that one by Tuchman? Yeah, oh, that was great.

He talked about your doctoral dissertation.

Yeah, he wrote that after *The Painted Word*. It went further than that. It was called "The Manchurian Candidate," and it said in all seriousness that I had somehow been prepared by the establishment, which he obviously thought existed at Yale, to be this kind of kamikaze like Laurence Harvey—I think that's who was in *The Manchurian Candidate,* wasn't it?—to go out and assassinate liberal culture. I loved that. And he's talking about Yale. When I was at Yale, William Buckley was writing *God and Man at Yale,* saying that it had been taken over by the Left and that the Left was pouring all this poison into the innocent vessels of the young. Tuchman's saying I turned on liberalism is amusing in itself, because it would indicate that I had either been or pretended to be a liberal and then had turned on my comrades for some devious reason. All I ever did was write about the world we inhabit, the world of culture, with a capital C, and journalism and the arts and so on, with exactly the same tone that I wrote about everything else. With exactly the same reverence that the people who screamed the most would have written about life in a small American town or in the business world or in professional sports, which is to say with no reverence at all, which is as it should be. And these days, if you mock the prevailing fashion in the world of the arts or journalism, you're called a *conservative*. Which is just another term for a heretic. I would much rather be called a conservative in that case than its opposite, I assure you. Of course, the word *liberal* in itself doesn't exist anymore. Nobody talks about liberals or liberalism.

The Left no longer exists in America. There *are* leftists, but they have no terrain. There is a swing away from the political fashion of the Sixties. It doesn't mean anything more than that. The disappearance of the Left is something that deserves book treatment, and I don't pretend to know exactly how it happened, but it happened in one year, in 1970. In May 1970, the Left reached a peak of power with the shootings at Kent State.

You've never really written about politics or wanted to. In fact, I heard that you advised Hunter Thompson not to, that if he did, he would lose it.

Oh, I think writing about politics was probably one of the biggest mistakes Hunter ever made. I believe he is interested in it, which astounds me. I think his gifts, which are tremendous, are wasted on American politics, except possibly in an event like Watergate—which he didn't write about, I don't think. Because this country is *so* stable politically. It really is an extremely stable country.

It doesn't matter who's president.

Oh, I don't think so either. That's why I'm not too concerned about who gets elected in 1980. The real lesson of Watergate was, what a stable country! Here you've got the president forced out of office, and yet the tanks don't roll, the junta is never formed. I don't think there was even a drunk Republican who went out and threw a brick through a saloon window! Everyone *enjoyed* it. That was the greatest show on earth. Everyone sat back and watched it on television and enjoyed it when Jerry Ford, who had been handpicked by the man they just threw out, stumbled from one side of the country to the other. And then they elected the guy who for three years wore picnic clothes [*laughs*]. Carter's *too much*. I think if they ever do the presidential portrait of him, they should take him to the bow of the *Delta Queen* in his cutoff Levis and Adidas shoes and have him lean against the railing with Rosalynn in her khaki harem pants! And there you have it!

Have you always been a real clothes horse, really careful about clothes?

The first time I remember being interested at all in clothes was after I saw *The Kiss of Death* [1947] with Richard Widmark as Tommy Udo. That was his first big role, he was the villain; Victor Mature was the hero. It was a gangster movie. I was at Washington and Lee, and there was a custom, I guess you'd call it, of conventional dress. It was an all-male school, and everyone had to wear a conventional jacket and tie. I guess I just wanted to put a *spin* on the custom without transgressing the rules, so I decided on these dark shirts.

Now when I think back on it, I have done the same thing *ever* since, which is to wear rather conventional clothes and put a little spin on it, such as to wear white where you'd ordinarily wear navy, black

or things of that nature. Style, men's clothing, has very rigid
presumptions about it, and if you really experiment, suddenly you're
out of the ball game. You could cerainly cut a striking figure by
wearing a royal blue caftan everywhere you go, but you would
remove yourself from most transactions of life. So if you want to have
any fun with it, it really has to be rather marginal. But the interesting
thing is that marginal things seem outrageous at first.

I also think I was the only person on campus who wore a hat. And
I know I was the only person who carried an umbrella every day.
When I got to my next stop, Yale graduate school, I fell into great
confusion, because the grad school was full of genuinely eccentric
people, and to try to be eccentric in the midst of a zoo full of
eccentrics was a lost cause. The currency was debased. At the same
time, it was no use trying to dress very conventionally because there
was a whole campus full of undergraduates who were dressed very
conventionally.

It was a very confusing time for me in terms of dress. My last
couple of years there I discovered long hair, and that was very
unusual. When I say long hair, I'm not talking about hair down to the
shoulder blades. That was still the period back in the Fifties, when
everyone's ears stuck out and the sun shone through them.

Finally, when I got to Washington, I started having clothes made
because I discovered a traveling British tailor. There were actually
several who advertised in the back pages of the *Manchester Guardian*
air-mail edition. They would set up shop in a hotel room. The
samples used to always be on top of the bureau. You'd go look at all
these samples books and pick some material. They'd make you
whatever you wanted.

Is that when you discovered real buttonholes?

Yes. Then, once I got into it, this tailor told me the names of his
customers, rather indiscreet of him, and some turned out to be very
famous people. That was the basis of a piece I would later write for
New York magazine, called "Secret Vice," about the buttonholes and
so on.

When I came to New York I decided I should start getting clothes
made in this country so I could get fittings, because there were some
rather bad mistakes, though not as bad as you would get with a
Hong Kong tailor. So I went to a tailor here in New York and picked

out a white material to have a suit made for the summertime. Silk tweed is actually a very warm material, so I starting wearing the thing in the wintertime. This was the winter of 1962 or 1963, and the reaction of people was just astonishing.

Long hair at that time outraged people. It was a real transgression. I did a story on Phil Spector in 1964, and he had hair about as long as the Beatles'. The things that were yelled to him on the street—I mean the *hostility*—were just amazing.

The hostility for minor changes in style was just marvelous. I had a great time. I was really getting into the swing of things. I remember my friend Bill Rollins, who was one of the great figures on the *Herald Tribune* at the time. Every time I came into Bleek's or one of those places where newspaper people met, he'd say, "Here comes the man with the double-breasted underwear." I rather *liked* that. In fact I loved the idea. I've always been waiting for someone in an interview to ask me what I sleep in.

Okay, I'll bite. What do you sleep in?

I think I would say double-breasted pajamas with frogging. In fact, it's not true. I actually wear nightshirts.

Brooks Brothers nightshirts?

No, my mother's made me a few that are really nice. I've also got these chain-store-look ones with the alligator; I don't know who makes those—they're like a long polo shirt. But I much prefer the idea of the double-breasted pajamas. I mean I *bought* some; they really aren't comfortable. They have a big lapel, you know, and piping around the lapel and collar.

Strangle you while you sleep.

The cinch drawstring on the trousers was always uncomfortable, and the big collar tends to make you perspire. But those things are so *beautiful,* with all the buttons and the frogging; that's the way people *should* sleep. Which brings me to one final note on style. It's still possible to have fun with clothes if you're willing to be pretentious. That still annoys people: pretension in dress. In fact, this summer I was in East Hampton visiting some people who took me to a party. I was wearing a four-button seersucker jacket that buttons up really high—I think it is actually Edwardian—with a little tiny collar and a white tie with small, far-apart black stripes, and I had on a collar pin and cuff links, white serge pants and white cap-toed shoes, which are

real English banker shoes, only I had them made in white doeskin. I
had on some sheer white socks with black stripes to pick up the
stripes in the necktie—I'm the *only* person who would confess all this
to somebody. Pretty soon I noticed that I was the only man in the
room—and this was a party of maybe sixty people—who had on
both a jacket and a necktie. I think everyone had an income far in
excess of mine. Finally this man came over to me; he was a little
drunk, but he was also angry. He asked, "What's the idea of the rig?"
I asked, "What do you mean?" He said, "The *tie, the pin,* all this
stuff." So I looked at him, and he had on a polo shirt and some kind
of go-to-hell pants, and he had this big *stain* down the front of his
polo shirt, right down the middle, right down to his belt line. I said,
"Well, gee, I guess I can't keep up with the styles in these parts. How
do you do that bright stripe down your polo shirt?" He looked down
sort of in surprise and said, "That's sweat, goddamn it, that's *sweat!*"
He suddenly was very proud of it. I could see that I had landed in the
midst of the era of funky chic.

You know when I write certain things and it turns out that I'm
correct, it amazes me, I must confess. When I wrote that thing, funky
chic, I never dreamed how correct that was.

On several occasions, most recently in the Polo Lounge in Beverly
Hills, I'd just be standing around and people would come up and ask
me if there's a table available, because I'd have on a suit and necktie.
It's really odd, but you can have fun if you're willing to be a bit
pretentious. Wear some trick outfits. If it's worth it to you.

Does it ever get in the way of your role as the observer?

No, most often the opposite has gotten in the way. In the beginning
of my magazine-writing career, I used to feel it was very important to
try to fit in.

To be the chameleon?

Yes, and it almost always backfired, most notably when I went to
do a story on Junior Johnson, the stock-car racer, one of the first
stories I did for *Esquire*. I was quite aware that he was from the hills
of North Carolina. A lot of moonshine and ex-moonshine runners
were involved with stock-car racing at that time, Junior being one of
them. I thought I'd better try to fit in, so I very carefully picked out
the clothes I'd wear. I had a knit tie, some brown suede shoes and a
brown Borsalino hat with a half-inch of beaver fur on it. Somehow I

thought this was very casual and suitable for the races; I guess I'd
been reading too many P.G. Wodehouse novels. I really thought I'd
fit in until about five days after I was down there. Junior Johnson
came up to me and said, "I don't like to say anything, but all these
people in Ingle Hollow here are pestering me to death saying, 'Junior,
do you realize there's some strange little green man following you
around?'"

I realized that not only did I not fit in, but because I thought I *was*
fitting in in some way, I was afraid to ask such very basic questions
as, what's the difference between an eight-gauge and seven-gauge
tire, or, what's a gum ball, because if you're supposed to be hip, you
can't ask those questions. I also found that people really don't want
you to try to fit in. They'd much rather fill you in. People like to have
someone to tell their stories to. So if you're willing to be the village
information gatherer, they'll often just pile material on you. My one
contribution to the discipline of psychology is my theory of
information compulsion. Part of the nature of the human beast is a
feeling of scoring a few status points by telling other people things
they don't know. So this does work in your favor.

After that, when I did *The Plump House Gang,* I scarcely could
have been in a more alien world. I did the whole story in my
seersucker rig. I think they enjoyed that hugely. They thought of me
as very old. I was thirty-odd years old, and they thought of me as
very stuffy. They kind of liked all that—this guy in a straw boater
coming around asking them questions. Then it even became more
extreme when I was working on *Electric Kool-Aid Acid Test.* I began
to understand that it would really be a major mistake to try to fit into
that world. There was a kind of creature that Kesey and the
Pranksters, practically everybody in the psychedelic world, detested
more than anything else, and that was the so-called weekend hipster,
who was the journalist or teacher or lawyer, or somebody who was
hip on the weekends but went back to his straight job during the
week. Kesey had a habit of doing what he called testing people's
cool. If he detected the weekend hipster, he would dream up some
test of hipness, like saying, "Okay, let's everybody jump on our bikes
and ride naked up Route 1. They *would* do that, and usually at that
point the lawyer, who didn't want an indecent exposure charge on
his life's score sheet, would drop out. Kesey explained this theory of

testing people's cool, his notion that there're lots of people who want
to be amoral, but very few who are up to it. And he was *right*.

How did you come to write Acid Test?

This goes back to 1966, the year after *The Kandy-Kolored
Streamline Baby* came out, and I had written a whole bunch of
articles that eventually became *The Pump House Gang,* but I didn't
want to bring out another collection. It just wouldn't seem like a step
forward. I was really casting about for another book to write. About
that time, Henry Robbins, who was my editor at Farrar Straus and
Giroux, had gotten Xerox copies of some letters that Larry McMurtry
had gotten from Kesey, who was then in hiding in Mexico. These
letters were marvelous, paranoid chronicles of his adventures and
lamentations about the strange fate that had befallen him now that he
was a fugitive. And I got the idea of going to Mexico, finding him and
doing a story on the life of a fugitive.

I bought the ticket for Mexico City, and somehow, before I went
there, Kesey sneaked back into the U.S. and was arrested by the FBI
just south of San Francisco. I went out to the jail in Redwood City
where they'd put him, and I met all these crazy-looking people
hanging around. There were people trying to get me to take books to
Kesey with I Ching coins slipped into the binding. They turned out to
be Pranksters. I didn't know anything about these people and what
they were up to. I knew that Kesey had been involved with dope,
because that's what he'd been arrested twice for. I assumed that dope
must be what accounted for their strange appearance. Stewart Brand
was one of the first ones I met. He wore a piet in his forehead. A piet
is a disc, a silver industrial disc; I don't know what they were used for.
They reflected the light in some strange way. They had a very
geometric sunburst design.

They had these white coveralls on with pieces of American flag
sewed on. Only a few of them had really long hair; it was more just
strange rigs and gear. They were very open and invited me to this
place, this abandoned pie factory where they were studying while
they waited for Kesey to get out. It was down in the skid-row section
of San Francisco, worst place I ever saw. Very *hard* on a boy like me,
that life. It got more and more interesting. I'd learned that some of
them had been down in Mexico with Kesey, so I started pumping
them for information—about the fugitive life. They kept saying,

"We'll tell you about that, but that isn't what it's all about." I said, "Well, what is *it* all about?" And they said, "It's the unspoken thing." It gradually began to dawn on me that this was a *religious* group, a religion in its primary phase. It began to seem even important to me. The sociology of religion is one of the things I'd picked up at Yale graduate school.

One learns that every modern religion, from Hinduism to Buddhism and Christianity on to the present, started with a primary group, a small circle of disciples, as they're called in Christianity, who have an overwhelming experience that is psychological, not neurological—a feeling, an overwhelming *ecstasy* that they have interpreted in a religious way and that they want to enable the rest of the world to have so it can understand the *truth* and the *mystery* that has been discovered.

The Pranksters were no exception. Their neurological experience had come through LSD, but that wasn't so unusual either. The Zoroastrians were always high on something called *haoma;* to this day no one knows what it was, but it was obviously a drug. By the time I met Kesey, he was already starting to promulgate the concept *beyond acid:* the idea that LSD could only take you to a certain level of understanding and awareness, but that you couldn't become dependent on it. Having reached the plateau, you must move on without it. He announced this new truth to the movement and was much criticized for it, because by this time, 1966, the rest of the movement was having a helluva good time still getting high. They didn't want to hear this. But this is exactly what Zoroaster ended up doing. He said, now boys, we've got to start doing it without this *haoma* stuff. A little astral projection if you please, maestro!

How did you come across the third great awakening and the Me Decade? Was that originally a lecture that you were doing?

I think I did it for *The Critic;* I used "the third great awakening" in that.

One of the few things I learned on the lecture circuit, which I have abandoned for the most part, was the existence of these new religious movements and some insight into what they were like. I would begin to meet members of religious communes who had come to my talks in hopes of hearing about Ken Kesey and the Merry Pranksters, whom I was not talking about any longer. I would talk about art, and the first question would be, "What's Ken Kesey doing now?" And I can't tell you how many times that happened. I began to see that I was perceived as a medium who could put them in touch with the other world. And all these people were patiently listening *just* to get to the question period, or to get me alone to ask, "What's Ken Kesey doing now? What's he really like? Where can I find a commune? Are we running our commune correctly?" *God,* I used to get all these letters—I could have started a column like "Dr. Hip Pocrates, Advice for Heads."

Well, the other question that everyone asks, I recall, is how many times you'd taken acid in order to do Kool-Aid Acid Test, *and you said you hadn't, which disappointed everyone greatly*

Yeah, I think they really wanted me to be on the bus. In fact, I never was.

You went off in private and took acid, just to see what it was like?

Well, I actually did it once during the writing of the book; I'd started writing the book, and then I thought, well, this is one little piece of reporting I haven't done. So I did do it; it scared the hell out of me. It was like tying yourself to a railroad track to see how big the train is. It was pretty big. I would never do it again. Although at several places I went to lecture in the years that followed, people would put things in the pie that was cooked for dinner—not LSD, but a lot of hashish, marijuana baked into things, or Methedrine. People would pop poppers under my nose, things of this sort. They thought they were doing me a favor. But one of the reasons I wrote *The Electric Kool-Aid Acid Test,* one of the reasons I thought it was important enough to write about, was that it was a religion; Kesey's group was a primary religious group.

And you could see how just such a group developed, as if you'd been able to have been a reporter when the early Christians were forming and then again, running into students who would tell me they had formed communes, and who were very frankly religious and would call themselves Jesus people. They said they didn't use dope, but they all *had.* In the beginning the whole Jesus movement was made up of former acidheads, and when they said they didn't use dope, in most cases they really meant they didn't use chemical dope. Anything you could grow was quite all right. That meant that marijuana was okay, peyote was okay . . .

. . . mescaline was all right, mushrooms, etc.

Yeah, if you would go to the trouble of making it. Those things were all okay. The people in the psychedelic world had been religious but had always covered it up. There was such a bad odor about being frankly religious. I mean Kesey would refer to Cosmo, meaning God; someone in the group used the word *manager*. Hugh Romney [a.k.a. Wavy Gravy] used to say, "I'm in the pudding and I've met the manager." Or they'd say, if they were getting into a very religious frame of mind and began to notice a lot of—what's the word when two people pick up the same thought at the same time? Probably *coincidence* is the right word, but they had another name for it—they would begin to say, "Well, there's some real weird shit going down" or "Brothers, this is the holy moment," or anything like that.

In the early Seventies, the mood of all this began to get more and more frankly religious, and the idea that this was the third great awakening popped into my head. Because I had remembered from graduate-school days the first awakening and second great awakening, out of which came Mormonism. Then I began to read about it. I saw that the Mormons, for example, had been just like hippies and had been *seen* as such. Just *wild* kids. They were *young* when they started. You think of Mormons as being old and having big beards. They were *children*. They were in their early twenties. Joseph Smith was twenty-four years old—he was the leader of the band. And they were just *hated, more* than the hippies were hated. And Smith was lynched. He wasn't hanged, but he was in jail in Carthage, Illinois, and it was invaded by vigilantes and they shot him to death. That's why Brigham Young took the group out to the woods of Utah.

And I think that movement is growing bigger and bigger. There's such a . . . yearning in everybody—there always has been—for blind faith. There's no such thing, I think, as rational faith. It isn't faith. And people always want it, one way or another, me included, although I hide it from myself, as do most people who think they are really sophisticated and learned. But this is something people really *want,* because blind faith is a way of assuring yourself that the kind of life that you're either leading or *intend* to lead is inherently and absolutely the *best.* That's really what it's all about.

Now is a great time for new religions to pop up. There are people who get religious about jogging, they get religious about sex, and you talk to some of these people who are avowed swingers—they'll *bore your head off.* God, it's just *painful* to listen to them. Fifteen minutes in a roomful of these people is like turning your head into a husk. Health foods have become the basis of a religion. Let's see, ESP, of course, flying saucers, *anything* is fertile ground now. There's a new messiah born every day. That's why Jimmy Carter made such a colossal mistake in not preaching. He'd gotten away with murder as it was, getting elected as a born-again Christian. *That's* what people wanted. If he had just ranted and raved for the last three years about the depravity of the people, they would have *loved it.*

You've collected an impressive list of critics and enemies.

That's not hard to do, as we mentioned earlier, if you're willing to treat the world of critics and artists and journalists the way *they* normally treat other people. If you really want to accumulate a list of enemies, you can get it soon enough. There were finally so many extraordinary insults in print about *The Painted Word* that I began having fun by putting them in categories. Tuchman's "Manchurian Candidate" critique was under a huge list of political insults, most of them saying I was a fascist, but some also saying I was a communist. There was another category of what I thought of as X-rated insults, which came about as follows: right after *The Painted Word* came out, a well-known abstract-expressionist painter was at a dinner at which he said, you know, this man Wolfe reminds me of a six-year-old at a pornographic movie; he can follow the action of the bodies but he can't comprehend the *nuances.* Which incidentally is rather a reckless metaphor or conceit to set up for yourself, if you're defending contemporary art, because that's pornography, and I become the innocent child. Quite aside from that, I loved the notion that there was someone in this day and age who professes to find *nuances* in a *pornographic movie.* The next thing I knew, in *Time* magazine there is a review by Robert Hughes—the art critic, I think he's called—and he says, "Wolfe is like an eleven-year-old at a pornographic movie." [*Laughs.*]

Regarding John Russell's review in the New York Times . . . .

This is the man who, at the age of, well, I guess he was in his late fifties, had risen to the eminence of first assistant to Hilton Kramer of the *New York Times.* I only mention his age because he mentioned *my* age. He rather flattered me by saying I was a little too young to understand all these things. He changed the image somewhat. He said I reminded him of the eunuch at the orgy who can follow the action of the bodies but cannot comprehend the nuances. I suppose he was afraid that some of his readers might find the image of the child in the pornographic movie somewhat sexy, so he changed it to the eunuch; nobody would find that very sexy.

It became indirect proof of a point that I was making in *The Painted Word*—just how small a world the art world is. As far as I know, neither of those men was at the dinner party. But this conceit, this metaphor, quickly passed around to the 3000 souls who make up the entire New York art world.

It became doubly funny when I really began to realize that in contemporary art, there is almost no sexual content *whatsoever.* It's one of the few major movements in art history where there is no sexual content. Even in pop art, what few sexual images there are, such as Wesselmann's nudes, are so highly stylized that there is no sensuality. In effect there's a very determind effort made to remove the sensuality, from nudes, for example. Let's see, there were a lot of psychoanalytic references.

Some [critics] were rather simple-minded, along the lines of how sick or neurotic I was. There was one woman who was much offended by *The Painted Word,* and she wrote to Bob Shnayerson, who was then the editor of *Harper's,* where the piece first appeared, and she berated him for letting *me* exacerbate my well-known mental affliction—psychosis or neurosis, I forget what she called it—by publishing this piece. And it was really more *his* fault than *mine,* because after all, I was *sick.* It was a shame, a terrible chapter in what had been the rather great history of *Harper's* magazine. I happened to see a copy of the letter and I ran into her at a party. So I said, "I must tell you, I happened to see a copy of what you wrote, and you could do me a great favor if you would explain my affliction to me, because I believe that prophylaxis is a good thing to aim for in mental health as well as in such areas as tetanus and diseases of that sort." At the very least, I expected a little dissertation on obsessional neurosis or something of that sort. Instead she suggested that I perform a crude anatomical impossibility on myself and then left the party. [*Laughter.*]

But that was the *passion* of the response to that piece. I found that
there are people who take art more seriously than politics. Everyone
seems to understand that underneath it all, politics is a game. But art
really is religion to some people. Creativity is the new godhead and
the artist is a receptor of emanations from the gods. It is the fulfill-
ment of a prophecy made by Max Weber, who said that in the
twentieth century, *aesthetics* would replace *ethics* as the standard for
moral conduct. I think we see a lot of that now.

*Tell me, where are you going to turn your eye next? Are you at
loose ends, or casting around?*

I'm doing something that I've had on my mind for a long time,
which is a *Vanity Fair* book about New York, à la Thackeray. When I
went to Leonard Bernstein's party, it was with the idea of gathering
material for what was going to be a non-fiction book, which *could* be
done, incidentally, if you could find enough events or scenes like that
to move into. My impulse now, though, is to try to do it as a novel,
since I've never done one, and to just see what happens. I'm also
very much aware of the fact that novelists themselves hardly *touch*
the city. How they can pass up the city I don't know. The city was a
central—character is not a very good way to put it, but it was
certainly a dominant theme—in the works of Dickens, Zola,
Thackeray, Balzac. So many talented writers now duck the city as a
subject. And this is one of the most remarkable periods of the cities.
Who has been the great novelist of New York since the Second World
War? Nobody. Or Chicago or Cleveland or Los Angeles or Newark,
for that matter. My God, the story of Newark must be absolutely
amazing.

So you're going to be out prowling the streets?

Well, I don't know if I'll be charging into people's houses, but I will
have to do a lot of reporting. There's more good material out there
than in any writer's brain. A writer always likes to think that a good
piece of work he has done is the result of his genius. And that the
material is just the clay, and it's ninety-eight percent genius and two
percent material. I think that it's probably seventy percent-thirty
percent in favor of the material. This ends up putting a great burden
on the reporting, and I don't think many fiction writers understand
this.

Wasn't that part of the first big attack on the New Journalism?

They said, well, the material is just there; it's the inspiration, the genius of the novelist that does something with it. If it's a reporter digging something up it's just journalism, raw material lying around; anyone can pick it up.

Yeah. I'm sure I went into this in the introduction of *The New Journalism,* but novelists in the nineteenth century understood that no one writer had enough material, and they would go out and do reporting as a matter of course. And Zola especially—he wrote a lot of his novels serially—would spend two weeks of the month doing reporting with a notebook, and the second two weeks he'd spend writing the episode. There's a scene toward the end of *Nana,* a very important scene at the races of Longchamps; he just went out there and soaked up all this material. It's not just a matter of your saying, "Here's the episode I want to write, so now I'm going to hang some accurate details on the story." The *material* leads you to the story. I don't know exactly what Zola did in that case, but I have a feeling that he came up with an entirely new and more exciting story because of the material he ran into.

I know that in one part of the book, there's the image of a golden bed, which is one of the great symbols in French literature, and he found it through reporting. He wanted to do a novel about a courtesan, Nana, so he arranged an introduction to meet a real courtesan, and he went to her house, and he was greatly disappointed to find out that she was far too urbane and cultivated to serve as a model for the kind of woman he wanted to present. He wanted really just an animal, a sexpot who had a tremendous power over men of all sorts. While he was there she showed him her bedroom, which featured a bed with golden posts done by goldsmiths at enormous cost, with all sorts of priapic cherubs and nymphs with shanks akimbo springing out of it. That stuck in his mind and he used it, he gave it to Nana in the novel. It became a symbol of the decadence of the Second Empire. You know, you wouldn't *dare* dream up such a bed, even if you had the power to dream it up in the first place. But the fact that he actually saw it gave him the idea in the first place, and then the confidence to use it.

Tom Wolfe

Joshua Gilder/1981

From *Saturday Review,* 8, April 1981, 40-44. Reprinted with permission of Omni Publications International Ltd.

Interrupted in the midst of finishing his new book, *Under the I-Beams** (to be published by Farrar, Straus & Giroux next fall), Tom Wolfe answers the door in his work clothes—a powder-blue suit, high tab collar ("I feel one should suffer for style"), flat-yellow tie, broad blue-and-white striped shirt complimented nicely by the blue piping running up his white socks, and glossy yellow shoes. The total effect is nothing less than . . . well, beautiful. Wolfe the renegade dandy has exacted his share of critical howls with devastating critiques of New York high society's flirtation with radical politics ("Radical Chic"), the soporific prose style of *The New Yorker* ("Tiny Mummies"), and the theoretical contortions of contemporary art *(The Painted Word).*

When not satirizing the social scene, the chief banner-waver of New Journalism turns his talents to what he has called "field work among the noble savages in search of a lifestyle." He chronicled the "happiness explosion" of the Sixties in *The Kandy-Kolored Tangerine-Flake Streamline Baby,* the birth of the psychedelic movement in *The Electric Kool-Aid Acid Test,* the society of surfers and racers in *The Pump House Gang,* and most recently the brotherhood of astronauts in *The Right Stuff.*

In contrast to his exclamatory, whammo prose, the 50-year-old Wolfe is surprisingly soft-spoken and gentlemanly in manner. We talked in the Manhattan town house where he lives with his wife of three years, Sheila, and their six-month-old daughter.

Q: Tell us about your new book, *Under the I-Beams.*

A: It's a sequel to the *Painted Word* that will be mostly about architecture, but it also brings in a little bit more about painting, about

*Editor's Note: This book was published as *From Bauhaus to Our House.*

dance, about serious music, structural philosophy, and other allied arts. I think in the arts and in all matters that relate to the intellectual, we still have a colonial complex. It's always better if it comes from France or someplace similar. It's really very funny. V.F. Calverton coined the term "colonial complex" way back in the Twenties, saying "now it's all over, we've found our own." Except it's utterly not true. Our painting—much that we've gloried in since 1943—will be seen by the historians of the 21st century as a footnote to French Cubism. Of course we have our own moves, but always within the tracks set by the French in painting, in philosophy and literary criticism.

Q: And in architecture?

A: It came directly from the Bauhaus. There's a very funny thing going on right now. The architects, the established people like Philip Johnson, talk about modernism almost as if they had nothing to do with it. They'll talk about "glass boxes" with a snigger. They realize that this is an exhausted form; quite aside from aesthetic considerations. It's old now, real old. But they only move a few steps off from the center track. They'll add an "historical reference," a slightly reinterpreted cornice stuck in always very archly to show it's a gesture rather than a conviction.

Q: It's kind of a comic self-reference, isn't it?

A: It's not meant to be comic. They're quite serious about it; the word that they use is ironic, or witty. But it's dead serious. That's something that is—sometimes willfully—misunderstood about *The Painted Word.* I keep seeing it referred to both by enemies and the few friends the book has as something that seeks to expose the fraud of modern art. And I kept trying to make it clear all through the book itself that it is the very opposite of fraud. You're looking at upland Baptists. You're looking at people who seat the men and the women on opposite sides of the church and have them wash each other's feet out of conviction. They're not going to go through a strange ceremony with the idea of "Oh, I'm going to put one over on anyone who might be watching." And that's to me, the exciting part—that these are *believers.*

The Painted Word was taken as an attack on modern art, an attack on the critics. In fact I don't believe there's a single aesthetic judgment passed. If anyone is implicitly attacked—there is such a thing as an implicit attack through satire—it's the painters, not the critics. It's

the artists who were very willing to give up personal vision to illustrate
theorems. The book is a history of the rise of theory. And this new
book takes that a bit further, in a historical fashion. People in the art
world tend to very much resist the type of social analysis they quickly
make elsewhere.

Everybody knows that there are forces of class and status that
affect the businessman, that in some places in history the military
have become the tools of economic interests. I try to tell people in the
arts that the same sort of social pressures can have an influence on
the course of art. They refuse to believe it, but I think that when they
unconsciously know it's true, they scream.

Q: The virgin artist complex?

A: Yes. The idea that what comes from the artist comes from the
Godhead, which is now known as creativity. I guess I'm saying that
there is no Godhead.

Q: How have your work habits changed over the years?

A: In the early days when I was working so steadily, the phone
didn't ring very much, I didn't have the money to travel anywhere,
and actually there was no impediment, no temptation to keep me
from devoting every spare moment to writing. It was at the *Herald
Tribune* in between assignments—I was a general-assignment reporter—there would be stretches when I was doing nothing, so I would
work on an article for *Esquire* and sigh deeply and grumble when the
people who were paying me interrupted to assign a story. And I
would often start work at night. That's the best possible way to work.
Except now, in addition to everything else, I'm married—and I
wouldn't give that up for anything. With a family you can't live like
an urban monk.

When I finally had to get *The Right Stuff* written, I didn't answer
the phone. I had to stuff cotton between the bell and the ringer. See,
the actual writing of a book never takes more than six months. I don't
care which book it is. People who are working on a book for five
years, six years, have often said they're "writing a book." Writing a
book doesn't take that long. They're doing a dance around the book.
I used to do that myself. The term "work in progress" means
"haven't started."

Q: Did you have trouble getting down to work on *The Right Stuff?*

A: Yes, years went by. I was intimidated by two things: The

obvious fact that no one was interested, and that I knew the routine
in terms of structure was going to be incredibly hard work. No one
figure, no hero—there was no Ken Kesey, for example. Through his
experiences, through Kesey's life and the Pranksters, you could show
the heart of the whole psychedelic experience, and the whole
religious movement of the Sixties. With *The Right Stuff,* you had to
keep filling people in on world history, which seems impossible to do
in an interesting manner. It isn't all that hard—once you decide on it,
you just tell them.

But it must have been 1978 when I decided I just had to write it.
And then came the period of stuffing telephones with cotton. I even
got to the point where I wore clothes in which I couldn't go out into
the street. Such as khaki pants; you know, I think it's demeaning. I
can't go out into the street in khaki pants or jeans.

Q: You own a pair of jeans?

A: I have one pair of "Double X" Levis, which I bought in La
Porte, Texas, in a place that I was told was an authentic Texas
cowboy store, just before I started working on *The Right Stuff.* I've
had them on, but I've never worn them below the third floor. So I put
on a pair of khaki pants and a turtleneck sweater, a heavy sweater.
When I'm writing I like to keep the room cold—I think between 62 to
65 degrees is the right temperature to write. It's another way of
boxing myself in. I wrote that and *The Electric Kool-Aid Acid Test*
both in the same amount of time. Six months of concentrated writing,
another few months for rewriting, checking facts.

Q: How do you organize your day when you're working?

A: I try to set a quota of 10 pages—I triple space on the typewriter.
For me it's about 1,900 words. Any time I'm finished with that I can
quit. I will quit even in the middle of a sentence at the end of the
tenth page. The hardest thing is overcoming the inertia of beginning
the next day. If I'm in the middle of a sentence or a paragraph, at
least I know how the next day is supposed to begin. And I'll try to do
a page or two before lunch. I always get up earlier than normal, but
nothing gets done until just before lunch. I do a page or two. At that
point I go outside, just walk around the block. I try to get five pages
done in the afternoon, so that working after dinner is not going to be
too much of a struggle. But I usually end up working late anyway.
This is not a very good way to do it. Ideally, as I always used to

gather Philip Roth does, one should get it all done before 2 PM. Then the rest of the day you can play tennis, go out in the evening, or whatever you like to do—just be a part of the world.

Q: Do you do a lot of revising or do you write straight through?

A: I usually write straight through. I think it's a good habit to revise first thing the next day. It's much easier than writing, sort of gets you started. The inertia is such a damned thing.

Q: Have you ever experienced writer's block?

A: I have, but I don't call it that. What is called writer's block is always here. It's me-fear, fear that you can't do what you announced. Maybe you only announced it to a few people, or only to yourself. The awful thing about the first sentence of any book is that as soon as you've written it you realize this piece of work is not going to be the great thing that you envisioned. It can't be. That's one type of fear. Another would be not coming up to the expectations of editors, authors, and all the rest. The other feeling is—fear is not the right word for it—despair. The realization that what you are about to do will be worthless no matter how well you do it. That it isn't worth doing. I think we've all had assignments—if you've ever worked for magazines or newspapers—where we have that feeling. Out of economic necessity you say, *"OK, I'll do it."*

In the case of *The Right Stuff,* it took a long time to do the research, but I would constantly find myself doing other things. Writing other things. That's always a problem, when you write something that's easier than the thing you know you should be working on. I published three books in that period: *The New Journalism,* which I dawdled over for months; *The Painted Word,* which was too long for a magazine piece and too short for a book.

The book *Mauve Gloves and Madmen, Clutter and Vine* was made up almost entirely of magazine articles done during that period, including one of the magazine pieces I'm proudest of, called "The Truest Sport," about carrier pilots in Vietnam, and the one short story that I'd written—since college anyway—called "The Commercial." I thought because it was fiction you could do it in a day because you could make it up. I must say I had contempt for fiction as a craft until I started trying to write this thing. I started in on it, and I soon found that to accomplish what I wanted to accomplish was not only technically more difficult than I'd ever dreamed, but I needed to go out and do some reporting.

Reporting is important for two reasons: To give one's work the flavor of life itself, but also because the reporting feeds the imagination. It gives the imagination something to work with. Human imagination isn't that strong; it can't work in a vacuum for very long. Most novelists ransack their lives for that first novel; it might be called involuntary reporting. They wonder why things are so rough the second time around.

Q: John Hersey wrote a piece in a recent *Yale Review* criticizing the New Journalism. He said that it's hard to distinguish between fact and fiction.

A: He could say the same thing about *Hiroshima*. There are not footnotes. To me, it's extremely important to be accurate, because a lot of the voltage of narrative nonfiction is that the reader is able to believe. I think there are very few readers who want to read fantasy. They read novels because they're getting a picture of the emotional life of human beings that they can't get in any way except in the best forms of nonfiction. But if people start to ask, "I wonder if he makes up the parts in between that he doesn't know about," that's when you're undercutting the whole enterprise if you indulge in it.

Q: So you make it a point not to fictionalize?

A: No, not even in the slightest. It's a tremendous mistake to do it. And also it's as if you violated the rules of your own game. There's a great satisfaction in taking the actual facts insofar as you can get them and turning this material into something that is as engrossing as fiction, and in some cases more so, when you succeed.

Q: Often you reconstruct someone's inner thoughts.

A: You have to do it by interview. You can argue that people who can't remember very well will lie. That's a risk. You have to have faith that the writer went conscientiously about doing this—believed his source was leveling with him. We do this in autobiography all the time. We tend to believe that an individual can remember his emotions and report them accurately. We hardly even blink. I feel that in a way the nonfiction writer is writing parts of other people's autobiographies. And what he comes up with should be given at least the credence that we give other autobiographies.

Q: Is there a different mind-set to reporting?

A: Oh very much so. I think you have to concentrate totally on it to the exclusion of being civil. That's one thing that's bad about being at all well known and doing reporting. It's not so much that it alters people's behavior around you, it's that they may want to engage you in conversation, and may make a fuss over you when you arrive, which turns your head. You become a guest at the party instead of an observer.

Q: How do your subjects feel? Did you get any feedback from the astronauts?

A: I've had varied reactions. Some of them really seemed to like it, or at least to have said that it's accurate, which means more to me than whether or not they really liked it. Alan Shepard, I know, doesn't like it because every time he's asked he says, "I haven't read it and I'm not going to." John Glenn, who in the minds of reviewers came out worst of the seven, wrote me a very funny, friendly letter. I was surprised, incidentally, that he came off the way that he did. In my mind, I was presenting a rare and strangely colorful figure of our time. It's very rare to see a man in our day—outside the Church— who is a moral zealot and who doesn't hide the fact; who constantly announces what he believes in and the moral standards he expects people to follow. To me that's much rarer and more colorful than the Joe Namath-rake figure who is much more standard these days.

Q: Do you feel ambivalent about "the right stuff?"

A: In the sense that to me it wasn't nearly so important to say "Here is this great quality" as to point out that this is the core of the competition for status that drives these people. It wasn't this great quality that everyone should aspire to. Since then, people have asked me: Wouldn't you say that one can also speak of the "right stuff" in journalism, in the business world, everybody's up against difficult moments; and I always said no, there is no analogy. It involves risking your life in an essentially sporting way. But there's no halo around it.

Q: You mention that you're so softspoken. Do you think that affects your interviews? Joan Didion said once that she's so incoherent that people just never take her as a threat.

A: I think you learn to work by the principles of Jujitsu; you know, the Oriental art that is based on the principle of using the opponent's force. (Not to say that all interviewed subjects are opponents.) You use the force of the person you're interviewing by constantly giving way.

There's no craft to reporting, I think. It's all personality, and having some idea of what you're looking for. So I think you have to use the personality you have to advantage.

Q: Do you try to adapt to your subject?

A: No, I used to. When I first started at *Esquire,* I made the mistake of trying to fit in. And given the kind of things I was sent to cover—stock car racing, the Peppermint Lounge, topless restaurants in San Francisco—not only did I not fit in no matter how hard I tried, but I would deprive myself of the opportunity to ask very basic questions that the outsider can ask. You just discover after awhile that people like to be asked questions they know the answers to.

I first approached Kesey in a blue blazer, white pants, necktie, and so on. Instinctively I began to dress up a little more as I stayed with him, and finally I remember for a good length of time I had a very pale gray suit, stepped collar vest, peaked lapels, and a big, blue corduroy necktie that I like very much. Finally one of the Pranksters, a girl known as Doris Delay said, "You know, you've got on the wildest costume around." The only time I ever got into trouble was when the Pranksters gave a party for Hell's Angels. I was the only person at the party with a necktie on or a suit. And I saw this guy— Pete the Drag Racer they called him—staring at me across the room. I tried to ignore it (these guys can really *stare*). I was sitting on a hassock and I suddenly see this pair of boots in front of me and he says very aggressively, "What's your trip?" I say, "I'm . . . I'm a writer." "What do you write about?" "Weeeell . . . Ken Kesey and the Merry Pranksters." He says, "How does it come out?" I say, "Gee, I don't really know—I'm just getting started." He says, "You're from New York?" I was so thankful that a neutral question had been asked that I said, "Oh, YEAH!" And then I suddenly realized that one of the various mortals that the Hell's Angels had earmarked for extreme treatment—in addition to homosexuals, Communists, and intellectuals—was anybody from New York.

So he looks down and says, "New York's a shitty town." And then it was very quiet all around. People could tell this was a confrontation. And I suddenly realized that everyone was listening to how I'd answer: You know, you can't let yourself be pushed but so far. So my brain's spinning, and I say, "You've got a point there. I don't know why I stay there. . . ." At this point he seemed to realize that he wasn't going to get a fight or at least not one that he could be proud of; so he suddenly changed completely, sat down and said, "I used to live in New York. And there are only two ways to live there. You can live on the bottom floor because it's easy to get to a little air and space—a garden maybe—but all day long, five flights up they'll throw shit on you. Or, you can live on the fifth floor and throw shit on everybody else, but you have to climb five flights to get there. That's New York." The guy was a philosopher: He had something there.

Q: You've said you're writing a novel. How far along are you?

A: I have to be honest about that. I haven't begun the writing, but I have a working title, *Bonfire of the Vanities,* after this 15th-century Venetian religious reformer, Girolamo Savonarola. He used to go about Venice and have people bring all their vanities out of their houses, pile them in the street and light them on fire. He was quite popular for a while, but ended up being thrown on one of these bonfires himself. . . .I'm not sure exactly where that leaves me.

Q: Why write a novel?

A: I've made so many comparisons between fiction and nonfiction, I have to see what it's all about. I'll have to box myself in. It's like announcing a duel. After it's public, it's hard to back out.

An Interview with Tom Wolfe

Martin Levine/1981

Reprinted from *Book Digest*, November 1981, pp. 60-61.

In From Bauhaus to Our House, *you make much of what you call
"the colonial complex"—our tradition of looking to Europe for what
is chic and bright and sensible and modern.*

It starts in the '30s with the German refugees. It picks up very
rapidly in the '40s, when a lot of painters, even from France, start
coming to the United States. After the Second World War it only gets
stronger. That's the beauty of it to me. The United States becomes
the most powerful nation in the world . . .

*And we're embarrassed about our roadside stands in the shape of
ducks.*

We feel terribly inferior in cultural matters. And this only becomes
stronger as the years go by. I think literature is a particularly fascinating
example, because in the '30s the American realistic novel became
much admired in Europe. In France they discovered Faulkner—not,
as we would, as a very complex and somewhat arty writer, but as a
primitive who had barely emerged from the ooze, somehow, to write.

At the same time they were admiring the energetic, classless and
low-rent, rude, animal side of American art, our artists were striving
like mad to shed all of that and to stop being hicks and rustics.

The greatest period of the American novel in terms of worldwide
prestige was the '30s: Farrell, Hemingway. Dos Passos had a great
influence on Sartre. But after the Second World War, ironically, our
young writers in the universities picked up such models as Kafka.

Who did that?

John Gardner—although he's backing off now—Pynchon, Barthelme. Roth succumbed after starting off as a realist. This happened
to Mailer, too. It hurt him tremendously as a novelist. It hurt Roth
also. Look at books like *The Breast, The Great American Novel.*

Did you like Mailer's The Executioner's Song?

I must confess I haven't read it.

It keeps a dozen balls in the air at once, like a novel.

167

Well, Mailer always does better when he is forced to deal with new, real material. There are few people who have enough material in their own lives to keep turning out great fiction. Nineteenth century novelists understood this; as a matter of course they went out hunting for material outside of their own lives. Dostoevski and Dickens did it. Zola worked two weeks of the month taking notes and would knock off his fiction in the second two weeks. This was not considered anything very unusual.

And now Roth, for example, writes increasingly about what it's like to be a famous author beset by psychological conflicts.

I call this the "Dissertation on Roast Pig" complex. You remember Lamb's marvelous piece?

A Chinese farmer's house burns down. In the house is his pig. He tries to rescue the pig from the fire; the pig is by now roasted. He burns his fingers and licks them. And the thing is that it tastes so exquisite that it haunts him for months.

He rebuilds his house, and he has his pig inside again. And one day the memory of that taste becomes too much for him, and he burns his house down again. To have some more roast pig.

Now, this is what our novelists tend to do. Without knowing it, they burn down, or ransack—cannibalize—the first 25, 30 years of their lives. They've done involuntary reporting, I call it, by just living. And perhaps they've come across something interesting. So they use this material, and they come up with one great novel.

Then they decide they want to do another novel, and so they burn down the house again—namely, their lives. By this time they've only lived two or three more years, and the only drama in their lives has been "Gee, how am I going to get this second novel written?" So you have this rather dreadful second novel by an intellectual in a bind somewhere. The only person that I can think of who really pulled it off was my namesake Thomas Wolfe in *Of Time and the River.*

"The second-novel problem" is well-known. But don't most people see it as a psychological problem?

It's the material. Writers like to think that talent is 95 percent genius, which is something that exists in a little brass crucible deep in the recesses of their sphenoid sinuses, and five percent material. I think the proportions are more like 35-65.

As someone working in nonfiction, this has become very clear to me. I've *had* to go out and get the material. Where I've tried to write without enough material, I see that it affects not only the gravity of the story but also technique. Writers just don't like to face up to this.

Does your namesake occupy a special place in your psychic territory?

Yes. I suppose because of the name. He was one of the first novelists that I read. I was just swept away by the sort of thing that he did.

I was always convinced, incidentally, that Thomas Wolfe was kin to me, and it was very hard for my parents to convince me that he wasn't. I was named for my father, in fact.

Among the architects you mention in your new book, you seem especially fond of the "primitives."

Actually, strategically, I have tried to avoid saying who I like in art and architecture, because in these fields people like nothing better than to be able to put you in a category. And once they can file you away . . .

I want people to pay attention to what I think is my sole contribution in these areas—showing how certain fashions, certain styles, certain trends come about. They're not like the weather. Most of our critics and historians seem to think that styles are like Bermuda highs. That it's the spirit of the age and so cosmic in nature that you don't have to think about how it happened. You just note that it happened, and if the weather is serious enough, you bow down. What I keep saying is that styles are created by people. And the task of a historian—which is all I picture myself as in these books—is to find out who these people are and what the competitions were that brought the styles about.

Why do you prize uniqueness and the bizarre in the arts? What's wrong with learning an accepted language and expressing yourself in that?

If you're going to be in some field where you can express yourself, you might as well leave the world with something it hasn't seen before. You might as well cut up a bit. As someone who has grown up in America, I've always admired the tremendous energy and momentum that you sometimes see in the arts.

One of your early Esquire *pieces was about the neon signs of Las Vegas. There's a kind of progression from your perhaps not-totally-*

*reasoned-out awe in the face of that to what you have now made
into a whole esthetic theory.*

That was my first excursion into the idea of some sort of American
forms that did not come from inside the orthodox cultural precincts.
(I had a little bit of the same thing in *The Kandy-Kolored Tangerine-
Flake Streamline Baby.*) These signs are done by people who don't
have art-history backgrounds but are technically very sophisticated.
Now they've come up with some I've only seen pictures of that go
beyond anything else that has been done. The Thunderbird has a
quarter-of-a-mile-long sign out front, with two streams of light coming
from either side, and they collide in the center and explode . . . Wild.

*For a man who writes admiringly of the American style of "Hog-
Stomping Baroque," your living room here on the Upper East Side
shows none of the excesses one might expect.*

In my imagination I've dwelled in fantastic-looking places that have
somehow never come about. I have no real interest in architecture or
interior design; my interest is in the sociology of such things. This
room is very eclectic, to dignify it. This table is strictly Bauhaus. These
chairs are imitation Bourbon Louis. The carpet is Wilton Weave
Restaurant. All the carpet I like is in hotel lobbies and restaurants. You
can't wear this thing out with jackboots; I could invite the remnants of
the Polish army in to bivouac.

*Your dress is much more expressive. Have you always been a
dandy?*

I've been very crazy about clothes and conscious of them for a
long time. I guess it started in college. When I was at Washington and
Lee, all students were required to dress in coats and ties. I used to
take great delight in wearing black or maroon shirts, silver-blue ties
and powder-gray camel's hair coats.

*Does it annoy you that Americans often assume that men who
dress flamboyantly are homosexual?*

Sensitivity to homosexuality is very much a New York phenomenon. It never came up back home in Virginia. There always was
the tradition of the honorable dandy and the honorable bachelor. I've
always felt that people should be highly respected, if not actually
rewarded, for long bachelorhoods. [Wolfe married in 1978, at 47,
and has a year-old daughter.]

How many suits do you own?

I don't know. I guess I could have 30 or 40 feet of them. I'm conscious of feet because I don't have enough closet space. You see, other people play golf, tennis, take vacations in the Caribbean; they use up a lot of time and effort and imagination in these ways. With me it's been clothes.

And remains so.

It's not as much fun now as it was. When I started really cutting loose in New York, minor departures from conventional dress infuriated people as well as astounding them. Now that's not so.

My defense of my tastes would be that most departure from convention is in the direction of being casual. So the only real fun you can have—it's minor fun, just a small kick—is going pretentious. That's why I enjoy these high collars.

And dressing formally and elegantly but extremely is more subversive than simply thumbing your nose at the world with jeans and so on.

It is in the literary world. To this day I'm amused by jacket pictures of writers—there's an awful lot of Lord Byron's locks flowing in the wind, and open shirts.

You're writing your first novel, aren't you—a New York City panorama?

Yes. I should say this publicly so I can't possibly do otherwise.

When will it come out?

I would dearly love to see it come out next year, but that's not likely to happen; '83 is more realistic. I've had a book a year for three years now—books of sorts—and I honestly think writers should have a book every year.

You've established a comfortable, even luxurious life style for yourself. Have you done it all on the proceeds of your books?

Yes, I have no other source of income. I was surprised how well it worked out when I went completely freelance in 1967. I discovered that the only path to any kind of financial security is to have something to sell. Fees won't get you there; it's not enough, even, to be a doctor anymore. A book is like a little factory that's out there chugging away. It may not do terribly well, but it's out there working while you sleep.

What Are the Social Pressures Affecting the Art World Today?

Lori Simmons Zelenko/1982

From *American Artist*, 46 (April 1982), 12-13, 82, 84, 86. Reprinted from *American Artist* Magazine with permission from
Billboard Publications, Inc. Copyright © 1982, Billboard Publications, Inc. All rights reserved.

A dandy vision in chocolate-brown and ivory, Tom Wolfe doffs his
matching fedora as he greets me in the crisply checkered foyer of his
Manhattan townhouse. Momentarily distracted, he stoops to play
with his toddler daughter, Alexandra. This low-key, loving parent
demeanor is a contrast to the biting tone of his social satires of the art
world, the architects, and the astronauts.

Infused with energy, he joyfully tackles my question, What are the
social pressures affecting the art world today? "When people talk
about the art world, they talk about it as if it is some sort of cosmos
where ineffable developments—styles—arrive like Bermuda Highs
from God. They settle over an area and, suddenly, there is
modernism, or minimalism, or conceptualism. There has never been
any realistic explanation of how these things work." Without taking
his eyes from my face, he continues his metaphorical answer. "We
never see the geology. We never see the earthquakes. We have no
analysis of the mountains. We dwell on the peaks. There is not even a
realistic picture of how Picasso became Picasso. This is the part of the
art world that intrigues me.

"I feel I have nothing much to offer to aesthetics. I don't pay
attention to other people's opinions of what is good or bad. I don't
think anyone should pay attention. People always ask me about my
taste in things," he says, grinning as he glances around the room's
multi-colored jumble of books, paintings, pillows, and furniture
representing a potpourri of interests and eras. "As you can see, it is
what is dignified by the term 'eclectic.'" Laughing, he adds, "It goes
under the better name of 'motley' or 'hodgepodge.'

"I can't tell you how bored I am with the question in the absolute.

I'm interested only in how certain tastes become established. I insist that they become established in a political fashion, using politics in a broad sense as various social pressures added together to produce a particular result, specifically in the case of the arts—painting, sculpture, and architecture. I think my major contribution is one that is seldom mentioned," he says, smiling ironically. "If I go by the reviews, it is my theory of compounds.

"We are in a period that is unique in the history of art. We are still in the first century where artists themselves have announced that they are going to band together and control taste. They will be answerable to no one but themselves. They will, in effect, create 'churches.' " Speaking with growing intensity, Wolfe discusses this phenomenon, which he feels finds its roots in the Sezession (Secession) movement in Vienna, Munich, and Berlin during the 1890s. The artists and architects of the Sezession, among them Gustav Klimt and Otto Wagner, rebelled against bourgeois academic strictures. They said, "We want out and we are taking artistic authority with us . . . we will tell you what is divine in art and you will take our word for it."

Wolfe calls the Sezession "a semi-religious art movement," feeling that this perception of art as religion still prevails: "Most people who become involved in art and architecture in a serious way come as believers. They are people who are already truly enthused and passionate about the subjects. They want to believe the most cosmic things about the arts, replacing religion as a system of belief for educated people. That was Nietzsche's prediction. Max Weber predicted that aesthetics would replace ethics as the standard of conduct for educated people. I think we see a lot of evidence of this development. Galleries and museums have replaced yesterday's churches as the institutions to which people of means devote their needs, their money, their time, and their passions. They leave their money to these places and not to their church on Fifth Avenue."

If art is the religion of the 21st century, it is not one for the masses. "The fervent congregation of the art world is no more than 10,000 people world-wide," declares Wolfe, "and no more than 3,000 people in the United States, with almost all of them in New York City, if not living here, visiting frequently, dining at Lutèce. That is presented as history. It's bonkers!"

Tom Wolfe sees himself as the first sociologist of the art world. He has been called a philistine, a term he says he feels comfortable with these days. "I took the trouble to look it up," he states proudly, emphatically adding, "which I am sure none of the people who have used the epithet have ever done. It is a term coined by Matthew Arnold about 100 years ago. He said in 1869 that the world was a modern society with three classifications. There were barbarians, by which he meant the upper classes; philistines, the unenlightened middle classes; and the populists, the lower or working classes. There were also enlightened members of the middle classes and an occasional barbarian with good instincts who would save culture, also a word he coined." To Wolfe, a philistine is someone who exists outside the compound, that small world of literary people and artists. "A person with impeccable theoretic models," he chuckles softly, "and I won't give you two guesses as to who that might be. This person will describe the walls, take you inside to show you the people who reside therein; and will also take you out again, giving you an analysis of that walled world. The person who is willing to do this is not going to be found inside that art world.

"Whenever people in the world of art try to tackle history, they get it totally backwards," says Wolfe, explaining that he is always accused of dreaming up theories of conspiracy in *The Painted Word* and *From Bauhaus to Our House*. Specifically, he says, he is misinterpreted. People believe that he believes "European conspirators came to America and forced their styles upon us. I am saying the opposite." Wolfe feels Americans have willingly abandoned personal vision and originality as they gladly worship European styles. "Creativity has been sacrificed in order to work à la mode."

Wolfe continues: "There are no conspiracies in the field of Modern Art, certainly not among the dealers, the critics, and the museum curators. Nobody would go into contemporary art as a dealer with the notion of making money. You would have to be an absolute maniac to do so. You go into it because you believe in it.

"It is almost a central assumption of the art 'aborigines'—the people who write the history and the criticism of art—that all of history is reflected in the great art of the period. It is more nearly true to say that nothing in the history of our times is reflected in the most prestigious art," he clarifies. "Nothing that is creative is present. Now I say that is nearly true, because there is no way that an individual cannot reflect something of the time. But I am talking about artists like Robert Rauschenberg, Jasper Johns, any of the famous names. De Kooning . . . how could you find an artist who has less to do with the age he lives in than de Kooning?"

Exulting in this illustration of his theory, Wolfe goes on: "He's not connected to this planet! Neither was Jackson Pollock. Not in terms of what they did as artists. Look at Andy Warhol. You would say his Pop Art is certainly connected. He used mass-produced forms—Brillo boxes, Campbell's soup cans—at precisely the time when the age of mass production had come to an end. The age of computerization had begun. It is amazing anytime there happens to be a connection. It is totally anachronistic. Rauschenberg's vision, his collages of the city, seem to have a certain connection, but look at the images and the colors. Always washed-out, dull, lifeless."

Sex is the major element missing from prestigious contemporary painting, Tom Wolfe vehemently observes, flashing his brown-and-white houndstooth check socks. "It does not exist. It's amazing. This is the most sexually amok age in American history," he observes, "probably in the history of any country in the history of the world. We are drenched in sex. We are treading water in it. We are going down for the third time in a sea of sexual hormones. But . . . in art . . . nothing! Zero! There is a blank, with the one exception of Tom Wesselmann's airbrush-style nudes and Ramos's *Chiquita Banana Girl,* which are done purposefully to remove the sexual content from the image. Wesselmann's nudes are done like the Doublemint twins of advertising fame. His technique consciously presents you with a sexual image and then removes the sexuality from it to complete the process of de-sexualization. It is quite marvelous how empty of contemporary life this type of representation is.

"There is no rule that art has to be influenced by the age in which it exists," Wolfe elaborates. "It is remarkable in the past history of art when you don't find it, and even more remarkable when the statement is made that all of our times are summed up in great art. When arguments for this idea are made, someone has to explain the point. But explanations are usually given in the most metaphorical language. It's crystal-ball reading," Wolfe exclaims, sitting calmly. "When you look into a swirl of paint by de Kooning and say, 'Here is a maelstrom of the events of our time . . . the chaos . . . the social clamor . . . ,' that's just tea-leaf reading.

"Writers don't hesitate to look objectively, sociologically, politically at American business life, American military life, or any other sector of the United States government. But somebody comes along like myself and tries to look at the art world the same way . . . everyone starts screaming." Wolfe shrugs, amused. "I've insisted I've done no more than a job of reporting, research, and analysis, which should be done in every field. Art and architecture people tend to take a sociological approach as an insult, reacting to it with, 'You can't soil us with your conceptual apparatus that you apply to the outside world.'" With mock seriousness, he adds, "I think that this world should be grateful to me. I have done the work that none of them care to do."

So why isn't the art world appreciative? "You would think that they would be, but it is taken as an affront, as an insult, as not accepting the religious standards of the world within the world. I am not trying to make what I have done sound any bigger than it is. It only has to do with American art and architecture, which are not the greatest subjects in the world.

"I have written the evolution of the species for American painting and American architecture. *From Bauhaus to Our House* and *The Painted Word* are the first books to show how the species actually evolved as opposed to the notion that they arrived in the Garden of Eden and just wandered out. The cries are the cries that were heard at the time of the Scopes trial. It doesn't make as much difference, but it is the same phenomenon. As I hear some of the shrieks, I can think only of Mencken's account of the confrontation between Darwin and William Jennings Bryan. I cast myself in the role of Darwin, not Darrow."

Will the art world simmer down long enough to consider the validity of Tom Wolfe's point of view? "Yes, I think it has already happened. If these books have served no other useful purpose within these worlds than to make the soup bubble a little faster, they are worth it." He grins, relishing the controversy in his cool Southern way. "Once someone presents the actual history of your own world, it is hard not to reflect upon it; even if you hate it, you think about it. I do think my books have been of benefit to these worlds, but I will get, and will expect, no thanks." He laughs at this pious pose. "I can't take credit for this, although I know I have helped the process along. There is a chaos of standards in both fields. I think it would happen with or without what I have written. The modern movement in each field has reached a point of exhaustion from overuse. You cannot do the same thing interminably. It just wears out of its own accord."

Heeding his own advice, Tom Wolfe does not plan another sociological dissection of the arts. "I promise not to write a book called *The Lost Chord,* about the world of serious music." He smiles slyly, looking something like the proverbial cat who swallowed the canary. "This is my last book about art and architecture." Satisfied, he smiles again as he says, "I feel like I have had my say."

CA Interview

Mary V. McLeod/1983

From *Contemporary Authors, New Revision Series*, vol. 9, ed. Ann Evory and Linda Metzger (Detroit: Gale Research Co., 1983), pp. 536-39. Reprinted with permission.

CA interviewed Tom Wolfe by phone August 7, 1981, at his office in Southhampton, N.Y.

You're credited with creating the nonfiction short story—the New Journalism—which has been criticized for being too personal, too unbelievable. Was this early criticism ever discouraging to you?

Only in the sense that when people referred to it as too personal or too impressionistic, I felt like they had totally missed the point of what I and a number of other writers were doing. Most of the major things that I have written, like *The Right Stuff* and *The Electric Kool-Aid Acid Test,* have not been personal. They've been completely about the lives of other people, with myself hardly intruding into the narrative at all. They were based on reporting, so a lot of it is impersonal and objective. It can be discouraging to see it described as implausible, personal, and unbelievable.

I very seldom use the first person anymore. I think it's a very tricky thing because whether you know it or not, if you use the first person you've turned yourself into a character, and you have to be ready to make that character an important part of the narrative.

In the introduction to The New Journalism, *you wrote about the very few novels that evolved from the 1960s, a period "the novelists had been kind enough to leave behind" for the New Journalists. With all that was happening socially and politically then, why do you think novelists shied away from writing about it?*

I think the main reason was because the realistic novel had gone out of fashion. This is part of what I call our colonial complex. In the arts, we're still the most obedient little colonial subjects that Europe could ever ask for. After the Second World War, there was quite a vogue for European fiction as practiced by Kafka, the Soviet writer Evgeny Zamyatin, the South American writer Gabriel Garcia Marquez, and the playwrights Harold Pinter and Samuel Beckett. They

178

were all influential among novelists writing what I think of as the modern fable, in which all of the trappings of realism are scrupulously removed. The realistic novel is considered old-fashioned, old hat. The idea was that after Balzac, Henry James, Proust, and Joyce, what was there left to do with the realistic novel? It had all been done. The flaw there is the fact that realism in prose is not just one technique out of many.

In my opinion, you can't advance the state of the art of literature by turning your back on realism. Due to sheer intellectual fashion you have a generation of young novelists turning their backs on the most potent devices in prose, namely the devices of realism. The only important realists in prose became the journalists. That's why I said that New Journalists had a field day in that period. For example, the three major books written about Vietnam were all by nonfiction writers—Michael Herr's *Dispatches,* C.D.B. Bryan's *Friendly Fire,* and John Sack's *M.* So you have about a thirty-five-year period from 1945 to the present in which the most talented young novelists coming from the universities steered away from the realistic novel. The publishers were dying for the great realistic novels that were going to be written and they just weren't forthcoming. I think the business of intellectual fashion is terribly underrated. I think it plays a much bigger part in the lives and careers of writers than any of the larger issues of the world.

Do you think the events of the 1960s were perhaps too painful for novelists to write about?

I think there are very few things writers find too painful to write about once they think that's the direction they should go.

In an article in the Los Angeles Times *[19 October 1979] you said, "At the risk of being immodest, I suppose I'm probably the most parodied writer in the last fifteen years." How do you react to the many journalists who try to imitate your style?*

Every now and then somebody will bring me a piece and say, "Here's somebody imitating your style," and I read it and I *like* it, I think it's pretty good. There's always an implied flattery in being parodied, even if the parody is meant to be an attack. That's why I seldom use parody as a weapon, because no matter how vigorous you attack, you're also patting your subject on the back. When I wrote the piece about the *New Yorker* in 1965, I got many people upset. The whole idea was based on a parody that Wolcott Gibbs had done of the *Time* magazine style back in the late 1930s, when *Time* was very new and very lively. I started writing a parody of the *New Yorker* style, but I could see that there had been so many parodies of the *New Yorker* that they were all compliments in a way; they were saying, "Here is a magazine with a recognizable style." If you parody a dull style—and the *New Yorker* style had become very dull—you can get away with it for about a page. For one page, a dull style is funny. For two pages, it just becomes dull and boring. So I opted for the antiparody and took a tone that was as far removed from the *New Yorker* as possible, which was a kind of screaming tabloid style, and I think it worked better.

Do you get many requests from journalists to read their writing and comment on it?

I get a lot of requests from all types of writers, but I've finally reached the point where I just can't accommodate those requests. Once somebody gives you a manuscript, they really want an answer *tomorrow;* they expect it. To tell you the truth, I think I get more requests from novelists than anyone else. One good thing about journalism is that you're being pressured to produce by a deadline and get it out of your system. The manuscripts don't seem to linger around as much, whereas often a novelist or a short-story writer is simply having a hard time getting published at all, and is just looking for any sort of reaction.

What advice would you give aspiring journalists who are just getting started?

I would offer what I think is very practical advice—to somehow understand very early in the game that there is no substitute for reporting. For that reason you should get a job on a newspaper, no matter how miserable it is (this country is mainly full of miserable newspapers) just to get used to the process of reporting and acquaint yourself with a few things that you wouldn't see otherwise, no matter how boring it may seem. I would also suggest that you not be bashful, particularly if you have an idea for a magazine story. You should get up your courage and approach the biggest magazine you can think of that might be interested in the subject. Approach a junior editor rather than the man at the top, because the junior editors are in competition with one another to discover new writers. Even if you've already written it, present the story idea to the editor, because editors like to feel that they're part of the creative process. Wait a decent interval of about two weeks and then send them a manuscript. Magazines will be in a receptive mood if you have approached them ahead of time. They'll want it to be good, they'll want to buy it, and they'll want it to be a success. There's a continual shortage of good writers and good journalists. It's really not an overcrowded field because there's not that much talent to go around. A lot of it is having the determination and perseverance to do the reporting.

You've illustrated most of your own books and have had several one-man shows of your drawings. Do the writing and the art influence each other? Is it hard to separate the two?

They *should* be two very different things because I have the feeling that they are different neurologically. At one point I used to try to illustrate newspaper stories that I had written myself against a daily deadline; so I would do both things in the same day. That was maddening because they're so different. All this business of the two hemispheres of the brain is probably correct. If you're concentrating on a design or a drawing, it's almost impossible to listen to words at the same time. And if you're listening to words for their content, it's almost impossible to draw at the same time. Now I often illustrate the stories after I've written them. Some of the things that I do for *Harper's* magazine, I do the drawing first, just because I've seen something that appealed to me, and then I think of the copy afterwards. I find that the drawings are more successful if they happen that way. If the illustration follows something I've written, I find it more difficult to give the drawing a life or a compelling design of its own. The words that I've already written are influencing the drawing in a bad way. I can't explain that, but I find that if the drawing comes to me first and then the words, it's better.

Reviews of The Right Stuff *were mixed—some critics missed your usual flamboyant stream-of-consciousness style, and others said it was your best book yet. Were you pleased with it?*

I felt that it was my best book. I very consciously tried to make the style fit the particular world I was writing about, mainly the world of military pilots. To have had a prose as wound up as the prose of *The Electric Kool-Aid Acid Test* would have been a stylistic mistake. I've always insisted that there was no set Tom Wolfe style, that I was trying to make a style fit the event. So many of the things that I wrote about in the 1960s were so wild in themselves that a wild style seemed to fit. The world of military pilots was different, a world that seemed to me to require a different tone.

The book was extremely difficult to write. There was no central character, no protagonist. There were seven Mercury astronauts, three or four pilots in the X-series of experimental flights, such as Chuck Yeager and Scott Crossfield. The problem of giving the book a narrative structure, some sort of drive and suspense, was quite tough. I finally adopted the technique of trying to make each chapter, particularly the early ones, like a short story, with the hope that if that chapter was effective, if the story was effective, then you would go on to the next one. It had none of the ordinary structure of the novel, including the nonfiction novel. Yet somehow I had to try to make it work and have a dramatic structure. I think I finally succeeded, but during the writing of it I became tremendously discouraged.

Is The Right Stuff *going to be made into a movie?*

Yes. The project is in the hands of the Alan Ladd, Jr., organization.

Will you have a hand in the production?

No, I will have no part in making the movie; it's out of my hands. I know the producers, and I have every confidence that they'll make a good picture out of it.

Is your work schedule still ten pages a day?

Yes, that's the way I worked on *The Right Stuff.* If you're writing nonfiction, there's no use getting into the schedule until you've done the reporting and you have the material. Once I've done the reporting, I've found that the only way to make myself get the writing done is to adopt the ten-pages-a-day schedule. I always make an outline, but if I try to make myself cover a certain portion of the outline each day, that's very dispiriting. It's psychologically crushing because a part of the outline that you thought would take a page may turn out to take six or seven pages. But if you set a quota, the pain can't last but so long. I do find writing a very painful process—I never understand writers who say it's enjoyable. I think it's the hardest work in the world. It's like having arthritis or something; it's a little pain every day and you have to press on.

I wanted the writing to appear buoyant, free and easy, spon-taneous. Creating the effect of spontaneity in writing is one of the most difficult and artificial things you can do. I was much relieved to learn that Celine used to spend four or five years rewriting his novels in order to achieve the effect of someone just sitting down across the table from you, spouting up the story of his life. Writing is an extremely artificial business; it's artificial by its very nature—you're taking sounds and converting them into symbols on a page. To make that transference from one sense to another and reinvest the words with vigor and rhythm and spontaneity is quite a feat.

How much revising do you do?

I tend to do as much revising as editors will let me do. I rewrote most of *The Right Stuff* and I rewrote *Radical Chic* a couple of times. But there was no revision at all with *The Electric Kool-Aid Acid Test*. I was writing against a book deadline and I sent in chapters as I finished them. I did a little bit of last-minute revision when the book was in galley form, but that was it. Sometimes the greatest favor an editor can do a writer is to trick him into yielding up the manuscript.

Has the critical reception of your work—both positive and negative—been helpful to you?

All writers like to say they don't pay any attention to it. I wish I had thought of Arnold Bennett's line, "I don't read my reviews, I only measure them." I don't think Arnold Bennett really meant it. Writers all wear their egos on their sleeves. It's irresistible, the business of reacting to reviews.

I was fortunate in that very early in my career, when I was unknown, I was severely criticized and denounced by very eminent people, particularly in the case of the *New Yorker* article. I was working at the *New York Herald Tribune* at the time and I didn't have a book out or anything—I was just a man who wrote magazine articles for the Sunday supplement. I suddenly found myself denounced by the likes of Joseph Alsop, Walter Lippmann (he called me an ass in print), Murray Kempton, a distinguished columnist for the *New York Post*. Richard Goodwin called up from the White House to denounce me; E. B. White; even J. D. Salinger, whom the press hadn't heard from for years, sent in a telegram denouncing me as a yellow journalist. I really felt that perhaps the world was coming to an end. All these eminent people descended upon me, and I felt the sky was falling in.

Then a few days later I woke up, and nothing had happened. It dawned on me that it's very difficult to get hurt in a literary fight. In a strange way, all the shouting and shooting and the explosions were part of the literary excitement. I took so much abuse at that time that I think it made me fireproof. So now if I am attacked in a review—and it happens quite often—I can't say that I like it, but I know that no matter what it says, the sky really isn't going to fall.

Are you working on a novel now?

I am. I hate people who say they're "working on a novel"; it means they haven't started. But I've begun to do the reporting. The novel depends on it. It's about New York City today. So like anybody else, I have to go out and see what's going on, because you can lose track of things so very quickly. The novel will be about New York, high and low.

Is that a hard transition to make, from journalism into straight fiction?

We'll see. I did one long short story in 1975 called "The Commercial." It's in the collection *Mauve Gloves & Madmen, Clutter & Vine*. It's about a baseball player making a commercial. I thought I was going to be able to do it in several weekends, but I was quite shocked to see that writing fiction wasn't all that easy. I thought that since you could make up things there was nothing to it, but it's not easy to make up things effectively. The imagination needs material. I had to put everything aside and do some reporting—how commercials are made, what athletes think about, and for that particular story, a little research about class structure in the black community, because the baseball player was black. That story was a good exercise for me because it showed me that I had to approach it with the same kind of reporting that would go into *The Right Stuff* or anything else.

Would you like to comment on the status of New Journalism today?

Fortunately, as a subject that people talk about and write about, it has largely died out except in the case of something like the Janet Cooke fiasco. Then everyone decides they'll blame it on the New Journalism. [Janet Cooke won the Pulitzer Prize for journalism in 1981 for a story she wrote about an eight-year-old heroin addict. She later admitted that the story was a composite, and the prize was relinquished.] That whole business really made me laugh.

It reminded me of when I first went to work on the *New York Herald Tribune* and they were still laughing over the ship-of-sin scandal from prohibition days. An informant had told the *Herald Tribune* that there was a ship of sin operating outside of a three-mile limit off of eastern Long Island. On board you could get liquor and dope and sex. So the *Tribune* sent a reporter out. He didn't find the ship, but he *did* find a saloon in Montauk, and he phoned in about five days' worth of the most lurid stories in the history of drunk newspapermen. Half of New York City gasped and the other half rushed out to eastern Long Island to rent motor launches, until it was discovered he had made up the whole thing. These things happen about every three or four years; some reporter gets caught piping a story out of his skull.

Today, it makes the newspaper industry and publishers and editors feel a lot better if they can blame it on some strange new Legionnaire's Disease, some new strain of bacteria, that is afflicting the young writers. Then all you have to do is develop a vaccine, and the problem is on the way to being cured. Phony stories are going to be written every once in a while, so long as you give reporters the trust that you have to give them. But to blame it on the New Journalism or any other new thing is ludicrous. There's nothing new about sham.

Other than that, the New Journalism was superceded in terms of publicity several years ago by the investigative reporting era, starring Woodward and Bernstein. I think that was all for the good as far as techniques in nonfiction are concerned. I was beginning to feel bad about having touted this thing myself so assiduously. I had the feeling I was beginning to make people self-conscious about the form and the techniques; one of the virtues had been that it had happened without any self-consciousness or tradition. There was a great deal of freedom and a great deal of experimentation with it when it started out. The best thing that could happen is what has happened now. The techniques are all known. The young writers who want to use them will use them because they know what they are. But it's not constantly talked about so that writers will look over their shoulders and wonder if they're doing it correctly.

GEO Conversation: Tom Wolfe

Ron Reagan/1983

From GEO, 5 (October 1983), 14-26. Reprinted by permission of William Morris Agency on behalf of Ron Reagan.

Tom Wolfe has been making people angry for almost 20 years now, ever since he decided that the novelists of the day were not properly capturing the era, not getting it all down right, so engrossed were they in "poor, frantic little exercises in form." The Sixties, a vast virgin territory of cults and subcults, trends, fads, rituals and fashions, were unfolding everywhere. Wolfe charged in with a style as outlandish as the times, and the result was *The Kandy-Kolored Tangerine-Flake Streamline Baby,* published in 1965. The New Journalism was born.

Wolfe staked out his own high ground, and from this ridge of iconoclastic conservatism he has brought to bear his considerable gifts for satire and criticism. A variety of cultural phenomena have felt the sting of his attention: glass-box architecture in *From Bauhaus to Our House,* arbiters of artistic fashion in *The Painted Word* and limousine liberals in *Radical Chic & Mau-Mauing the Flak Catchers.* Whether these books were timely lampoons of what is foolish in American culture or merely polemical expressions of an archconservative point of view remains a matter of lively debate.

Wolfe is quite capable of putting aside his slings and arrows, however. In books such as *The Electric Kool-Aid Acid Test* and *The Right Stuff* (the movie version of which will appear in theaters this month), he combines his reportorial skills with his flamboyant style to re-create portions of the American experience that eluded day-to-day media coverage. And he is currently at work on his first novel.

Thomas Kennerly Wolfe, Jr., was born in Richmond, Virginia, in 1931. After receiving a Ph.D. in American studies from Yale in 1957, Wolfe went to work as a reporter. He served as Latin-American correspondent for the *Washington Post* before moving to New York to write for the *New York Herald Tribune* and numerous magazines. After 18 years and 10 books, Wolfe's writing remains

unfailingly popular. His singular sartorial style is also un-
diminished. When Ron Reagan met him at his townhouse
in New York City, Wolfe was wearing a double-breasted
gray-and-white houndstooth-check suit with a lime-green
tie and the inevitable high-collared shirt.

GEO: After so many years devoted to journalism, why have you
decided to write a novel?

Wolfe: I'm not abandoning nonfiction. I still consider myself
primarily a nonfiction writer. But every time I've done a long piece of
nonfiction, I've said, "I'll never do this again. It's too hard." I've
always had the idea of writing a novel in my head.

GEO: Is it the research that makes working on nonfiction so
difficult, having to deal with veracity and detail?

Wolfe: Well, I'm finding that fiction and nonfiction aren't at all
dissimilar as far as the research goes. I find that to get the kind of
detail I want—not just the kind of detail but the kind of information—
I have to do reporting. So in a way it's turned out to be just as big a
job. In nonfiction, there's a marvelous discovery that's forced upon
you by the facts. For example, when I was researching *The Right
Stuff,* there were always these stories about a woman—sometimes
she was described as a nurse, sometimes as a cocktail waitress—who
eventually went to bed with all seven Mercury astronauts and went
around saying, "Four down, three to go." Well, I had looked and
looked into that thing, and as far as I could tell, there wasn't any such
person. But the general attitude of the astronauts toward what we call
groupies was interesting. There were some, such as John Glenn, who
were dead against the whole business of messing around with these
girls and others who had different attitudes—it was a problem to
some, not to others. In fact, for my money the different approaches
to that temptation made a much more interesting and complicated
story than the yarn about this cocktail waitress.

GEO: You've chosen New York as the setting for your novel?

Wolfe: Yes. The idea is to do a novel with a city in the forefront,
the way Paris was in the forefront in the novels of Zola and Balzac.
I'm choosing New York because it happens to be *the* Western city of
the second half of the twentieth century, just as Paris was in the 1840s
or London in the 1860s or 1870s. It's the city where things happen,

meaning where people go if they're ambitious and want to breathe the same air that other illustrious people breathe. My idea is to write a novel of the city of ambition.

GEO: Did *From Bauhaus to Our House* spring from some negative, visceral reaction to the architecture that has changed the character of American cities?

Wolfe: My interest in writing *From Bauhaus to Our House* was not to express aesthetic preferences in architecture but to present an intellectual history of how ideas take hold in the United States, which is still a little colony of Europe when it comes to ideas. One of the latest European ideas to take hold here is the nuclear freeze. People have accepted it the way surfers accept a wave: it doesn't matter what formed it, what storm out there kicked up this lovely wave, they just want to catch it and go with it. But in the intellectual area, *where* it came from, the fact that it came from Europe, remains all important.

GEO: Was there a point when architecture began to free itself from the dictates of European taste and the desires of the so-called common man?

Wolfe: I think it upset things tremendously here that the working class started making so much money and was in a position to express itself. When I wrote a piece about Las Vegas years ago, the thing that interested me about the city was that it, the *new* Las Vegas, had been created by gangsters. This in turn was interesting because they were uneducated; so here was an entire city built according to the tastes of uneducated people. Leaving aside the fact that they were gangsters, that's a big version of what took place in many smaller places all over the country: uneducated people having the money and also the freedom, the social freedom, to express themselves in architecture and in many other ways.

GEO: What do you mean by "social freedom" in this case?

Wolfe: I say social freedom because to this day, the United States is one of the few countries in which people—as long as they're not in cultural areas—have no hesitation whatsoever about expressing their own tastes without looking over their shoulders to see what people of elegance and refinement might think. In the cultural areas, being good little colonials, they still do that; they look for approval from Europe. In Europe, to this day, everybody who achieves wealth immediately wants to convert it into aristocratic bearing. That continues to be true in New York, but almost only in New York. The new fortunes in the computer and microprocessing businesses are being made by people who are completely different. One of the fascinating things about the Silicon Valley fortune is that it doesn't seem to produce the same type of rich person. I get the impression that they're not as comfortable with limousines and chauffeurs and doormen. It's interesting that the impulse toward aristocracy in this country becomes more and more attenuated the farther west you go. Sure, people want to live a fancy life, but they don't really want to do it in the European aristocratic way.

GEO: Fashions in art, architecture and thought aren't the only ones that come from Europe. What about youth trends like punk?

Wolfe: The history of punk seems to go as follows: It was picked up by young English people and used in somewhat the same way that Los Angeles teenagers used the word *rotten* to mean good. Punk had a certain genuine quality at the outset in England as a kind of version of the great gob of spit in the face of the class system. So there was this elaborate glorification of things rotten, as in the name Johnny Rotten. Then it was brought to this country in magazines. It had no roots in this country whatsoever. Young people read about it, and the shops existed before the phenomenon. It just caught on as a fashion. This is what I think of as information ricochet. The Hell's Angels, for example, didn't exist until the movie *The Wild One*. They looked at *The Wild One* and said, "Oh, that's the way it's done." So they took their own name and insignia and stuff, and Roger Corman came by and said, "Oh, that's the way it's done," and made a movie called *The Wild Angels*. And the Hell's Angels came by and said, "That's a nice idea; we'll do that." That's information ricochet. Punk was developed the same way, and the only genuine thing about it is a general impulse among people in their late teens to thumb their noses at the ongoing attempts to make them act like adults, which begin to seem like an imposition and rather boring. So you glorify wanton, impudent violence.

GEO: I suppose long hair and marijuana were threatening enough for a parent, but when your son comes through the door with safety pins through his nipples and a mohawk and he's carrying a chain, isn't that the ultimate gob of spit?

Wolfe: But I get the impression that the boys and girls involved don't feel the original punk emotion. They don't know what the class system is. There is no class system here, and I don't think they'd know what you meant if you brought up the subject, which is probably all to their good. You might say they feel nihilism, but I don't think they do. It's interesting to watch the cable music channel and see the mental atmosphere of the recording stars. It's this mindless frenetic race of young people walking through de Chirico landscapes of barren high-tech alleyways. This is all a wonderful pose. The wives of the male stars are on the telephone all day to Bloomingdale's or I. Magnin trying to get the order for the polished chintz or the Austrian shades done right.

GEO: If punk is an empty fashion that amounts to little more than clothing and music, what do you see as a real youth trend?

Wolfe: There is much more openness about expressing status among young people now than there was, say, in the Sixties or Seventies. College students, a certain segment of them, had an orgy of *nostalgie de la boue,* nostalgia for the mud, and attempted, like Louis XVI in his last year, to get closer to the people. Louis XVI began sleeping on the floor to be closer to the people—of course, he was still sleeping in a castle. The style the students developed began to be picked up by the people they pretended to be identifying themselves with. For example, when long hair began to be picked up by actual working-class youth, the children above the bachelor's degree line, where the father has a bachelor's degree from a good college, recoiled. So now that hair, which was very much the hair of the educated classes ten years ago, is almost exclusively that of guys working in the lube pit at the service station. You see it at the construction sites, but you don't see it in Harvard Yard. People, no matter what age, never lose their sense of status divisions. They only playact at losing it.

GEO: Do you see any signals that we are replacing the principles on which Americans governed their lives in the past?

Wolfe: In a piece I wrote called "The Me Decade," I presented the notion that the next assumption of Western civilization to be challenged would be the idea of serial immortality—the assumption that you live on not only through your children but through the children of your society. Even people who are single make wills, because there's an assumption that even after you're gone, you should do something nice for someone you care about. The assumption is that life goes on, the great stream goes on. People sacrifice for their children without thinking of what the consequences are because there's an assumption, although never stated, that what comes after is important. I predicted that this would be the next great assumption to be challenged. You can see it in the rise in child killings and abandonment. People are expressing the notion, "Why should I have to sacrifice for a child who is going to do nothing for me?" It's as if the prophecy has come true too fast. There's a hint of it in the increase in divorces. The idea of keeping a family together for the sake of the children, that is, for the sake of the great stream, doesn't cut much ice.

GEO: Do you think that the nuclear dilemma—"We're all going to be blown to hell in the next decade, so who cares?"—has anything to do with the upset of our past assumptions?

Wolfe: I don't believe anyone thinks that. The nuclear-freeze movement is by and large an intellectual fashion, and I don't think its roots are very deep. I attended the rally in New York last year. I noticed that with the exception of Arthur Miller, none of the big names or semi-big names or even junior-welterweight names that had signed the manifesto turned up for the big event. The nuclear-freeze movement has very little sex appeal. It's like being against typhoons. A repoter came up to me during the rally and asked me if I was there to be a part of the freeze movement. I said I was there to take a look at it, and he said, "You mean you don't support it?" I said, "I support the idea of peace, but it seems to me that if your objective is peace, you might examine a couple of other possibilities for preserving peace."

GEO: Such as?

Wolfe: So far as I know, no democracy has ever waged war against another, certainly not in the twentieth century. So I said that it seemed to me that the way to work for peace was to insist upon democracy. It's not as much a pie-in-the-sky idea as it might seem. Even to this day, I don't think anyone interested in peace and good things for mankind insists on democracy enough for, say, a country like Poland. These things are seldom actually said.

GEO: It seems that we're selective in our concern for the political futures of other countries. How can a Pol Pot sweep through

Cambodia and slaughter millions of people and the story end up as just a media blip?

Wolfe: So much of the political thought and fashion among writers and other commentators in the United States is based on the idea that liberty has always existed in a kind of mist over the left. In this country there have been very few idealogues, but there has often been a Marxist mist, the idea that there is something wonderful about socialism that if pursued correctly will lead to liberty, peace, harmony and the betterment of man in a way that nothing going on in a modern industrial nation can. In the past ten years it's been discovered that socialism, when put into effect by experts, leads only to extermination camps. This has been a terrible blow to a very fashionable idea. That's why it's embarrassing to dwell on Pol Pot. Pol Pot is not a maniac. He's a man who studied the future for his country for years starting in France, and the whole Khmer Rouge movement was probably as rational an undertaking under a Marxist ruler as has ever occurred. Everywhere the experts have put socialism into effect, the result has been the gulag. Now to point this out is to be regarded as right wing. I regard it only as obvious—so obvious, in fact, that you have to be crazy to avert your eyes from it.

GEO: Did the Marxist mist drift over here from Europe?

Wolfe: Mannerist Marxism is one of the reigning fashions now, and there are a lot of latter-day curlicues of Marxism here and in Europe. One of the nuttiest expressions of mannerist Marxism is the vogue that has swept through most of our major universities—structuralism, which now dominates both philosophy and English.

GEO: Can you explain structuralism?

Wolfe: The premise of structuralism is that the structure of the language is part of the baggage of capitalism. The bourgeoisie has dominated the very syntax of the language so that no matter what the people say, they are given the opportunity to learn nothing else. The idea is to take the structure of the language apart to expose these mechanisms. So far as I know, there isn't a single example of the kind of political construction of language that they insist exists. Nevertheless, this dominates the philosophy and literature in this country's major universities today, to the point where philosophers who concern themselves with the psychology and fate of man are looked upon as the most reprobate idealists. The whole notion of being an academic of prestige, an intellectual, has become more and more dependent on the art of separating yourself from the bourgeoisie and other influences to ensure your semidivine status. It's as it is in any religion: you constantly have to purify, cut ties, to maintain the integrity of the religion. That's why I like to use the term *clerisy* instead of *intellectuals*. The clerisy is a nonreligious clergy.

GEO: In a way, you've separated yourself from this clerisy by satirizing it. Do you get a thrill out of being a rebel?

Wolfe: I shouldn't confess to saying yes to that because it makes it seem gamelike, but that's true. I have enjoyed that. Don't ask me why I have, but I have. I have enjoyed the game because it seems to me that people in my bailiwick—journalism, literature, the arts—are lucky to be able to look at their own world with the sense of fun and mockery and cynicism with which they properly look at business, the military or any world. I think there's absolutely nothing wrong with skepticism and a good healthy send-up now and then. But when exactly the same attitude is directed toward writers and artists, they tend to scream in a way that is now much louder than the way anyone in business screams.

GEO: Do you ever run into people whom you've skewered?

Wolfe: Nothing that marvelous has ever happened. I do hear, every now and then, that somebody has promised to punch me in the nose or something. Actually, nobody has ever been hurt in a literary fistfight in New York.

GEO: Given that writers are assumed to be intellectual and not terribly physical, they seem to have a fascination with people who are at the other end of that spectrum. For example, Hemingway and Mailer were interested in fighters, murderers, people who got their hands dirty.

Wolfe: For this analysis, I go to Sigmund Freud. He said that writers and artists are people who discovered as youngsters that they lost out in the hurly-burly of the playground. They discovered, however, that they had the power to fantasize about such things, about the fruits of power, such as money, glory and beautiful lovers. In a way, that resonated with the fantasies and dreams of other people who were not so talented. When they are successful in presenting these fantasies to the public, they end up achieving through fantasy that which they were previously able to achieve only in fantasy. But somehow it's not enough to be known as someone who is a skilled fantasist. That is second best; it would have been much better to have ruled the playground. So they constantly try to prove to themselves that they can rule the playground if they really try. But only rarely do you run into an obsession like that. It's all part of the nostalgia for the mud, the idea that you should be at home in the mud. For some reason, this seems to appeal to writers and artists. I should make a distinction. I don't think that female writers and artists are nearly as concerned with the mud as males are. At any rate, it seems to me that the opposite should appeal. When I got to New York, I decided that there was something about the notion of the artist as Bohemian. The arts are extremely artificial. The brilliance of writers is in no small part their mastery of artifice. Why not face up to that and head in a different direction and dress up, not down, and so on?

GEO: Do you have a gun?

Wolfe: No. I have a baseball bat. I've thought about getting a shotgun. I think pistols are really bad news. I hesitate to have guns in the house at all, and it's not just because there are children there. Guns are something you should really know how to use if you're going to have one.

GEO: How do you feel about gun control?

Wolfe: After living in New York for twenty-one years, I would now like to see handguns outlawed totally. I no longer see any justification for selling them. They're only used as weapons against people. This is an extremely emotional issue, and I know people who share my ideas on other things who are horrified to hear me say that I'm against handguns. The standard argument is that there are so many of them already that the bandits are going to get them and the nice guys aren't going to be able to. I don't think that's true. I think that if manufacture and sale stopped, the price of the ones remaining would go up on the black market. If it became a felony nationally to possess a handgun and there was a public call to turn them in, I think you'd be surprised at how many would be turned in.

GEO: Your writing style depends to some extent on patterns of speech. In "Mau-Mauing the Flak Catchers," for instance, you borrow from ghetto talk. Does capturing those speech patterns have something to do with how close you get to the characters you're writing about?

Wolfe: It does, and sometimes you have to condition yourself to turn on your radar set and devote as much of your mind as you can at the moment to absorbing the other person and the scene around you and cutting out your own normal feelings. The question people ask themselves all day long is, "How am I doing?" If you're always asking, "How am I doing? How do I look? What do they think of me?" then it's very hard to concentrate on what you need as a writer. That's why I find the worst thing about being a publicized writer is going into a situation in which not only am I recognized, which creates its own problem, but I feel myself onstage, so that I'm saying, "How am I doing? Am I really being Tom Wolfe? Am I sparkling?" That really gets in the way of the task.

GEO: Has being stereotyped as a pop commentator bothered you?

Wolfe: The work *pop* was one of the great curses of my literary life. *Pop* is a word you cannot win with. There's no other meaning for it other than "trivial." I never used the word myself, and I soon dreaded being called a pop commentator. *Time* magazine called me America's foremost pop sociologist. It may seem great to be the foremost anything until you ask who else is on the list, and it's an extremely sad list if you can even make a list at all. It ends up being trivial, and it's a signal that you can enjoy this, but you don't have to take it seriously. A commentator is somebody who is spouting off the top of his head about life, and I'd much rather be thought of as a reporter or as somebody who is discovering a slice of life.

GEO: We were talking about getting close to your subjects. Do you ever think you're getting too close?

Wolfe: If you stay with a person too long, you're likely to establish a friendly relationship, and when the time comes to be candid, that can be a problem. When I wrote *The Electric Kool-Aid Acid Test,* Ken Kesey was asked what he thought of it. He said, "It was okay. It was accurate, except for where he tried to be nice." Then he put his finger on the one place in the book where I had pulled my punch a little bit. This was in a scene with a gang bang with the Hell's Angels. I couldn't bring myself to name the member involved or her former husband. It's a horrible scene. Kesey said that by not naming the individuals, I turned this tragic moment into a scene of low comedy. He was right. I just couldn't bring myself to do it, and it had nothing to do with libel. For some reason, I couldn't walk over that line. But strictly in terms of the standards I set for myself in writing now, I should have.

GEO: In researching *Acid Test* did you ever drop acid?

Wolfe: Not with Kesey and the Pranksters, although I did before I wrote the book as part of my reporting. It was something I never want to do again. It was like tying yourself to the railroad track and seeing how big the train is, which is rather big. The drug is so powerful. At one point Kesey and the Pranksters were taking it every Sunday. It was like a sacrament. That's one of the things that interested me about the Pranksters: their acid tests were designed exactly the same way ceremonies were designed in the early days of Christianity, the early days of Buddhism, the early days of Zoroastrianism. Another thing I was interested in was the business of an ecstatic religion. All the successful modern religions started out as religions of ecstatic experiences. First comes the ecstatic experience, then comes the theology. What they're after is the psychological, neurological experience. All these things fascinate me. Here I had a chance to look at a primary religion in its early stages, though this is not to put the experience of Kesey and the Pranksters on a par with that of Jesus or Buddha.

GEO: How does the drug experience relate to organized religion?

Wolfe: What is so ironic is that it was the ecstatic nature of the psychedelic movement, ecstasy achieved through drugs, that eventually appealed to young people in the Seventies. In the Sixties, the established churches were trying to reach young people through secular movements. They would align the church behind the civil rights movement or open a coffeehouse in the church basement and have hootenannies down there. This had practically no appeal to the young people. What did was talking in tongues and all the other things associated with fundamentalism that came out of the psychedelic movement.

GEO: How does all of this fit in with the more political religious movements such as the Jerry Falwell type of fundamentalism?

Wolfe: It fits in pretty closely. This is something I'm sure Falwell would disagree with, but it was the hippie movement and the acidheads that made fundamentalism attractive to young people. Before this, fundamentalism was an old people's style of religion.

These religions and the people who follow them are generally not politically motivated; their moral concerns are on a higher plane. So where the issues are moral and fit in with the church, people can get excited. They can become excited about anything from abortion to feminism—things that affect the family particularly. But the point I want to make is that because a Falwell can galvanize a following on those issues, it does not follow that he can galvanize them in any political direction he wants. These religions are schismatic by nature. They are not ecumenical. They don't make alliances. None of the preachers can shout "Onward, Christian soldiers" and expect other groups to follow.

GEO: But these groups can apply serious political pressure. For example, some schools have been pressured into teaching creationism.

Wolfe: Well, politics affects education all over the place now, particularly in the rewriting of history. In that case, creationism would be rewriting science, not for academic reasons but for reasons of contemporary pressure. On the other side of it is the current decision in New York State to abandon conventional teaching of American history and teach courses on social trends in American history instead. One segment would be economic trends; another would be social in the sense of manners and mores and might include a section on the role of women in history. That is also the kind of thing that's affecting education, and there are all kinds of immediate political pressures that get into it. It seems to me that there'a a real need to give educational systems some autonomy so that they're not always caving in every year to the latest pressures.

GEO: You seem to lean pretty hard on liberals but not on conservatives. How do you answer charges that you're politically one-sided in your satire?

Wolfe: The subject in pieces like *Radical Chic & Mau-Mauing the Flak Catchers* is not politics. I'm not mocking the left; I'm mocking the whole world of the arts and Culture with a large C, whose orthodoxy at that time, less so today, was liberal or left. This is the kind of enterprise that is shocking the people in that world. The idea of making fun of the left orthodoxy that was very much a part of the Sixties and early Seventies is not something they would want to do— it's heretical. There was one crazy piece written about me in *The New*

Republic that said—and not metaphorically—that while at Yale I had been brainwashed by the Establishment, with a large *E*, presumably by Allen Dulles, who was then head of the CIA, and then sent forth to assassinate liberal culture. This thing was serious.

GEO: Are you a compulsive writer?

Wolfe: No. I find it very hard to do. I very seldom enjoy the process. The hope of applause will keep me going.

GEO: Do you write mainly for that kind of recognition?

Wolfe: I was once asked that when I was giving a talk at a college in Ohio. The talk had nothing to do with writing, but the first question was, "Why do you write?" I had never thought about why I wrote, and I was under pressure on this stage to say something quickly. Then I suddenly thought of the Presbyterian catechism, which I hadn't had a look at since I was seven years old. The first question in the catechism is "Who created heaven and earth?" And the answer is "God." The second question is "Why did he do it?" And looking back on it, the answer fascinates me: "For his own glory." That's quite an answer. That was the answer I came up with, so maybe that's it.

GEO: Any regrets so far?

Wolfe: Chiefly that I haven't written more, that I didn't get started earlier. I was thirty-three before my first book came out. A professional writer should have a book out every year; I haven't. Those are things I regret.

GEO: I almost forgot—how would you characterize the Eighties?

Wolfe: The Eighties will be the Decade of Cultural Amnesia.

The Evolution of Dandy Tom

Toby Thompson/1987

From *Vanity Fair,* 50 (October 1987), 118–27, 160–64. Reprinted by permission of Toby Thompson.

It's out. It's finally being published—Tom Wolfe's big novel of New York's high life and low life, *The Bonfire of the Vanities.* Writing it has changed the dean of the New Journalism—or at least the world's perception of him. Toby Thompson digs beneath the image of Wolfe as dandy and social satirist to find the man who has always viewed himself as an outsider.

It's raining in New York, on one of those spring nights when a light shower contains all the blessings the city might bestow. The white umbrella Tom Wolfe unfurls against this patter does little to conceal his glee at a stroll down Park Avenue—past those great co-ops where apartments sell for $4 million apiece and for which one must pay cash, showing a portfolio of $30 million to even apply. Wolfe himself has shopped for such an apartment, but, he says, laughing, "anyone can shop." The homburg and spatted shoes he protects with this circus tent of an umbrella suggest a man who fritters his life away at Le Cirque or in private dining rooms overlooking Central Park. But this is a writer—a worker happy to see the publication of his first novel after three years of backbreaking effort. *The Bonfire of the Vanities* is a big book, 560-odd pages, with a first printing of 150,000. And Wolfe is a big author. Still, he steps through the streets of Manhattan with some reserve.

"New York feels very much like home now," he says hesitantly, and with a touch of irony. "But it took a long time for me to feel that way . . . like it was *my city.*"

When I was nine, I started writing a biography of Napoleon. He was small, and I was small. I was nine years old. It bothered me that the world was run by large people, and Napoleon was this little guy who, at one point, ran the world."

Tom Wolfe pauses, sipping his iced tea. "I also did an illustrated children's book at that time, about Mozart—a child prodigy—who gave concerts to *tremendous* applause. Then I had a long fascination with sportswriting. But I think that was bound up with my aspirations to be an athlete. That's who got applause in school! Not writers!" he says with a slight smile. "At one point I went to a tryout camp for the New York Giants, and they told me, in *not* all that polite a way, that I didn't have a chance. I just didn't believe them. The denial is rampant."

Tom Wolfe has flown down to Virginia to accept the John Dos Passos Prize for Literature from Longwood College. He's at lunch, a few blocks from the Richmond neighborhood where he grew up—in the Art Deco bar at Benjamin's. It's a room with a wide oval mirror set into its mahogany, so that genteel Richmonders may check out their neighbors as that most subtle of southern drawls, the Richmond drawl, wafts around them. Despite Wolfe's fame, despite the arrestingly gangsterish elegance of his white slacks, white shoes, and baby-blue jacket with exaggerated lapels, no one at Benjamin's appears to take notice of him.

A tablemate remarks that Wolfe is one of a few serious authors never to have written about his childhood, and asks why.

"I don't know," Wolfe answers thoughtfully. "I probably need a psychologst to tell me." He glances up, appraising the room. "It's true, though. I've never written about Richmond, for example." His eyes narrow. "Maybe I want a safe harbor to come back to."

Status is one of Tom Wolfe's great themes. It is safe to surmise that he was profoundly affected by his family's move in 1927 from the rural Shenandoah Valley to a city with one of the haughtiest and most closed societies in the South. Wolfe was born in Richmond in 1931. Though his parents were gentry, they were country gentry. They were enlightened, Jeffersonian democrats who felt themselves above the fripperies of Richmond society.

"My father was the editor of *The Southern Planter,* a farm magazine," Wolfe says, driving toward Longwood College. His voice is full of Richmond, but his hands are thick as a plowboy's. "He was an agronomist and the director of a farmer's cooperative, but I always thought of him as a writer. He kept the novels of Thomas Wolfe on his bookshelf, and for years I thought he'd written them."

Thomas Wolfe Sr., a Cornell Ph.D. and a professor at Virginia Tech, died in 1972. He had moved to Richmond to run the *Planter*, which was geared to the squirearchy and to the elitist philosophy of the agrarian South. Wolfe's mother is now ninety and living near his sister, Helen Evans, in North Carolina. "My mother's interests are artistic," Wolfe says fondly. She is remembered by one Richmond neighbor as "delightful . . . and a liberal Presbyterian lady of the intellectual variety." In her youth, she studied social work in New York and was accepted at medical school but did not attend.

The family lived in the Sherwood Park section of Richmond, far from the fashionable west end: "We had professors living there, working people . . . everybody," Wolfe's sister remembers.

Wolfe attended public schools until the seventh grade. But that year his parents enrolled him in St. Christopher's, an Episcopal prep school where boys were taught "math and manners, Latin and lineage," as one friend describes it. There were nineteen sons of the conservative Richmond elite in Wolfe's graduating class.

Wolfe was still spending weekends and summers on his father's farm in the Shenandoah Valley; he was also actively Presbyterian, and "from the north side," remembers John Page Williams, his headmaster. "Not the part that was moving out to the country club." Perhaps from loneliness, Wolfe bragged to a Sunday-school teacher of the eight brothers and sisters he did not have. He was a sensitive boy who studied tap and ballet, and who became an overachiever. He was an honors student, chairman of the student council, a fair athlete, and co-editor of the school paper, for which he wrote and illustrated "The Bullpen," a column already crackling with his style: "Different spectators have suggested motorcars, bicycles and rickshaws for keeping up with Coach Petey Jacobs' live-five," he wrote of the basketball team.

Notice me was the subtext of these early accomplishments. *Applaud.*

At fifty-seven, Tom Wolfe has received more applause than any other literary journalist of his time. An author who has truly influenced his era, he's perhaps the best and best-known nonfictionist

in America. As a humorist "he's the funniest fucking guy *standing,*
when he's on," says novelist Tom McGuane. As a phrasemaker Wolfe
is nonpareil: "radical chic," "the right stuff," "the me generation,"
and other idiosyncratic designations have entered the language.
McGuane calls him "our Thackeray. His style has been imitated so
much that he has the burden of having to live it down."

It's surprising to hear Wolfe speak of writer's block and of the
terrible time he's had producing *The Bonfire of the Vanities:* "I
remember something Red Smith said when someone asked him how
he managed to turn out a column five days a week. 'There's nothing
to it,' he said. 'You sit there at your typewriter and you think, and if
that doesn't work, you open a vein.' "

For about six months Wolfe had sat there, "and absolutely nothing
was happening." Believing that pressure would be helpful—as it had
been when he began *The Right Stuff* in *Rolling Stone*—he'd decided
to compose his first draft on deadline, "to put myself in a vise and
force it out." Publisher Jann Wenner jumped at the prospect of a
Tom Wolfe novel appearing in twenty-nine consecutive issues of
Rolling Stone, and offered a contract for close to $200,000. "No
question," Wolfe quips, "that spurs you on." The public reaction to
the *Rolling Stone* serialization was mixed. There was a rave from the
ultraconservative *American Spectator,* but one major New York
editor, a Wolfe fan, described it as "just dreck." Few of Wolfe's
colleagues responded to the book. "I don't think they're reading it,"
he commented at the time.

In *The New Journalism* (1973), Wolfe declared that "the most
important literature being written in America today is in nonfiction,"
and predicted that journalists "would wipe out the novel as literature's
main event."

But "the road has been built," he says now of literary nonfiction.
"We're seeing what's traveling down it. Which is not as exciting as
building the road.

"And I didn't want to be in the position where at the end of my
career I looked back and said to myself, 'Wonder what would have
happened if I'd written a novel?' "

The wind is utterly out of the sails of New Journalism," McGuane
commented recently. "The art juice is in fiction."

Wolfe first discovered fiction writing at Washington and Lee, a private university in Lexington, Virginia, where Lee served as president after the Civil War. "The kind of boy that goes there is the boy whose family still believes in the Confederacy . . . planter money from Mississippi, big money from the Delta, from Memphis, and Texas," says Marshall Fishwick, one of Wolfe's teachers at W&L. The tobacco executive Smith Bagley is a fellow alumnus, as is Herb Hunt, the oil billionaire. Hunt's father bought him the local Texaco station after Herb suffered a slight there as a student. Wolfe found he could compete against W&L's wealth and its adoration of sports by writing about sports for the school paper—and by publishing short stories. He pitched for the varsity team, pledged a Richmond-boys' fraternity, and flouted the dress code "out of contrariness," he remembers, with styles that were both hyper-English and Hollywood-tough-guy.

Wolfe used W&L as a laboratory to polish his innate manners, for as his friend Clay Felker, who is now editor of *Manhattan, Inc.*, says, "Formal manners are a marvelous way of fending people off—without offending them."

George Foster conducted a fiction seminar once a week in an off-campus taproom called the Dutch Inn. "We would read our work aloud," Wolfe recalls, "and that could be brutal." He was disquieted by the credo that "the only valid subject matter was something you knew very personally within your own life." Or, as his classmate novelist William Hoffman put it, you had "to undress to write fiction."

Two of his stories appeared in *Shenandoah,* then a campus literary magazine. In one, "Shattered," a freshman football player dreams of "a wonderful someday hero worship by the whole university," but his hopes and a weak knee are smashed in the first game. "It has actually happened," he thinks, "these dumb goddam people are gawking at your helplessness."

Bill Hoffman, a war veteran from the mining country of West Virginia, was even more of an outsider than Wolfe. The two became close friends. Hoffman found the younger writer full of contradictions. He'd confide about St. Christopher's, for example, that "I didn't really belong to that group—I didn't move with that crowd," and would talk about status "in practically every other sentence." Yet he persisted in his dreams of playing professional baseball—hardly a gentleman's occupation. Hoffman remembers Wolfe's early stories as being "filled with fireworks and astonishing, huge detail."

"Tom had from the very first," Hoffman says, "a real sense of the absurd. I hated to go to the movies with him. He'd see something ridiculous like Elizabeth Taylor in *Ivanhoe* and call out in the theater, 'You can't beat Hollywood!'"

Wolfe was galvanized in his senior year by Marshall Fishwick, W&L's popular-culture guru. "He gave a course," Wolfe says, "which in effect was all of American studies compressed into one year— American architecture, American art, theories in psychology, history, across the board." "I tried to baptize the proletarian," Fishwick explains. "Tom immediately took the bait." Fishwick organized field trips to hear country music, taught his students how to rebuild old farmhouses, and even how to lay mortar. To Wolfe the course was an epiphany. He learned to respect his father's rural heritage, and found he could use the discipline of sociology creatively, turning his sharp literary eye away from himself. "He saw through the facade of the small, elite college," Fishwick says, recalling Wolfe's student papers, "and demonstrated that everyone was of the same pattern."

Though Fishwick had persuaded Wolfe to pursue American studies at Yale (instead of a career in baseball), Wolfe continued to write fiction. "I was the sort of person who from a certain moment *knows* that he's going to write novels. You just know you're going to do it. But when that's going to happen is another question."

Tonight—some twenty-five years later—as Wolfe accepts the Dos Passos Prize at Longwood College, it's his fiction that he's showcasing, rather than the journalism that made him famous.

"This award means a lot to me because the last of the Wolfes living in Virginia, Frances Roberdeau Wolfe, went to Longwood . . . and because I've been thinking a *lot* about Dos Passos. . . . I undertook as my project a work of contemporary fiction that would somehow encompass the life of the modern metropolis.

"Sometimes I thought of it as a *Vanity Fair* written 150 years later, or, if I was really feeling good about myself, something on the order of *Manhattan Transfer*. . . .The high life I felt I knew cold . . . because I lived in Manhattan . . . but, for the low life, I decided to go to the Bronx. The Bronx to me was sort of like the Arctic Circle: it was north of where I was, and you didn't go there."

The audience titters. "The lowest of the low life of New York is in the Bronx," Wolfe explains. Then he reads a chapter of *Bonfire* that turns upon the unmasking of his protagonist, Sherman McCoy, a Park Avenue liberal who will be exposed as an adulterer when prosecuted for disabling a black youth in a traffic accident in the Bronx.

At one point in the novel, in a scene of profound humiliation, Sherman is herded through the Bronx courthouse and penned in a holding cell with the black and Hispanic low life that, as a liberal, he has romanticized. Once released, he assures his lawyer, "I'm not going back inside that . . . place . . . ever, and I don't care what it takes to keep me out. Even if I have to stick a shotgun barrel in my mouth."

Wolfe leaves his Longwood audience in a park opposite the courthouse, where, "just last week, some poor devil was stabbed to death at ten A.M. . . .for his portable radio, one of the big ones, known upstairs inside the Island as a Bronx attaché case."

There is shocked silence in Farmville, Virginia.

Then thunderous applause.

When Wolfe moved to New York, in 1962, he dropped a letter to a friend, Hugh Troy, that hints at his ambivalence:

"The first thing I knew I was on the 1:20 A.M. bus with 15 colored brethren, all of us, no doubt, out to make it in New York. . . . Whether I am moving on to bigger and better things, I don't know, but I knew I wouldn't be happy until I gave it a try. This is one big sonofabitch of a town, I have found out, but I guess they are used to boys from the foothills coming in here, and they are probably even tolerant."

Today, Wolfe is still edgy about New York, but for a different reason: it won't let him alone. He is at his Manhattan tailor, Vincent Nicolosi, for a fitting, and his customary politeness becomes strained when he runs into two New Journalists who have been Anglo-dandiacal to the extreme since he published his 1965 piece on "the secret vice" of custom tailoring. He's delighted, however, when his close friend Richard Merkin, the "post-Pop Expressionist" painter, turns up with a silver *The Right Stuff* promo bag. Merkin is dressed in orange slacks, pink tasseled slippers, a striped boating shirt, and a double-breasted jacket.

"Dandyism is a mask," he observes, "but underneath, Tom's not flashy. He does it for effect. Remember Tom Buchanan's outrage at Gatsby's pink suit? I think that's Tom Wolfe in a nutshell: Gatsby in a pink suit. He's a very sensitive creative . . . and I've never met anyone so responsive to people's feelings. The last thing he would *ever* want to feel is that he's hurt you. Writing is a tremendous escape. What you do there is to assert yourself in a way you can't in real life. It's the invented part of life."

There's a male clubbiness at Nicolosi's this afternoon redolent of Savile Row—or, in Wolfe's case, his father's Victorian tastes.

"I see certain things of my father in me that I never was aware of," Wolfe says. "He always had his clothes made in Richmond. It was not considered a big deal. I started having mine made in Washington. Unlike him, I became very conscious of it. Then I started wearing large hats. That's something he did, also. . . .And he wore white suits, in the Norfolk style, with a belt in the back and pleats over the shoulder."

Wolfe stares toward the street. "Never underestimate how much of your childhood is sewn into the lining of your garments when you go to New York."

Wolfe came to New York to become a writer following an unhappy six-year hiatus in graduate school at Yale—"tedium of an exquisite sort."

Wolfe would blow off steam by visiting Bill Hoffman, who was then living in New York. Hoffman recalls that Wolfe would check into a welfare hotel on West 103rd Street, and "we'd go down to Greenwich Village to these crummy dives—Tom was very much interested in Bohemia then and he liked engaging these people in talks. But he didn't look like he *belonged* there."

He did not belong at Yale either. It was a rich Yankees' school, liberal and stuffy. "I was a Stevenson man," Wolfe remembers, "but everyone was so liberal and patronizing to Eisenhower that I acted more conservative than I was. I'd kid them by saying, 'You know,

Eisenhower's really very bright. He reads seven foreign papers a day. He *has* to. And there's that one from Belgrade.'"

"The professors didn't know what to make of him," Hoffman says. "He was supposed to present scholarly papers, and he would write them in this fireworks style of his and just drive them crazy."

Finally Wolfe buckled down and wrote his American-studies dissertation, *The League of American Writers: Communist Organizational Activity Among American Writers, 1929–1942*. "My theory was that writers, who think of themselves as loners in pursuit of a great goal . . . actually are lonesome. It's a socializing influence to join these organizations."

Increasingly he questioned the enterprise of writing fiction. The regurgitation of an author's deepest fears, hang-ups, and secrets onto the page still went against the grain, and he had begun to find it suspect as art. He wondered if "creativity in prose wasn't embedded in material" and if *reporting* wasn't the key to unlocking it.

After enduring reportorial stints at the Springfield, Massachusetts, *Union* and the Washington *Post,* where he won awards for his writing, Wolfe made it to the New York *Herald Tribune* in 1962. It was *the* experimental paper in town. Its Sunday magazine, *New York,* was edited by Clay Felker, just over from *Esquire,* and his mandate was liveliness at any cost. Wolfe had been hired as a general-assignment reporter, but soon was writing weekly features: "I looked out across the city room of the *Herald Tribune,* 100 moldering yards south of Times Square, with a feeling of amazed bohemian bliss . . . Either this is the real world, Tom, or there is no real world."

He rented an apartment in Greenwich Village and hit the streets.

"The idea," he later wrote of his fellow feature writers, "was to keep body and soul together, pay the rent, get to know 'the world,' accumulate 'experience,' perhaps work some of the fat off your style—then, at some point, quit cold, say goodbye to journalism, move into a shack somewhere . . . and light up the sky with . . . The Novel."

Though Wolfe derided this plan publicly, he kept it as a hidden agenda. "He always had an idea of doing a novel about New York, á la *Vanity Fair,*" Felker remembers.

In the early sixties, as Wolfe point out in *The New Journalism,* "the literary upper class were the novelists . . . the middle class were the 'men of letters' . . . the lower class were the journalists . . . As for people who wrote for popular ('slick') magazines and Sunday supplements . . . they weren't even in the game. They were lumpenproles."

Wolfe toiled as a lumpenprole, writing lively if conventional journalism, until a Hot Rod and Custom Car Show gave him a fundamental insight into the American class system and the 1960s. He talked *Esquire* into sending him to California, where he could further examine the phenomenon; it was his first national-magazine assignment. Back in New York, he had a terrible time lashing the piece together. His editor, Byron Dobell, remembers fearing they would be "stuck with having to write something based on the author's notes, because the author was having a nervous break-down." In desperation, Wolfe typed up his ideas in the form of a memo to a friend and found a conversational tone that unblocked him and proved exactly right. He wrote all night, listening to manic rock on WABC, and turned in the memo the next morning. Dobell struck out the "Dear Byron," plus "a few Chrissake's and the things that were too blatantly Holden Caulfield, and we rolled with it."

That was "The Kandy-Kolored Tangerine-Flake Streamline Baby," whose thesis was that the American class system could be beaten, that a reverse snobbery was afoot, in which the old elite was imitating the new. Wolfe characterized the California custom-car designers as artists outside any "ancient, aristocratic aesthetic," free of "the amoeba god of Anglo-European sophistication that gets you in the East." Because of postwar wealth, this new elite had been able to form its own status group.

Wolfe identified other maverick prole groups of the 1960s—rock 'n' rollers, D.J.s, gangsters, publishers like *Confidential's* Robert Harrison, stock-car racers, record producers. All were constructing artifacts that polite society considered "vulgar and lower-class-awful beyond comment almost," but that were having a profound effect. He might have been describing his own status as a journalist—and anticipating the furor New Journalism would cause later in the decade.

Wolfe took the techniques of realistic fiction (scene-by-scene construction, dialogue, point of view, and meticulous status detail) and applied them to this new way of reporting. Gay Talese, Tom

Morgan, and others had been doing the same thing in *Esquire*, but Wolfe took the form and pushed it to its limits, writing from *inside* his characters like a novelist; his best characters were outsiders—projections of himself. He was hip, the Lenny Bruce of letters. He wrote of the record magnate Phil Spector:

> All these raindrops are *high* or something. They don't roll down the window, they come straight back, toward the tail, wobbling, like all those Mr. Cool snow heads walking on mattresses. The plane is taxiing out toward the runway to take off, and this stupid infarcted water wobbles, sideways, across the window. Phil Spector . . . America's first teen-age tycoon watches . . . this watery pathology. . . .

The pieces were supereclectic. "If you'd never seen one before, they were fabulous, really exciting," recalls Tom McGuane. They incorporated the electronic beeps and chatter of TV, of rock radio; they moved like the spontaneous bop prosody of the Beats; they had a visual quality, on the page; and they were scholarly, with bits of art history and sociology. Wolfe flung this pastiche at a baby-boom readership raised on television and Top 40 radio, the best-educated generation in the history of the world.

"The sixties were a period when fictionists seemed to have abandoned the city as a subject," reflects Wolfe. "Nonfiction writers had a field day." In New York, styles and manners were changing faster than anyone could record them. The Social Register and Four Hundred crowd joined the rabble—in clubs like the Peppermint Lounge and Arthur—and mimicked their dancing, their dress. The new café society, or "Pop Society," as Wolfe preferred to call it, was "made up of people whose status rests not on property and ancestry but on various brilliant ephemera." It accepted Wolfe, the southern émigré, as its chronicler.

Wolfe's first book, *The Kandy-Kolored Tangerine-Flake Streamline Baby*, a compilation of articles written in that first, manic, fifteen-month period, hit the best-seller lists. He became the Journalist as Superstar, part of an independent statusphere that included Jimmy Breslin (also of the *Trib*), Rex Reed, Pete Hamill, Truman Capote, and Norman Mailer—writers as vilified or adored as rock stars.

"It was a very curious time for me," Wolfe recalls. "I'd spend the day at the *Herald Tribune* getting other people through the publicity mill, and after work I was being interviewed. Suddenly *I* was getting publicity." In 1966, he was photographed by Irving Penn for *Vogue*, and interviewed by a girlfriend, Elaine Dundy, who was Kenneth Tynan's ex-wife and a novelist. Penn caught Wolfe's arrogance of dress and attitude, but Dundy got below the surface flash to what was a driven and isolated young man. She noted his "country air," describing him as "Tom Sawyer drawn by Beardsley." She remembers him today as "pretty wary, and scared of people putting him on. . . . He was very much the Southerner trying to get it right in New York." Meanwhile, Wolfe had moved to an apartment at 2 Beekman Place, one of Manhattan's swankiest addresses—"When I came up North, I didn't come here to fool around"—but kept its interior bohemian and sparsely furnished.

Wolfe told Dundy that "perfect journalism would deal constantly with one subject: Status," and admitted that what made him angriest was "humiliation. I never forget, I never forgive." He said he'd always wanted to be a writer, but "didn't actually become one until I was thirty-two," the year of *Kandy–Kolored*—"I suppose there was a lot of fear involved." He complained that he had "taken more physical punishment from writing than . . . from any sport I've ever played." He felt that his greatest talent was for drawing (he'd illustrated the first book, and had had a one-man show in New York), but that he was least talented at "creating stable ties with other people."

Wolfe stayed untied to anything but ambition throughout the mid-sixties (though "a lot of girls were chasing him" remembers Clay Felker), and traveled helter-skelter across America and England in search of new trends or status groups who were "starting their own league," as he had. He "moved constantly," Richard Merkin remembers. "Tom must have lived in fourteen or sixteen different places in New York."

Gay Talese, who has known Wolfe since they were "young men on the street of journalism" together, describes him as "very much the Southerner who feels distance as he moves through the New York scene. It doesn't touch him. He doesn't *want* it to touch him."

Professionally, Wolfe ensured this distance from "the Kentucky colonels of both Journalism and Literature," as he put it, by publishing a two-part *Tribune* article, in April of 1965, characterizing William Shawn, editor of *The New Yorker*, as a "museum custodian,

an undertaker, a mortuary scientist" in charge of the magazine's
staff—themselves no better than zombies in the liveliness of the copy
they produced. E. B. White responded that "Mr. Wolfe's piece on
William Shawn . . . sets some sort of record for journalistic
delinquency." Muriel Spark commented that Wolfe's style of attack
"is plainly derived from Senator McCarthy," and even J. D. Salinger
emerged from his New Hampshire woodshed to sneer that the article
was "inaccurate and sub-collegiate and gleeful and unrelievedly
poisonous."

"That piece put *New York* magazine on the map," Clay Felker
says, "and it put Tom on the map too."

"There are two ways to make reputations," Wolfe says today.
"Build up yours, and tear down everyone else's."

America west of the Hudson beckoned. Wolfe got out of New York
to write a series of articles for the *Trib* about Ken Kesey, a novelist on
the lam in Mexico. Kesey had been arrested on drug charges and had
jumped bail. He was a good old boy in the mode of stock-car racer
Junior Johnson, whom Wolfe had profiled in "The Last American
Hero," a protagonist of the sort Wolfe was finding increasingly
attractive. Kesey's father, like Wolfe's, had headed a farmers' cooperative, and both writers were committed to experimental realism
in prose. They were outsiders who had gathered around them
revolutionary constellations. Kesey's was the Merry Pranksters, post-
Beat proto-hippies of a literary bent. One of them was Robert Stone,
who had landed an assignment with *Esquire* to write about the group
himself.

"Wolfe didn't know where Kesey was in Mexico," Stone remembers, "and I did. I immediately got on the phone and told everybody
who knew where Kesey was not to tell Wolfe. So Wolfe's sources
promptly dried up." When *Esquire* rejected Stone's piece, he
bequeathed his notes to Wolfe and agreed to be questioned by him.
"He's a dangerous kind of interviewer," Stone observes respectfully,
"because he really does put you at your ease."

The *Trib* articles resulted in a contract for *The Electric Kool-Aid
Acid Test,* Wolfe's first book-length work. He had begun to work on it
in New York, when his father became seriously ill. "I came home to
sort of help my mother out," Wolfe recalls, "thinking that I would say
good-bye to this book for a while. I was going to the hospital three

times a day—and the darndest thing happened. Since I had maybe a couple of hours in the morning, an hour in the afternoon, and maybe an hour at night to work, I was *religious* about it. I never missed those hours. I would sit right down and start writing."

Coming home had unblocked him. Even after Dr. Wolfe recovered, Tom stayed on in Richmond, completing the book in four months.

The Pranksters' experiments with LSD were on the cutting edge of theories about the mind that Wolfe had been exploring for some time. He'd developed a technique "that I thought of as a controlled trance," he says. "I'd review my notes for a certain chapter, then I would close my eyes and try to imagine myself, as a Method actor would, into the scene . . . going crazy, for example . . . how it feels and what it's going to sound like if you translate it into words—which was real writing by radar."

Eventually he decided there was one essential bit of reporting he'd failed to do: take acid. "I had a friend in Buffalo who had access to LSD, so I went up there and took 125 milligrams. At first I thought I was having a gigantic heart attack—I felt like my heart was outside my body with these big veins. . . . As I began to calm down, I had the feeling that I had entered into the sheen of this nubbly twist carpet—a really *wretched* carpet, made of Acrilan—and somehow this represented the people of America, in their democratic glory. It was cheap and yet it had a certain glossy excitement to it—I even felt sentimental about it. Somehow I was *merging* with this carpet. At the time, it seemed like a phenomenal insight, a breakthrough."

Though Wolfe dismisses this insight today as not meaning "a goddamn thing," it seemed to free him to write *Kool-Aid* as a love song to America. The book was American to the core, imitating the workings of the contemporary mind by incorporating stream of consciousness, poetry, and multiple points of view. And it was unreservedly hip. It remains the best book about 1960s America, and it is emotionally free in a way Wolfe's writing has not been since.

Kool-Aid was simultaneously published with *The Pump House Gang* in July of 1968—"Two books!!!!!!! Heeeeeeeeeeewack! The same day!!!!!! Too-o-o-o-o-o freaking much!" said the New York *Times* review—and became an immediate best-seller. All across the country, students in creative-writing programs stared at the photo of

Wolfe on its jacket—Tom in a dark shirt, white tie, white step-collared vest, white shoes and suit—and said, "Hey, that ain't Allen Ginsberg." And turned toward the New Journalism.

In the mid-sixties, "fiction moved a long way toward New Journalism," Tom McGuane says. Today "there's a kind of weird, natural meeting ground. All novelists are trying to fool readers into thinking it's real, and all adventurous journalists are trying to seize the flexibility of fiction."

The New Journalists had seized that flexibility, effecting at the very least a revolution in style. And, as Robert Stone remarks, "a revolution in style can be called a revolution in consciousness. . . . Wolfe reflected it, as I think Kesey reflected it."

Yet *Kool-Aid* had finished on a somber note. Despite a revolution in consciousness, the Pranksters had failed to liberate America with their vision of "now." The hierarchical status groups still reigned. "WE BLEW IT!" the Pranksters chant in Wolfe's final chapter, "WE BLEW IT!" "WE BLEW IT!"

By 1970, Wolfe thought he had cleared the decks for his big book about New York. In search of material, he crashed a fund-raiser for the Black Panthers' legal-defense fund at the Park Avenue apartment of Leonard and Felicia Bernstein. What he found at the Bernsteins' was such gold that it resulted in another postponement of his fiction.

Radical Chic is brilliantly executed and marvelously funny. "As a piece of sheer writing," Wolfe says, "it's my favorite book." In it Wolfe remains the outsider. If he identifies with anyone, it's with the Black Panthers, whom he characterizes as hip, stylish, and aghast at the hypocrisies of Park Avenue liberals. *Radical Chic* demolishes New York's rich socialites for their pandering to radical causes (it was authentically damaging, having its effect on both "radical chic" fund-raisers and the reputation of Leonard Bernstein) and analyzes the whole shebang, once again in terms of status. As Ellen Willis commented in the *Village Voice,* the piece's "underlying assumption is that political action is inherently ridiculous and irrelevant. . . . The very idea of social conscience pisses him off."

Suddenly the apostle of Pranksterism was being labeled a right-winger. Wolfe blames this on "my having gone against the prevailing orthodoxy" of high liberalism. He had always felt about politics "the

way the hippies who were asked to make statements felt about the
F.B.I. *Who cares?* I'm a democrat with a small *d*. I think it would be
perfectly O.K. to have an electrician or a burglar-alarm repairman as
president."

Today Robert Stone characterizes Wolfe as "a southern conservative of a very sophisticated kind. I think he sees New York, and
political liberalism, as wimpy and posturing and hypocritical."

He was feeling pugnacious in the early seventies. What seemed to
anger him most was the Vietnam War and the public's gloom over it.
Not only had Vietnam curtailed the "Happiness Explosion" of the
1960s, it had severely divided Wolfe's natural constituency, the
college-age baby-boomers. In a 1983 piece about the Vietnam
Veterans Memorial, he would note of the war, "The sons of the
merchant and managerial classes in American sat this one out, in
college, graduate school, Canada and Sweden," and would assert
that "the unspeakable and inconfessible goal of the New Left on the
campuses had been to transform the shame of the fearful into the
guilt of the courageous." Despite Wolfe's conservatism during the
early 1970s, he was a huge draw on the campus lecture circuit.
"What's Kesey doing now?" became a ritual inquiry that nearly drove
him crazy.

Once again during these years, Wolfe was deflected from writing
his New York book. "The Truest Sport: Jousting with Sam and
Charlie" was an article that presaged *The Right Stuff*, comparing
bomber missions over Vietnam to jousting. Later he'd comment,
"Sports were . . . a way of training young men to be warriors in a
relatively harmless fashion. . . .If we want to get into the psychology
of it, I think we'll find that men, not so many women, *love war*—and
they love sports."

The Right Stuff took him six years, during which time he
conducted voluminous research and cranked out three other, shorter
books to avoid finishing it. "I was stuck with how to handle point of
view, I had no main character—no one you could just tell the story
through. . . .I was obsessed with the notion that this book would
have no suspense, because everyone knew how it came out."

Changes in his life may have contributed to this block. Wolfe was
affected deeply when his father died, and he had become seriously
involved with Sheila Berger, a magazine designer whom he'd met in

the art department at *Esquire*. And he was unsettled by the desire to write his Manhattan book instead of *The Right Stuff*.

He finally created a suitable protagonist by digging within, presenting the Southerner Chuck Yeager as the very embodiment of that good-old-boy, knock-'em-dead spirit which had invigorated his portraits of Kesey and Junior Johnson. The book is a brilliant dissection of the status pyramid in the modern officer corps. At its apex stand the Mercury astronauts: modern knights locked into a Cold War struggle with Soviet cosmonauts for supremacy in the heavens. The right stuff emerged as an amalgam of bravery, style, patriotism, and masculinity. It was the spirit of the rural South, and of his father.

With the publication of *The Right Stuff* in 1979, Wolfe became a mature statesman of American letters, a literary oracle reflexively consulted on any number of national events, from the space-shuttle tragedy to the Statue of Liberty's hundredth birthday. The conservatism of *The Right Stuff* did no harm to either Wolfe's sales or his reputation. "You might say," Clay Felker observes, "that Tom anticipated the whole American conservative movement."

The Right Stuff certified Wolfe as a historian, and he abandoned his seat as pop-culture critic of the moment. The Victorian collar climbed his neck in *Bauhaus* and *The Painted Word* as his abhorrence of moderism intensified.

"The reaction to *The Painted Word* [in which he outlines the status hierarchies of the art world and argues that modern art would be devoid of meaning without the criticism of the New York culturati] was the most violent of anything I've done," Wolfe remembers, "much more so than *Radical Chic*. The things I was called in print *amazed* me."

Wolfe's annual retreat from Manhattan is reminiscent of the one his family made from Richmond each summer. The white frame house he rents in Southampton from May through September is late Victorian in style, with gardens out back and an enormous expanse of rolling green yard to Agawan Lake. Though grand in a way, the house offers no competition to the Gatsbyesque mansions that typify Southampton, but is extremely livable, with room for Wolfe's wife,

Sheila, and the children (Alexandra, seven, and Thomas, two), and the requisite help, and enough privacy to write.

"I really do a lot of work out here," Wolfe says. "Southampton's an old town, and it's a *real* town. . . .There aren't that many people I know in a literary sense." But, as Richard Merkin quips, "Tom can *dissect* the population of Southampton for you. The Real Stuff is there."

In June of '86, Wolfe's friend Ed Hayes married the fashion model Susan Gilder in Bellport, and Wolfe attended. "Tom doesn't have that many close friends," Merkin says, "and Eddie's as good a friend as Tom has, maybe his best."

The thirty-nine-year-old Hayes, an ex-Bronx D.A. now practicing law in Manhattan, is from an Irish working-class family in Queens. He came up the hard way. Wolfe's friendship with him seems an unlikely one. Yet, as Hayes observes, "Tom is fascinated with New York ethnic life, and I'm fascinated with this Wasp warrior class from the South. The real English dandies were aristocrats who were usually soldiers, and aggressive and athletic. Tom sort of represents that. It's that Protestant warrior mentality . . . similar to what you find in the street life of New York."

Beautifully dressed, Hayes exudes the elegance of a young Cagney. Wolfe has a fatherly affection for him. He is the model for the lawyer Tommy Killian in *Bonfire,* and has served, with Bruce Cutler and others, as Wolfe's guide through the criminal-justice system of the Bronx.

"The hard guys," Hayes says, "without exception love Tom. He's extremely manly in his way of dealing with things. . . .Actually, he's a police reporter in a nice suit."

When not writing, Wolfe will spend entire afternoons at Hayes's house in Bellport, or Hayes will drive out to Southampton. "I'll kill the day there," he says. "We eat, we talk . . . I'm the only Irish guy from Sunnyside who got crazed for gardening, and I'll go down to his house and prune his trees for him."

"I think Tom's life in Manhattan is glamorous," Gay Talese says. "And he's found glamour in family life." The years of loneliness when, as Wolfe recalls, he would "haunt the halls of a magazine you're writing for like an odor" are gone. With his children, he gets all the company he needs "at quarter to seven every morning." Wolfe did not marry until he was forty-seven, or become a father until he was nearly fifty. When his son was born in 1985, "it was all I heard about," laughs Hayes. "They climb all over him. They drive him crazy. It's tough to be a father in a white suit."

Despite the extramarital affair so painfully outlined in *Bonfire*, there appears to be no parallel in Wolfe's life. "When I got married," says Hayes, "I had an extensive discussion with him about wearing wedding rings, and about vows. Women really like this guy . . . but he's one of the few I know who's genuinely faithful. He and Sheila have been together about eighteen years, and the guy comes home nights."

Though Wolfe has friends from most strata of Manhattan life, his closest friends—Hayes and Merkin—are native New Yorkers from different ethnic heritages. Sheila is Jewish. "She's not from a wealthy background," Hayes says, "she's from the Bronx—but 99 per-cent of the women born to privilege should have her manners, and her looks to boot." He adds that "it's hard to be married to a very famous man, especially in New York. Sheila does that well."

Now forty-one, Sheila was twenty-three when Wolfe met her. "She's very feminine and refined," says Gay Talese. "Tom has a woman who cares greatly for him, and can protect him from a lot of the distractions of New York. She appreciates his need for solitude. Sheila Berger has good judgment. She's no Zelda, in other words."

The East Side town house that the Wolfes own is an 1868 brownstone, and with its block shaded by sycamores and its azalea-filled backyard is as close to a southern milieu as one might construct in Manhattan. Wolfe's second-floor study is colorfully functional: high white bookshelves lined with the classics, Chinese-yellow drapes, a word processor (his wife's gift, unmastered), and the galleys to *Bonfire* spread about. Wolfe's production quota on revising *Bonfire* for publication in book form has been a fierce two thousand words a day. To overcome inertia, he's kept a clock on his desk "to see if I can do a page and a half an hour."

It has taken him a year and a half to revise his novel. His anxiety about the book caused him to consult his first *Esquire* editor, Byron Dobell. "I frankly read it with great dread," Dobell reports. "I said, 'Oh shit, the guy always wanted to write a novel and can't'—but I was thrilled, delighted, and somewhat surprised. I told him, 'Absolutely this is a book to be published.'"

Bonfire has been altered substantially since its serialization in

Rolling Stone. Wolfe has changed the nature of Sherman McCoy's crime, heightened the female characters, and made Sherman a career man on Wall Street rather than a writer. "Maybe the writer was too close to him for comfort," says Jann Wenner, who edited the *Rolling Stone* text. "And maybe if he distances himself from Sherman McCoy, he'll write Sherman McCoy with a little more fervor."

"I can see why he's having trouble with it," Bill Hoffman says. "Tom's great strength is his intellect. And intellect almost always finds its greatest satisfaction in the satirical. But a lot of times you've got to have real *feelings* for people who are less well equipped than you are."

This afternoon Wolfe seems exhausted by the toll of completing his novel. He is pencil-thin, sniffly, and obviously on edge. We have tea in the elaborate Victorian sitting room off his study; silver-framed photographs of his mother and father look on. Wolfe ushers me to an Art Deco settee he designed as "a memory from my teenage years of what looks swell," and talks about rewriting the ending of *Bonfire,* "making it more complete, and more beautiful."

One of his difficulties with the reportorial novel has been that he's repeatedly been scooped by breaking news. "I guess I just have to write faster," he says. Before the Bernhard Goetz incident, he'd composed a subway scene with nearly identical events, which he had to discard. "Here was this great piece of city life that I thought I'd introduce. But Bernhard Goetz did it for me—in style. He shot up everyone in sight."

The urge to retreat to pure journalism has been strong: "Often in the midst of writing this novel there were so many resonances with the Goetz case that I really would say, 'Well, why don't I just write about the Goetz case?'" But he's persevered in his drive to join the literary upper class.

"I see the coincidences in the news as an upside-down compliment to my reporting. I'm hitting upon the things that are happening."

Like the Goetz case, *Bonfire* crackles with racial tension. "If the city's going to be in the foreground, you can't duck the factor of ethnic hostility, which is so much a part of life in all our cities." He sniffles, takes a sip of tea. "The point I'm trying to make about status in the novel is that it's so different now from what it might have been fifty years ago, because the ethnic lines in New York, ironically, are

more sharply drawn now than they were before World War II. The
black population then was hardly a factor at all politically. Now it's
very much a factor."

It's because of this "resort community" paradox, Wolfe explains,
that wealthy interlopers (whites) control New York's high life, while
the townies (blacks, Latinos, and the new-immigrant New Yorkers)
have the real political power.

"Somebody like Sherman McCoy, who you'd think is on top of the
status hierarchy in America—he's white, Protestant, old family, best
schools, Wall Street—is odd man out once he gets into a political
situation. He becomes a victim, a fat turkey to be sliced up."

Ed Hayes has explained it thus: "People with a lot of money and
social connections in New York have a power that is very
disconnected from ordinary life. You can wake up and become
involved in an incident like this in Tom's book, and the people you
come in contact with in the criminal-justice system, who are powerful,
are so different from you. They're smart, competent people who
really give a fuck about what they're doing. And they can hurt you."

Wolfe has given Sherman McCoy a family with roots in Tennessee:
"His grandfather was a man of no particular standing, but made
some money and came to New York. Sherman's father goes to the
right schools and becomes a pillar of Knickerbocker society."

In the first chapter of the book, Wolfe writes of a classmate of
Sherman's named Pollard Browning, "who at the age of nine knew
how to get across the astonishing news that McCoy was a hick name
(and a hick family), as in Hatfields and McCoys, whereas he,
Browning, was an Episcopalian Knickerbocker. He used to call
Sherman 'Sherman McCoy the Mountain Boy.' " Although there are
strong overtones here of Wolfe's early sensitivity to his family's
outlander status in Richmond, he seems oblivious to this connection.
"Sherman's from New York, but Pollard's family has been here
longer," he snorts.

The status of an individual within a group is still his first interest as
a writer. "I try to make the characters in this book inseparable from
that notion. The psychological development of a person is utterly
inseparable from the status that surrounds him. The task of a writer is
to show how the social context influences the personal psychology."

Wolfe's passionate feelings about New York's status hierarchy have resulted in a novel that is venomously critical of the city. "New York really is a bonfire of vanity. But there is no villain in my book—unless you consider the human condition villainous. And I don't. Everyone in the book is vain, though. This is the human comedy!" Wolfe says, gesticulating. "We're right in the middle of it. Every ethnic group is mocked equally in *Bonfire*; just about everybody is hypocritical— everybody is 'doing well by doing good.' Everyone is equally shown as a creature of vanity."

This sounds like yet another addendum to Wolfe's diatribe against New York. When I make this assertion, he puts down his teacup and stares.

"I don't see any antipathy at all! It may come out as mockery and so on, but, God, I *love* the cities—I love New York! And often it's hard for me to get across the idea that I don't want it to change. I don't want people like the Bernsteins to stop giving parties like the radical chic. And I really don't want people like the characters in *Bonfire* to act any differently."

He's nearly out of his seat. "I don't have an arcadian bone in my body," he says in outrage. "I'm Addison and Steele, or the early Thackeray! Look at Dickens' *Sketches by Boz*. Are there any sympathetic figures in *Sketches by Boz?* Not really. It's full of mockery, raillery, irony. And yet there is a love of the city. My relish of life in the cities is the very fabric of what I have done! Look at Balzac, who was extremely critical of Paris. Who can say Balzac didn't love the city? He wallowed in the city. He would have *died* anywhere else. And I feel the same way."

Tea, apparently, is over.

Once Wolfe has regained his composure, I ask the key status question: How might he categorize his own reputation among the hierarchical statuspheres of New York?

"I was afraid you'd ask that," he replies morosely. He deliberates a long moment, then says, "I'm either going to make it as a writer . . . or nothing."

"Never Try to Fit In," Tom Wolfe Advises Young Writers

Heath Hardage/1987

From *Richmond News Leader*, 3 November 1987, sec. Young Virginians, 27. Reprinted with permission of The *Richmond News Leader* and Heath Hardage.

Dear Heath,

Mr. Wolfe would be delighted to talk to you during this weekend's fall festivities. He has requested the interview be conducted during dinner at "La Maison Couillarde," located at 832 Shield Place. Mr. Wolfe has read a few of your stories in *The Richmond News Leader* and is impressed with your editorship of your school paper. He will meet with you Friday at the restaurant at 7:00.

Sincerely,
Mary Hall Brett

I felt a gigantic scream of joy filling my lungs as I read the note. I walked into my American History class and announced the news to everyone.

However, I quickly noticed that two of my friends were laughing hysterically.

"You are so gullible!" they said. They had written the letter on the word processor as a joke, knowing that I had been trying to arrange an interview with Tom Wolfe, the famous author and American guru of pop culture, for the better part of the week. Wolfe was scheduled to autograph his new novel at St. Christopher's School, his alma mater, Oct. 17.

"Ha ha," I muttered as I blushed furiously.

I couldn't set up a specific interview time, so I had to approach him unannounced. After walking around the St. Christopher's Field House three times and doing several deep breathing exercises, I finally found the courage to approach Wolfe.

The slim, fragile-looking man wore a yellowing, white three-piece suit, a blue and white-striped oxford [shirt] and a maroon tie overrun by oddly shaped blue figures. White and grey lace-up shoes, reminiscent of the kind of footwear you can rent in a bowling alley, completed his ensemble. A round but emaciated face peered at me, the lowly reporter, through plastic white rimmed glasses. Displaying the manners of a latter day Ashley Wilkes, the great author smiled benevolently and granted me an interview.

Wolfe was born in Richmond in 1931. He attended St. Christopher's School from the seventh through the 12th grade. As a senior, he became editor of the school newspaper, "The Pine Needle."

After graduating from St. Christopher's, Wolfe went to Washington and Lee University and then to Yale, where he received his doctorate. He became a well-known reporter and satirist in the 60s and 70s, working for such distinguished newspapers as *The Washington Post* and the *New York Herald Tribune.*

In 1965, he published his first book. *The Kandy-Kolored Tangerine-Flake Streamline Baby,* a collection of essays which established him as a popular author on non-fiction works. Since that time he has produced such books as *The Electric Kool-Aid Acid Test, The Right Stuff,* and *Radical Chic and Mau-Mauing the Flak Catchers.*

With the publication of his latest book, *The Bonfire of the Vanities,* which is his first novel, Wolfe has been hailed in *Newsweek* as "Tom Terrific" and was the subject of other articles in *Vanity Fair* and *The New York Times.* He spent three years doing reporting and research on the novel which is about "Wall Street and the criminal justice system in the Bronx."

What advice and expertise can a successful author like Tom Wolfe offer to young, aspiring writers?

"It's a Catch-22 situation. You need experience to get a job, but you need a job to get experience," he said.

If you are interested in newspaper writing, Wolfe commented that "most newspapers want to employ stringers. If you take the initiative, they'll probably let you do it (a story)."

If you are pursuing magazine writing, "Come up with an idea that you have unique access to." Wolfe's example, "Scandal involving high school decadence, something you have entree to. . . . Call up or

write a middling editor . . . as opposed to the chief editor because
. . . the underlings are in competition to discover new talent. Write
them as if you haven't written the piece yet. They want to be in on
the creative process."

Wolfe, who once was an English major, suggested that anyone
considering writing as a career also should major in English or, better
still, history, because it provides a "broad, factual and analytical
view. . . .The most valuable things for me were the American studies
programs at W & L and at Yale."

Most importantly, though, Wolfe said, "you have to have talent. . . .You have to be willing to do the reporting." Wolfe finds
reporting difficult "mainly because it's an embarrassing undertaking."
However, he feels that "reporting is the heart of successful prose in
any form."

Being a stereotypical "pushy reporter" is not necessary, insisted
Wolfe.

"I'm just the village information gatherer. I'm not shy, but I'm also
not aggressive." He cited another famous writer/reporter, George
Plimpton, as an example. "He doesn't charge out aggressively. He
waits to be invited in," Wolfe said.

Wolfe also advised that would-be reporters "never try to fit in: it's
sheer folly. . . .Be an odd, eccentric character . . . people will
volunteer information to you."

His ubiquitous white suit seems to fulfill this requirement nicely. "I
found it annoyed people tremendously," he said. "It's a signature—
sometimes I wear a hat, too."

According to Wolfe, making the transition from reporter to novelist
was done "very slowly. I had become curious about what would
happen if I tried it." He used techniques similar to those of authors
Emile Zola and Sinclair Lewis—immersion in the topic and extensive
reportorial investigation. "I went wherever the stories were," he said.

He was attracted to topics such as the California acid heads of *The
Electric Kool-Aid Acid Test* because of "the fact that it (the topic) was
alien. . . .I'm attracted to things I don't know about."

In the 60s, Wolfe wrote for *New York*, the Sunday magazine of the
New York Herald Tribune. Since the supplement often was thrown
away unread, Wolfe had to find "something to grab readers." Thus,
he began to develop an offbeat, wacky style coupled with imaginative

narrative points of view. "I started one article off by yelling at the character," he said. "Some stunts work, some didn't." Basically, Wolfe tried "anything to keep them reading!"

That Wolfe's style often is parodied doesn't bother him. "Every parody contains a germ of tribute."

What does the author do to dissipate a mean case of writer's block? "I go out and buy suits. (He thinks he has about twelve white ones at this writing.) Then I have to write more to pay for them," he said.

Contrary to popular belief, Wolfe is not a health food fanatic, he said. He enjoys Arabic food, but is unable to cook. He did divulge his recipe for a power breakfast, though. He eats Alpen cereal with wheat germ, 100 percent bran and stewed apricots with water poured over the mixture instead of milk.

From what he writes, wears and eats, Wolfe seemed to be summing up his philosophy of life when he declared, "Who wants to be rolling with the majority anyway?"

Tom Wolfe's Walk on the Wild Side

Alvin P. Sanoff/1987

From *U.S. News & World Report*, 23 November 1987, 57–58.
Copyright, 23 November 1987, U.S. News & World Report.
Reprinted with permission.

In his first work of fiction, *The Bonfire of the Vanities*, the
founding father of "new journalism," author of such memorable works as *The Right Stuff*, looks at the high life and
the low life of the city that is now his home, New York

People don't often confront the racial and ethnic hostility that is so
characteristic of New York today. But if you're going to write a book
about New York, you can't duck these issues. New York now is
actually a Third World city. The ethnic groups that rule—mainly
Italians and Jews—are fast fading. White politicians realize that there
are changes in racial makeup and respond as best they can without
giving up power.

But the day is soon coming when the Bronx, where so much of my
new book's action takes place, is going to be run by a majority of the
population—which is to say, Latins and blacks. Until that happens, a
person like the main character in my novel, a WASP bond trader
named Sherman McCoy, is actually at a great disadvantage, despite
all of his worldly advantages, once he gets caught up in the criminal-
justice system. He provides a convenient target for those white
politicians trying to win favor with blacks and Latins.

When I started the novel, I wanted to have the criminal-justice
system as a major setting because that's an area in which I could
bring the high and the low of New York together. I went down to the
Manhattan criminal court and just began sitting in on trials and talking
to lawyers. I was getting some good material, but I kept hearing
stories about the Bronx and how wild it was.

I shifted my reporting there and became fascinated, particularly
when I discovered that the white rulers—the Democrats—of the
Bronx are holed up in this fortress of a building, and they're afraid to

go out to lunch. Well, sometimes they go out to lunch, but they drive over to City Island, which is up on the Westchester line. And at night, if the trials run past dark, they have a recess. Courthouse employees go out and get their cars, and they pull them up around the courthouse like a wagon train making a circle at night in case the Indians attack. They don't want to walk three blocks in the civic center of the Bronx.

I don't find this kind of stuff awful; I find it rather marvelous. Mostly what's going on is part of the human comedy. New York is a carnival that never disappoints.

In doing reporting for the novel, I was taken down to the holding pens of central booking in the Bronx. I was getting good, colorful material but needed some interior reporting. I met a lawyer who had a client who had been inside; I looked this fellow up. He told me about being led over and over again through a metal detector. He said that the most horrible part of the experience was being treated as an object. The police took great delight in the fact that the fillings in his teeth set off the detector, and they had him go back and forth hunched over so that just his head went through. That's the kind of detail only reporting can provide.

What maintains a certain stability in New York now is that power, insofar as people can exercise it, is veto power. The ability of groups to stop things is greater than the power of anybody to get something done. That is why to a considerable degree the job of mayor is a charade. The mayor really can't lead anybody anywhere; he can only make people feel better about the fact that nothing is being done. That's been Ed Koch's greatest talent. The more racial and ethnic hostilities increase—and they're increasing all the time—the less likelihood anybody can lead.

Money is a fever in this city right now in a way that it wasn't in the '70s and '60s, when it was considered quite vulgar for an educated person to show his wealth. Now, you can't be vulgar enough. Look at the "plutographic" publications that are coming out. Pornography was the great vice of the 1970s; plutography—the graphic depiction of the acts of the rich—is the great vice of the 1980s. Now that *Playboy* and *Penthouse* are on the skids financially, what rises in their place? *House & Garden, Architectural Digest, Town & Country, Art & Antiques, Connoisseur.* And there's a new one called *Millionaire*—I love that.

Let me describe a marvelous scene. There's a pasta restaurant on
Third Avenue up in the 70s. They do not take reservations. It's this
week's "restaurant of the century." You see young investment
bankers drive up in limousines. They ask for a table. They write their
names down like everyone else. While they're waiting, they order
drinks from the bar and bring them out and drink them in their
limousines. And this is considered a great night on the town.

I see myself labeled a lot as a social conservative, and it doesn't
bother me, particularly when I consider the alternative. Usually what
brings that characterization is going against the orthodoxy of the
intellectual world. I use the term *intellectual* rather broadly to include
the world of journalism as well as literature, theater and so on.

I went to the 25th anniversary party of the *National Review,* and a
reporter came up to me and said, "Is this a clan meeting of the
neoconservatives?" First, I asked him how he was spelling *clan,* just
to be sure I had that part right. When he assured me it was with a *c,* I
looked around the room and said that as far as I could tell, most of
those in attendance had never seen each other before but all in one
way or another have thumbed their noses at the prevailing intellectual
orthodoxy over the past quarter-century. That's sort of the position I
see myself in—and I'm comfortable with that.

Every time I start a book, I plan to write it in nine months, and it
always takes years. I started *The Bonfire of the Vanities* in 1981.
Finally in 1984 I put myself into a vise by doing it serially for *Rolling
Stone* in 27 straight installments. Then I spent more than a year and
a half rewriting it. It's terrible to take that long on a book. Balzac and
Zola, who happen to be my idols of the moment—as is Sinclair
Lewis—wrote incredibly fast. Balzac published more than 60 books
in his prime. Zola berated himself for writing only 25 novels in 28
years. He figured that if you had anything going for you at all, you
ought to do at least one novel a year. I don't know why it takes me so
long. I'd have to ring up Dr. Freud's night line for the answer. I know
I was intimidated by the idea of writing a novel, and I'm sure that
slowed me down. At this stage in my career, writing a novel was really
taking a big chance, particularly after I had gone on about how little
regard I had for contemporary fiction.

When I wrote *The Bonfire of the Vanities* in serial form, I found
that I had made a lot of mistakes, particularly structural ones, which I

later corrected. In that version, Sherman McCoy was a writer. He's now a bond salesman. When I told people I was going to change him to a bond salesman, they said: "Are you crazy? They're the most boring people in the world." But they're not. I had never seen a portrayal in print or on film of the daily life of these people. I went down to Wall Street to just hang around. I tried to be the fly on the wall and worm my way into investment houses to get the material.

This is a book that turns on scandal, and I found it was a big mistake to have the main character a writer because scandals don't hurt writers all that much. In an odd way, a scandal can help a writer if heinous crimes have not been committed. But a bond salesman is in tremendous jeopardy at even a breath of scandal.

Realism is important in fiction, but I see so many really talented novelists following fashions that lead them away from realism into literary cul-de-sacs. There's a current fashion of the "anesthetic" novel: Nobody in these books has any feelings.

There's a rural anesthetic and an urban one. I was puzzled about why there are so many rural anesthetic novels, because I know a lot of the writers and none have rural backgrounds. What happens is that to make a living they go to work at a large state university teaching English. They rent a house out in the countryside, and after about their fifth conversation with a plumber named Lud, they feel that they know the rural psyche. So they write these novels.

The urban anesthetic novel is always about either Los Angeles or New York. Cincinnati and Cleveland don't exist. And if it's New York, the action always takes place on 14th Street and below. Most of it is in SoHo, NoHo, Tribeca, where wild things take place and nobody feels anything.

But I don't think writers can back off from realism, just as an ambitious engineer cannot back off from electricity. You can't say: "Ah, it's been done. I'm going to head off in another direction." It wouldn't work, because electricity gets down to the nature of matter. And realism in prose gets down to the nature of how writing triggers the memories of a reader.

The realism factor in the novel was such that I found I was anticipating real-world events. One character, an assistant district attorney, was introduced to the reader in a 1984 *Rolling Stone* segment. He was in disguise on a subway—a nervous wreck, eyes darting this way and that. You were supposed to wonder what had reduced him to this neurotic state. And in April of '85, you were supposed to learn that he had been surrounded on the subway by a cluster of young men who had demanded money and he had given them everything he had. I had talked to people in the Bronx to whom this had happened and thought I was really onto something people didn't know about.

Then in December of 1984, Bernhard Goetz finds himself in a predicament, pulls out a .38 and shoots everyone in sight. So how could I, in April of '85, go on with my plan? People would say: "Oh, this man Wolfe—he reads the newspapers, gets his ideas, and then he gives us this wimp who gives up all of his money. What kind of a book is this?" I jettisoned the whole thing. Reality had scooped me because I didn't break the news soon enough.

Now, Sinclair Lewis did it the right way. *Elmer Gantry* came out about 1925, and the reporting he did was amazing. He actually organized Bible classes and organized study groups for preachers. He gave sermons from pulpits in Cincinnati. In the last two chapters, Elmer, the great evangelist, is caught *in flagrante delicto* with a church secretary who is in league with an entirely unscrupulous lawyer. And they extort the equivalent in those days of $265,000 from Elmer. He turns the tables on them at the very end and gets out of it. But, you see, Lewis had the wit to publish it 60 years before the actual event, more or less. So I've got to work on my timing a little more.

Tom Wolfe

Brant Mewborn/1987

From *Rolling Stone*, 5 November–10 December 1987, 214–20.
By Straight Arrow Publishers, Inc. 1987. All Rights Reserved.
Reprinted by permission.

*As one of the chief architects of new journalism, you put such terms
as "good old boy," "radical chic" and "the right stuff" into the
language. Did you also come up with the term "new journalism"?*

No. As far as I can tell, it was created by Pete Hamill. He was going
to write an article about Gay Talese, Jimmy Breslin and a few other
writers for *Nugget,* when Seymour Krim was editing it. Remember
Nugget? It was a skin magazine that turned into a literary magazine
[laughs]. Those things happen to a lot of people. Anyway, I don't
know if he ever wrote the piece, but Krim says that Hamill was the
first to use the term. I don't know how conceptual he was being, but
the phrase stuck.

Who or what influenced you to go in this new direction?

It wasn't just me, although I was there at the founding. I remember
watching and reading Talese and Breslin very closely. And what was
exciting was technique. It had nothing to do with stating your
opinions, which Jimmy does all the time now. In those days it was
almost always a third-person scene. And the technical bravura was
what stood out. Never did Gay Talese write in the first person. Never
was he impressionistic. It was in the third person, written like a short
story. There were a few others, but those two were the standouts. It
was one of those things that was in the air.

*You may have followed their lead, but didn't you also elaborate on
the technique and consciously stretch the boundaries of conventional
reporting?*

I really made a concentrated effort to get in the game. I adapted a
lot of things I had run across in graduate school. For example, there
were these early experimental Soviet writers like Aleksei Remizov,
Boris Pilniak, Andrei Sobel and the Serapion Brothers. One of them,
Yevgeni Zamyatin, was best known for *We,* the book that Orwell's
1984 was based on. From Zamyatin, I got the idea of the oddly

punctuated inner thoughts. I began using a lot of exclamation points and dashes and multiple colons. A lot of dots. The idea was, that's the way people think. People don't think in well-formed sentences. Anyway, they were writing about the Russian Revolution with the techniques of the French symbolists, and it was just electrifying. So here was the perfect thing. They were writing about a real event— usually it was fiction, but it was quite realistic. From the outset, I borrowed heavily from them, and that's a pretty funny thing to do when you're writing for the Sunday supplement of the *New York Herald Tribune* [*laughs*].

And then I began to develop my own techniques. One of the things I used, which I now see has spread everywhere, is the historical present—I don't know how I hit upon that—where you just write an entire story, a nonfiction story, in the present tense. Today most serious first novelists write in the present tense—have you noticed? It does give you a wonderful sense of immediacy.

One recent first novelist, Jay McInerney, made a splash by embellishing the immediacy of the historical present with the second-person singular.

The second-person-singular narration was, as far as I know, introduced by Jimmy Cannon, who was a sports columnist for the *New York Journal-American*. I think it's a dreadful device. But I'm not one to speak, because in *ROLLING STONE* I introduced the first-person plural as a story-telling device.

The royal "we"?

The *astronaut* "we"! When I wrote the series on the astronauts, I used it because I had this miscellany of figures to write about— seventy-two astronauts—and I had to do it very rapidly. And if you use one of these hokey techniques, like second-person singular and first-person plural, you solve the problem of point of view very neatly. And it wasn't bad—well, actually, it *was* bad, but it was fun to do. Now, even though I made the historical present my trademark at the outset, I find that it's self-parody for me to lean on it. This can happen. Your own inventions can become deflated currency. How can you start another magazine piece with "Madonna sits there fidgeting with a forelock that just won't act right. She pouts, she pivots on her seat, she gives me a look through tiger-tongue lick-on eyelashes and says . . ."? Somehow, you just can't start a story that

way anymore. Well, maybe it's a good thing, because then you try
other things.

*The power of new journalism seemed to lie in the way it blurred
the lines between fiction and nonfiction. And now your latest book,*
The Bonfire of the Vanities, *is a novel. Was it an inevitable progression for you? And isn't your first fiction still heavily rooted in
nonfiction—a* roman à clef?

I certainly always used novelistic techniques, but I also felt that the
boundaries between fact and fiction should never be blurred. Not in
the sense of making you wonder whether you're reading something
that's true or made up. For that reason, in writing a novel—which I've
done out of curiosity as much as anything else—I haven't wanted to
write a *roman à clef.* I figured if you want to write about real people,
do it with nonfiction. It's exciting to write about real, living people—
in nonfiction.

For years, I thought about writing a novel. In fact, when I was in
college, if you were going to write, it was just *assumed* that's what
you'd write. If you were serious, you'd write a novel. I went into
newspaper work the way a lot of people did, with the idea that I'd
work on the newspaper for a while and get a little experience, maybe
work some of the fat off my prose style—and yes, I believed in that
mystical stuff about immersing yourself in life—and then leave the
newspaper business and write a novel. Instead, I began to get more
and more excited about what was being done in nonfiction as a
literary form. That became my great passion.

So, by the time I was thirty-four, which is really when I began
writing—nobody should wait that long!—I was completely wrapped
up in writing nonfiction. But I was very consciously using devices that
hitherto had only been used in novels and short stories. The game
was to be absolutely truthful and yet to have the *absorbing* quality of
fiction. By absorbing, I mean that power that some fiction has of
making you feel that you are in the story. You are inside the minds of
the characters.

And it's done by using four devices. At one point, I even isolated
the four—I think I'm the first person who ever did this. The reason I
pat myself on the back is that they are so concrete. They can be
clearly defined. I'm not talking about *zeitgeist* now, or spiritual
matters or other things that people tend to talk about when they're

talking about literary matters. These are very specific techniques. To me, it was always the technique that was important. And in non-fiction the technique was based on reporting. You can't pull these things off without reporting. Where do you get the dialogue without the reporting?

Of course, there's also the temptation to say what you know is on someone's mind—what you can't get them to say. But in nonfiction you really have to resist that temptation. In writing *The Bonfire of the Vanities,* I indulged that a lot. I was writing fiction that was based on reporting. So maybe I got that out of my system.

Briefly, what are the four basic techniques you refer to?

The first is scene-by-scene construction. In other words, telling the entire story through a sequence of scenes rather than simple historical narration. Second is the use of real dialogue—the more the better. The third, which is the least understood of the techniques, is the use of status details. That is, noting articles of clothing, manners, the way people treat children, the way they treat servants. All the things that indicate where a person thinks he fits in society or where he hopes to go socially. The fourth is the use of point view, which is depicting the scenes through a particular pair of eyes. It's really rather simple to do in a novel. Even bad novelists do it very well. Until the new journalism got going, it wasn't believed that you could do this in nonfiction unless you were writing autobiography.

Do you think the stylistic innovations of new journalism have been abused during the twenty years that it's been around?

No, it really wasn't used that much. There weren't that many magazines and publications that would *indulge* in it. ROLLING STONE would. *New York* magazine in another life did. *Esquire* did and perhaps still would. But the techniques still seem to be well understood by young writers. It pops up in strange places. Pick up any airline magazine, for example. But it was superseded as a topic among the young by investigative journalism, thanks to Woodward and Bernstein. In fact, it's interesting to me that they wrote *All the President's Men* in two forms. First, they wrote it as straight news-paper journalism for *The Washington Post.* Then they did it in the form of the new journalism in the book. You can take your choice. And I think you would choose the latter.

Unfortunately, new journalism became so confused in terms of

definition that after I edited the New Journalism anthology, I vowed
never to talk about it again. That was in 1973, and I didn't for years,
but I guess I can talk about it now. After a while, I began to regret that
I had written about it the way that I did, because it began to look like
a codification. You know, here are these techniques, and here's what
you do, and here are the rules, here's who does it well.

You really didn't intend to set up the Institute of New Journalism.

That was the problem, which had already become the problem for
the novel and the conventional essay—there were too many
standards. And it makes writers, particularly young writers, too self-
conscious.

Why do you think your take on the Ken Kesey saga in The Electric
Kool-Aid Acid Test *captured everyone's imagination?*

For two reasons. One, Kesey was a rather prominent literary figure
who got involved in a bizarre adventure. And two, it was *the* right
story of the whole psychedelic hippie movement. All of the changes
that movement brought to the country generally—which we're still
feeling—can be felt and sensed in his story. After all, the story of Ken
Kesey is not just the story of some disturbed young man from the
fringe who sets out with a bandoleer full of resentments to disturb
American society. Here's somebody who is from the salt of the earth,
from a farm family that moves from the heartland to the rich
Willamette Valley of Oregon, who makes good and does all the right
things: joins Beta Theta Pi fraternity and the drama club, becomes
both an A student and a wrestling star. He was just the best sort of
Joe College. And it is *he* who becomes the leader of a religion based
in large part on LSD. The changes in him are on the heroic scale, in
a literary sense, and they're the heroic version of changes that were
going to affect a lot of children over the succeeding twenty years.

*So Kesey was representative of the emerging youth culture of the
Sixties?*

Yes, and when you talk about the Sixties, in most cases you're
talking about things that young people did or were responsible for,
except for Vietnam. There's a dark side of the Sixties and a happy
side. And the happy side was dominant. Do you want to know the
truth? Ninety-five percent of the young people in the United States in
the Sixties didn't give a damn about Vietnam. If you could make a

survey, you'd find that the number of those who cared was very small. They were having too good a time. They didn't have enough leftover energy to be down in the mouth.

I insist that the way the young people changed life in this country was the big news of the Sixties. It overshadows, in importance, Vietnam, the riots, the racial collisions, the space program. Any of the big historical events of the Sixties are overshadowed by what young people did. And they did it because they had money. For the first time in the history of man, young people had the money, the personal freedom and the free time to build monuments and pleasure palaces to their own tastes. And they created styles. That's what the psychedelic, or hippie, world did. It created musical styles. Without that world, without Ken Kesey and the Grateful Dead, there would have been no serious music by the Beatles. They take off from the Grateful Dead, starting with that album *Revolver*. Everything from *Revolver* on comes out of the American psychedelic world, to which they were turned on by Bob Dylan—in person, in private. Not by listening to his records, but by getting involved with him personally.

One of the things the youth culture did was to break down the walls of formality between people of different status, such as the wall between faculty and students in universities. Ironically, today the faculty members look more like children than the students, because many of the faculty members were children of the Sixties, and they still dress that way. The whole breakdown of formality between the old and the young—it changed universally, just like that *[slaps his leg]*. It comes out of that period.

What effect did that breakdown of formality have on the country?

We can't even calculate the effects, good and bad, of that yet. When you sweep aside the structure of maintaining divisions between people of different status, you've done a fundamental thing. You've done a radical thing. And that's a big part of the story of this country in the second half of the twentieth century.

Look at what's happening in religion today. All the new religions— their strength is seen indirectly in the scandals—are evangelical, charismatic religions. This would have never happened without the hippies, or "the psychedelic world," a term I prefer. "Hippie" was completely a *Newsweek* magazine creation. The term within Haight-

Ashbury was "acidheads." But if you're going to pump a subject for
journalistic excitement, you can't keep having these people called
acidheads. It sounds like corroding batteries.

Anyway, without the psychedelic folk making ecstatic religion hip,
there would have been no resurgence of charismatic religion in the
last quarter of this century, which there has been—and it's a big
thing. Insofar as young people are attracted to religion in this country,
they are attracted to ecstatic religion. They're not attracted to the
Episcopal church or the Presbyterian church. They're not even
attracted to the Roman Catholic church unless it's in an ecstatic
offshot—and there are some. There's even an ecstatic branch of
Judaism. This all came out of the youth culture of the Sixties.

*And of course rock & roll, which has roots in gospel music,
emerged as a major force in the Sixties.*

Rock & roll itself—I mean, it's so obvious, it's so big and
everyone's so aware of it that people tend not to realize the effect of
rock & roll. Rock & roll was a socially radical form of music. Rock &
roll demolished the ballroom-dance hegemony of popular music—
Glenn Miller, Frank Sinatra. . . .And ballroom dancing is one of the
support structures of the conventional status system. It's good
manners. Presley, and later the Beatles and the Rolling Stones,
demolished the status structure of popular music. When Presley came
along, the fact that he was of low-rent origins and had a low-rent
sound—a black singer who happened to be a poor white boy from
the hills—was very much a part of his importance, musically and
socially. This is Marshall McLuhan's insight—and it's quite valid—that
it was of crucial importance to the influence of the Beatles that they
were lower-class boys from Liverpool, or thought of themselves as
lower-class. I guess most of them qualified. The same with the Rolling
Stones. Even if they had to manufacture a lower-class background for
themselves, it was important that they have it. This was a social
revolution.

*Because they were among your most celebrated subjects, you are
forever linked with the Sixties and all the flamboyant characters of the
youth culture. But did you ever really feel a part of if?*

I was very much unlike most of the people that I wrote about.
When I wrote about the surfers in *The Pump House Gang*, I thought
I was pretty young. I was thirty-four, I guess. They were anywhere

from fourteen to about nineteen. To them, I was ancient. I was a little odd to them, particularly since I came out on the beach with white ducks and a seersucker jacket and a necktie *[laughs]*. And this was almost always the situation I found myself in. I arrived in a suit and tie to work on *The Electric Kool-Aid Acid Test,* and I never took that necktie off. Never. I quickly realized that it would be folly to pretend for a moment to be "on the bus" with the Merry Pranksters. Because it was a commitment that led—you know, you didn't just present your tickets and sit in your seat and watch *[laughs]*. Once you pretended to be or somehow assumed that you were a part of what was going on, you were swept into the maelstrom! So I was never really in any of these scenes. Although it has been odd that the people I have felt close to over the years and kept in touch with are often people very much unlike me. People like Phil Spector. I wrote a piece about him called "The First Tycoon of Teen," in which I made the case that he was the first man to become a millionaire creating a product—which was rock & roll—that had solely to do with the life of teenagers.

So you were always the detached and satirical observer?

I have been pretty much the outsider in my stories, but I've always rejected, at least consciously, the tag of "satirist." In my mind, I was never satirizing anybody. My intention, my hope, was always to get inside of these people, inside their central nervous systems, and present their experience in print from the inside. That can come out seeming like satire in some cases where people are leading wacky enough lives. Now, *Radical Chic* had to do with the disparity and the tensions between the socialites and what they regarded as their pet primitives, the Black Panthers. It ended up as satire, perhaps, but never have I sat down and said, "I'm going to write a piece of satire." Certainly *The Right Stuff* is not satire, although English critics in particular took it to be insanely satirical: "Oh, wow, boy, what a sendup of all these crazy Americans!" But that's because they think America is a walking joke.

I really felt that the discovery of these forms of life in the Sixties was so exciting that the discovery was the thing. Why put them down? The world didn't even know about them yet.

What are the Purple Decades?

I originally used the phrase—and I could kick myself—in the

singular, on a television show on New Year's 1979, just as the new decade was about to begin. Tom Brokaw, who was then on *The Today Show,* said, "Okay, you named the Seventies the Me Decade. What are the Eighties going to be?" And I said, "I predict it'll be known as the Purple Decade." I said "purple" in the sense of royal purple, that in this decade people are going to become much more blatant in the pursuit of status than they were in the Seventies and the Sixties, when it was rather bad form to make your ambition naked—you had to cleverly cloak it. And I turned out to be right, but my term was superseded by a better term, "yuppie," which says the same thing. I wish I had thought of yuppie. It's a brilliant term.

I later used the Purple Decades to characterize the Sixties and Seventies, using "purple" in the Victorian sense, as the color symbolizing rebellion. In any case, that's how that phrase started, but if only I had followed up that little proto-insight, I could have claimed the Eighties the way I claimed the Seventies *[laughs].*

If you were to write Radical Chic *today, who and what would it be about?*

You couldn't write it today, because there's no radical movement that's chic, not that I'm aware of. Someone wanted me to write about the current fund raising for AIDS in the vein of *Radical Chic,* but the whole concept is wrong. *A,* there's nothing funny going on, there's nothing funny about it. And *b,* there's nothing radical about wanting to save lives. It's just not radical in that sense.

There's nothing really radical going on anywhere, and certain things that *are* radical on campuses have no chic. There's nobody on Park Avenue, or any street leading therefrom, interested in South Africa and divestiture. Believe me, you couldn't get a party of any social wattage organized against nuclear war. You'd just get a big yawn.

What about the youth culture and the social revolution today?

In *Bonfire of the Vanities,* I mention that this is the generation in which the deltoids, the trapezius, the pectoralis major, the latissimus dorsi, are all better known than the names of the major planets.

But more young people today—and most of the rockers—keep their social consciences in high profile. Witness Live Aid and the Amnesty concerts.

Yes, but that's Community Chest stuff. Remember the Community Chest?

Your style of dress is as distinctive and famous as your style of writing, and it hasn't changed much since the Sixties. What's your fashion statement on the state of fashion today?

I had started dressing in white suits around 1962, when I first came to New York. I found that it really annoyed people to wear white in winter. *Why* I wanted to annoy people is another question. You'll have to call Dr. Freud's night line to get an answer to that! *[Laughs.]* My white suits, as I began to get a little publicity, created quite a stir, and I had a great deal of fun with them. And then it began to be pretty common. There were so many wild things going on in men's clothes that no one was raising their eyebrows, and I began to feel like just part of the backdrop. But today I see something else happening, which makes me feel good. Most of the adventures in dress still go in the direction of the casual. Today in the Hamptons— to which I admit going—there is such a fashion of the casual among men of all ages. I mean, men who should be covering themselves up—to their bald pates if they could find a way to do it, who should be wearing wigs, who should be wearing *powdered* wigs—they go around in the most casual clothes they can find. To show up the way I show up, with a high, starched neo-celluloid collar—in fact, you're looking at one; you can't bend this thing with a hammer—and a tab collar and a necktie and a suit! There are no suits in the Hamptons, except for mine. *I have the only suits in the Hamptons!* It's very abrasive—and oddly satisfying *[laughs]*. Again, don't ask me to psychoanalyze myself and say why I should enjoy this, but I do.

But with all the talk of the new conservatism, aren't people moving more toward the formal, the classic?

Not true. I think it will happen, but it's not happening now. The only place that happens is in New York City, which is a more conservative place by far than, say, Los Angeles, where men are spending a lot more money on their clothes and trying to get better clothes. But once they leave the city limits, they go to great lengths to look pathetic.

It's a very eclectic time now. People seem to be mixing the styles of all periods from the past couple of decades: you see long, hippie-

length hair right beside short, spiky punk cuts. What does all this mean?

To be absolutely honest, I don't know. This seems to me like a postpunk period, in the sense that there's a post-modern period in architecture. I think you're right: there are all these eclectic fragments. I was unaware of the new fashion of long hair among men. Well, then, I guess information ricochet is getting more rapid.

Could you define "information ricochet"?

When you have a new version, a retread, a recycling of something that is itself only born yesterday, that's information ricochet. In the art world, for example: last year's style of the century in art was neo-expressionism, this year's style of the century is neo-geo. Last month's style of the century was neo-conceptualism, last week's style of the century was neo-minimalism, and last night's was neo-process and neo-appropriation. And maybe that's happening in the styles among the young as well. And you and I, in this interview, are feeding the process. We're pouring oil on the flames by talking about all this. You see, immediately, as soon as we mention neo-processing, neo-appropriation, neo-punk, all these things become suspect and have to be reacted against, simply because *they've already been mentioned! [Laughs.]*

So, looking back from this twenty-year vantage point, are you saying that it's actually harder to get a fix on things?

Well . . . we don't understand the human animal any better from living in the last part of the twentieth century. I am convinced that human understanding of the human condition never improves, and it doesn't matter how many schools of psychology and anthropology and sociology are created. We don't understand the human animal any better now than we did four thousand years ago. Technically, we understand a lot more, but we don't understand people any better.

That's what's nice, actually. That's what keeps all of us journalists in business.

The Police Reporter at the Garden Party
Hilary DeVries/1987

From *Christian Science Monitor,* 14 December 1987, 1, 6. Reprinted by permission from *The Christian Science Monitor* © 1987 The Christian Science Publishing Society. All rights reserved.

Flaubert would love this guy.

Even with the screaming Notice Me! white suit, there's still the wife and two kids, the East Side Manhattan town house, the polished politesse. Talk about a bourgeois life. And then there is the work, which from the get-go is as original as any in the past two decades. Just take the titles: *The Kandy-Kolored Tangerine-Flake Streamline Baby; Radical Chic & Mau-Mauing the Flak Catchers; the Right Stuff.*

Yeah, Tom Wolfe is Flaubert's kind of writer, one who cottons to the creed of that 19th-century French novelist: Live life for art's sake.

And Mr. Wolfe did just that: the ordinary beat reporter who jammed novelistic techniques into the "pale beige tone" of conventional journalism, turning an entire genre on its ear 25 years ago; and who, having now written The Big First Novel that has critics aflutter, remains a quintessential Southern gentleman who happens to sport spats—spats of his own design.

"I call them my faux spats," says Wolfe, peering past his knees clad in perfectly tailored gabardine (white, of course) to let his gaze rest on his equally perfect two-tone shoes. "Real spats are OK. But they're too hot. They really make your ankles hot. So I designed these."

This is some verisimilitude from the author who insisted that a writer's only moral duty is to record "the right details"; that the writer's one true subject is "status"; and who has spent his career chronicling cultural revolutions through recorded minutiae.

Such was the crux of the New Journalism of which Wolfe was a chief pioneer back in the '60s, when the then Brat Pack of American Letters—Wolfe, Gay Talese, Jimmy Breslin, and the like—changed the face of nonfiction. Such is the crux of Wolfe's first fiction, *The Bonfire of the Vanities*—a modern-day remake of the 19th-century

241

novel of manners that is meant to do for today's New York what Thackeray's *Vanity Fair* did for pre-Victorian London.

In short, a satirical skewering of society's mores.

In other words, the same old Wolfe is at the door.

And here in his hotel suite during a recent interview, Wolfe is that same Dixie-accented, double-breasted dandy. He resembles a TV test pattern at the neck and ankles (a kaleidoscope of stripes and pin dots), but in between remains impeccably Thackerayesque—all custom tailoring and flawless decorum. With an appearance that beggars comment but a demeanor that belies it, Wolfe remains the anomaly he's always been: a police reporter dressed for a garden party.

Despite his much-heralded, late-in-the-career change of literary vehicles (the novel was four years in the making), Wolfe is still prowling his favorite beat: the status seekers' turf. And he is still writing with a Waugh-like savagery coupled with a journalist's instincts.

"I feel comfortable if the subject hasn't been written about and I've just heard about it in conversation. That's the journalist in me," says Wolfe. "In the case of *The Bonfire of the Vanities,* I started hearing about the Bronx [District Court], and I just went up there day after day. . . . I went out and did the same kind of reporting I would have done for nonfiction."

One of the era's most distinctive prose stylists and an acute observer of America's mood swings, Wolfe has, in his novel, turned his satirist's gaze and technical virtuosity to the high roads and low roads of New York.

Bonfire, which exploded out of the starting gate to land near the top of the *New York Times* best seller list, is a tale of two cities—one that pits Manhattan's rarefied stratosphere against the belly of the beast, the Bronx. It's page-turning fiction populated by the kind of relentlessly observed characters that dominate Wolfe's nonfiction. Sherman McCoy, millionaire bond trader, runs afoul of New York's criminal-justice system and cut-throat news media after a bizarre accident involving a Bronx ghetto youth. Other larger-than-life players include Larry Kramer, the hungry district attorney; Peter Fallow, callow yellow journalist; Tom Killian, the jaded Irish defense lawyer; and Reverend Bacon, a big-time Harlem scam-man.

It's an explosive mix in Wolfe's take-no-prisoners style, one that without the cushion of journalistic fact has set book critics to baying. Assessments range from "hilarious" and "brilliantly plotted" to something, well, far darker. "What subway-rider Bernhard Goetz aimed at with his gun, the more gently conveyed Tom Wolfe aims at with his novel," said the *Los Angeles Times*.

"A nervousness creeps into one's laugh when Wolfe makes sport of current black sensitivity . . . ," seconded the *New York Times*. "A racist, in this case, is a satirist who plays favorites," stated the *Boston Globe*.

Wolfe, ever the gentleman in his hand-tailoring and Southern affability, bristles. Just a bit.

"Never in *Bonfire* did it cross my mind that I was writing satire," says the author with a faint smile, who also insists his novel is no *roman á clef.* "Some things that strike people as mockery or hyperbole were, to me, instances of my barely being able to keep abreast of what was occurring. . . .

"I throw the critics a challenge," he continues. "If you don't think this is a correct picture of New York today, then do your own reporting. I say you'll come back with what I did."

In this instance of life imitating art, Wolfe maintains he had "started my research before [Ivan] Boesky, before the [stock market] crash, before Goetz. . . . In fact, I had this strong urge to put the fiction aside and go do a book on the Goetz case. I mean, I was the one who had said fiction was a secondary form [to journalism]. Why was I doing this novel?"

Why, indeed?

Wolfe's journalism had already served as a palimpsest of American pop culture. With his caricaturist's eye and reporter's nose for news, Wolfe had chronicled, albeit satirically, a couple of generations' worth of social change: '60s-style activism in *Radical Chic*; self-awareness movements in *Mauve Gloves & Madmen*; the US space program in *The Right Stuff*. Even modern art (*The Painted Word*) and modern architecture (*From Bauhaus to Our House*) did not escape Wolfe's Emperor's New Clothes approach to cultural revolution.

Many of the decade's most telling buzzwords—"the me decade," "radical chic," "the right stuff"—are bons mots of Wolfe's making.

So why a novel now?

"I had always contended that the two approaches [fiction and nonfiction] should be the same. But I had never done fiction and . . . I always had the feeling that people were saying behind their hands, 'All this big talk of Wolfe's is just an elaborate way of avoiding it.' "

So Wolfe summoned his courage and plunged in. Yes, even this champion style-breaker had to take a couple of deep breaths at the typewriter. "I was surprised I was so intimidated by fiction. The great thing about journalism back then was that nobody cared enough to make rules." Wolfe turned to one of his favorite novelists, Sinclair Lewis, as proof positive that writing a "modern-day Babbit" could be done. "Lewis proved my theory long before I did," says Wolfe. "He was an inveterate reporter. I had always felt that today's fiction writers were passing up great devices and material and turning to those private concerns that Virginia Woolf called 'the psychological glow.'

"[But] I believe the 'psychological glow' comes out of your experience in society at large and that much of our intense personal feelings are not private, but are the result of where and how you live," Wolfe says. "These are all the theoretical things I wanted to explore and prove to myself in this novel."

Indeed, Wolfe's preference for charting the inner man through the public persona has long been at the core of both his work and his personal life. Born in Richmond, Va., in 1931, the only son of an agronomist and farm journal editor, Wolfe studied literature at Virginia's Washington and Lee University. He tempered his Jeffersonian roots with graduate work in American studies at Yale, a stint Wolfe later characterized as "tedium of the exquisite sort."

After cutting his journalistic teeth on a handful of newspapers, including the *Washington Post,* Wolfe moved to the now-defunct *New York Herald Tribune,* where his wit and hyperbolic style began to jell as the New Journalism. It was his trip to California in 1963 to cover a customized-car show for *Esquire* that eventually turned into the best-selling *Kandy-Kolored Tangerine-Flake Streamline Baby* that set Wolfe on his way as a seer of the American scene.

Although he has been a fixture on the New York literary circuit for 20 years, Wolfe remains at a partial remove, owing as much to his background as to his perpetual journalist's stance.

"I consider myself a Southerner more in terms of personality than

in terms of ideas," says Wolfe. "But in terms of New York, I'm
outsider because everyone is."

Indeed, Wolfe's love of journalistic inquiry remains intact. Scratch
the surface of this new novelist, and the spirit of the veteran reporter
surges to the fore. "Today is much wilder than the '60s. Because
today's social trends started in the '60s, they no longer seem so
novel.

"I think the yuppie is a normal human being," adds Wolfe. "In
fact, I wish I had coined the term. It's brilliant. We went through two
abnormal decades, the '60s and '70s. Now it's no longer bad form to
flaunt wealth. It makes today much more like the '20s. . . . But there
is a big change coming. I call it 'The Great Relearning.' I think the
'90s will be dull."

What does Wolfe see as the big new subjects? "Universities. High
schools. Religion. We're just getting a glimpse of it through the PTL
scandal."

It is not surprising, however, that Wolfe's love of the '60s remains
uppermost in his mind. "What is extraordinary is the way people
swept aside standards that were in place for a millennium . . . It was
an exhilarating time," says Wolfe, with a touch of Flaubert's
reasoning.

"As a writer, who could ask for anything more?"

Tom Wolfe

Bill Moyers/1988

This is the transcript of an interview broadcast on *Bill Moyers'
World of Ideas*, 26 January 1988. Copyright © 1989 by Public
Affairs Television, Inc. Used by permission of Doubleday, a divi-
sion of Bantam, Doubleday, Dell Publishing Group.

Bill Moyers: [on camera] Good evening. I'm Bill Moyers. It's the
nature of journalism to occupy itself with the bad news in life, the
fires and the traffic jams, the depressions and the wars. It's the nature
of some journalists to turn a sharp eye and a biting pen on the follies
and vanities of everyday life. It's all the more surprising, then, to hear
one of those acidic journalists tell us there's never been a greater
moment to be alive or a greater country to be alive in. Join me for a
conversation with Tom Wolfe.

[*voice-over*] Tom Wolfe dresses like a dandy from the 19th century,
but his beat is the popular culture of the 20th, the follies of modern
times. With *The Kandy-Kolored Tangerine-Flake Streamline Baby*,
his first collection of essays, Wolfe in the 1960s helped to invent a
new journalism. It snapped, crackled, and popped with exclamation
marks, word pictures and dialogue that bounced and cavorted like
some of the exotic characters Wolfe found growing in liberated
America.

Other books followed. *The Electric Kool-Aid Acid Test*, which took
on the shenanigans of Ken Kesey and his merry pranksters and their
romance with psychedelic drugs. *Radical Chic*, with its unforgettable
portrait of piety on Park Avenue, *The Right Stuff*, and why America's
space-age test pilots had it. For a year now, Tom Wolfe's novel,
Bonfire of the Vanities, has been on the best-seller list, carrying
readers into the depraved, amoral and absurd life of New York City in
the age of acquisition.

Wolfe has eyes like blotters, soaking up what others look at but do
not see, and like the 19th-century novelists who are his literary
heroes, he is first and foremost a reporter of the life around him. We
talked at his townhouse on the East Side of Manhattan.

[*interviewing*] Many of us through the last 25 years haven't known

246

what we were seeing until you told us what we had seen. But you were right. You caught radical-chic on the fly in the sixties, the Me Decade was right on for the seventies. The eighties have been the Purple Decade, in the sense of the royal pursuit of ambition. What are you seeing now makes you think you can give a name and time to the nineties?

Tom Wolfe: Well, I'm beginning to see a lot of different trends that were so spectacular in the sixties and seventies beginning to run into a stone wall. Just to use the most obvious example, pornography. Which became an everyday business in the seventies. The court decision that enabled pornography to be widespread and absolutely legal came in 1968. It was in the seventies that you began going to towns of about 200,000 and finding about 14 theatres of which about 11 were showing so-called-X-rated, or pornographic, movies. And of those, there'd be two that would be outdoor drive-ins with these screens seven, eight, nine stories high, you know, the better to beam all these moistened folds and stiffened giblets to the countryside.

This has actually been a tremendous change in a country like this. This is a very religious country, or it has been. It's a very rapid and remarkable change in the country. And now it's run into something I don't have to elaborate on. It's run into AIDS. And this is in effect a stone wall that stops a very wild trend.

Moyers: You said in this regard, hitting a dead end, that the 21st century may well become known as the 20th century's hangover. In what sense?

Wolfe: Well, let me put it this way. This has been an extraordinarily free century, particularly in the United States. Free not only in the conventional sense of political freedom, but also free in the economic sense of practically everyone who works having surplus income with which to express one's self, to live a life of some kind of slack in the line, some kind of luxury, if you will, some kind of real recreation. It has also been extremely free in the sense that people are not bound by the most ordinary religious standards, or things that were ordinary for centuries, if not millennia.

Moyers: Every person an aristocrat, as you said? Every person his own law? His own fashion?

Wolfe: Well, it's every person an aristocrat in that you now find what we used to think of as the ordinary people taking on the privileges that in the past only aristocrats could help themselves to. For example, divorces. This idea of being able to help yourself to new mates, new lovers, whatever you want to call them, has always been the aristocrats' prerogative. Henry VIII's prerogative. Now if you go down to Puerto Vallarta, or St. Kitts, or Barbados, you'll run into factory workers, electricians, people we used to think of as working-class—to use another term that's disappeared—down there with their third wives, or their new girlfriend, wearing their Harry Belafonte canecutter shirts to allow the gold chains to twinkle in their chest hair, living a rather really luxurious life. Now this is two sides of the same coin. And one side, which is quite glorious, is prosperity and almost absolute freedom.

Moyers: The other side?

Wolfe: The other side is all the hazards of freedom in sexual activity. Divorce is one of them, which does have its penalties, does have its effect on children. Now this is all—I think that the down side is beginning to become clear. And so we're entering into this period that I think of as a period of relearning, in which we're busily relearning things that everybody knew 75 years ago.

Moyers: Namely?

Wolfe: Well, such as the fact that promiscuity has its price. But this is also, I think, something of a world wide phenomenon. In Europe—we've been blessed in a way. We haven't gone through any political upheavals in this country. This is a very stable country politically, very stable. Richard Nixon thrown out of office, forced out. Not only was there no junta rising from the military to take over the situation, there wasn't even one demonstration by Republicans or anybody else. In fact, as far as I know, there wasn't even a drunk Republican who threw a brick through a saloon window.

Moyers: Republicans don't drink and they don't throw bricks.

Wolfe: Instead, everybody sat back and they watched it on television. They said, "Look, he's crying now. Isn't that fascinating? He's crying now. He's leaving the White House now." I mean, this is a stable, this is a really stable country. But in Europe they've gone through communism—that's an impolite term now, incidentally, you're supposed to say Marxism, Leninism, or monolithic socialism—but they've been through communism. And the thing that was so radical about communism was not that it swept aside the old order.

All revolutions do that. It was the fact that it reinvented morality, as in the Maoist expression, "Morality begins at the point of a gun."

Moyers: Are we relearning morality? We're certainly learning, as you said, that promiscuity has its price. What else has its price, and what are we learning from it as a result?

Wolfe: We're relearning the nature of debt. I never will forget in the 1970s, people started telling me, "You've gotta leverage yourself." And I said, "What do you mean?" "You gotta get into debt. You gotta get into debt up to here." I said, "Why?" They said, "Because debt is the lever that moves the world." And there was some strange logic to it that worked.

Moyers: Did you get leveraged?

Wolfe: Oh, I got leveraged out of my mind. I never will forget one night I was in Texas, I was at dinner with some strangers, and I was sitting next to a man I never met in my life. And he says to me, "Son—" I thanked him for the compliment. "Son," he said, "I went down to the bank today and I borrowed $1.8 million." He said, "It wasn't for my company, it was a personal loan. No security, unsecured loan, $1.8 million." And I found myself in all sincerity clapping almost, "That's great. That's terrific. $1.8—" If he had told me that he had made $1.8 million that day, I would have probably yawned, because you're always hearing about people—But, golly, he could leverage himself in one day, $1.8 million—

Moyers: Let that be a lesson to you, never go to dinner in Texas with strangers unless you're prepared to borrow money from them.

Wolfe: I may be prepared. Now that's—I think that since a year ago, since October 19, 1987, there's been more and more talk about the virtue of liquidity, which means having cash, which means not being in debt. Now, this is a form of relearning on what is oddly enough an ethical level. It used to be considered unethical to be deeply in debt. It was considered to be showing a lack of discipline.

Moyers: The Bible, where I grew up, preached against it. Not that it had any impact in Texas, but the Bible preached against usury, against—

Wolfe: Here's another thing that's now like a foreign notion. The seven deadly sins are all sins against the self. And this is an idea that's vanished pretty much. Lust, for example. The reason that lust in Christian religion was—particularly in the form of Catholicism that originated the seven deadly sins—was considered a sin was not that some man would be leading some nice girl from Akron into white slavery, or the pages of the pornographic magazines, but that he would be hurting himself by wasting his spirit on this shallow and pointless, base passion. And the same with anger, which is one of the seven deadly sins. It is not that your anger might hurt someone that it's directed against, the idea was that getting angry hurts you. Again, it's a waste of your spirit.

That idea has vanished. And today one of the typical forms of absolution is to say, "Well, it's not hurting anybody but me." You know. "Why do you object? It's not hurting anybody but me." It's hard to believe that 100 years ago, people didn't say things, didn't say things like that. You know, we've actually gone pretty far into this program without mentioning deTocqueville. It's very hard to talk about—

Moyers: I'm sure we would have gotten to it, we have in all the other fifty.

Wolfe: But I think it was 1835, deTocqueville said the only way that the United States can afford the extraordinary political and personal freedom that people have is the fact that the American people are so intensely religious. And at that time we certainly were a religious people. It was very hard to rise to the level of assistant feed-store manager in a Midwestern town without belonging to the dominant Protestant church of that community. And there was this internal monitor, in the Calvinist sense, in people throughout this country; if you can believe the history that we read. And that is what tends to, it doesn't disappear, but it slackens if there isn't this internal monitor. Now, I'm sounding like a theologian. I'm just a social secretary. I just take notes on what I see going on. I have no agenda. I have no spiritual agenda for anyone, but this is what I see.

Moyers: But you did say in your Harvard Class Day speech recently that we're celebrating the age of freedom from religion. The implication of that, I seem to perceive, is there ought to be restoration of the ethical framework which grows out of religious roots?

Wolfe: Well, if you've had every form of freedom that has been known before, been known to man, and then some, the only freedom, the only freedom that is left is freedom from the internal monitor, is freedom from religion. It has been an experiment that perhaps at some point man had to make. Ken Kesey, whom I wrote about in *The Electric Kool-Aid Acid Test,* once said, in effect, "No one can be godlike without trying." Which was an interesting idea.

Moyers: Do you think that's what we've done in this century?

Wolfe: I think just as—that has been sort of the idea of being the ultimate master of your own fate. I mean, for most of the history of man, nobody would dare assume that you could be master of your own fate. That's what that whole concept of God was about.

But as Nietzsche pointed out, God died about 100 years ago. And then people began to see just how far the mastery of the world could go. And you know, it's been a marvelous experiment in this country, and one that I have greatly enjoyed writing about. But when you take a headlong leap into the unknown, and a lot of it has been that, you can crash, and you can also find great heights. And I think we've done both. So I'm—you know, what I worry about is you get into this area, and people think that you're painting a gloomy picture and that there's hell to pay. And I don't believe that. I don't think in this— There has never been, I think, a greater moment to be alive and a greater country to be alive in.

Moyers: But don't you think that the religious restraints were thrown off in part because people learned there wasn't hell to pay? That hell disappeared?

Wolfe: I think you're right. It seemed to—at least it certainly seemed to.

Moyers: And yet you've been suggesting that there's a different kind of hell to pay, which we're reaching at the limits of our permissive, autonomous, self-exploratory dive.

Wolfe: Well, then, there may be in certain areas. AIDS is pretty forbidding stuff. It could occur in the economic area, but it hasn't yet. We've now been through a forty—I'd say a forty-five year boom. I think the boom that we're in right now, the economic boom, started about 1943, in the middle of the Second World War. And it hasn't stopped. Now it took a terrific jolt on October 19, 1987, but the other shoe has never dropped, and it may never. It may never drop.

Moyers: But something is happening to the old idea that you and I, when you and I were growing up, was certainly the notion at the heart of the dream, which was that we were moving toward a more equitable distribution of goods. Now that's happened to most of us, but at the same time it's happened for the majority, it hasn't been happening for an increasing underclass, as you yourself have written about. Do you think that notion is finished?

Wolfe: No, I think it has happened for an awfully large majority. I think money in the last 45 years—affluence, if you will—has come down to most parts of the working population of this country on a scale that would have made the Sun King blink. I mean, it is extraordinary to see—it started in California, working people, factory workers, buying first a car, and then a home, and then maybe a second car, and then maybe having a weekend place.

I was amused—I don't know why I was amused—but when one of the surveys was taken after the Republican National Convention to see how the voters were going to go with Dukakis or Bush, they decided to have the respondents identify themselves by social class. And 85 percent said they were middle class. And I was only sorry that the news item I read didn't tell how the other 15 percent characterized themselves.

Moyers: What do you make of that?

Wolfe: It's a sign of wealth. I mean, it's a sign that the term working class can't be used in this country, because working class indicates that somebody is a slave to a job and is defined by a job. That just isn't true in this country any longer. I've talked to one of the heads of one of the big advertising agencies recently, and he told me that it's driving the advertisers crazy, that these large blocks that they used to be able to pitch ads to no longer exist. There isn't the factory worker, there isn't the housewife any longer. And to reach the factory worker, you may have to isolate his hobby. And his hobby may be anything from hang gliding to handcrafting of Venetian boats. And so there's this constant market segmentation, as they call it, to try to reach these little, these little special interests. Because here are people who have the free time and the money to cater to very esoteric, aesthetic interests.

In so many ways we are now alive in the period that the Utopian Socialists of the 19th century dreamed about. People like Fourier, and St. Simone, and Owen. They foresaw that industrialism would give the worker the free time and the personal freedom and the political freedom and the surplus money to express himself, and to somehow live up to his potential as a human being. They thought it was going to take place under socialism, and it didn't. It took place here. Under what is now called capitalism.

Moyers: I recently did for this series an interview with Noam Chomsky. And he repeated what he and Herbert Marcuse were espousing in the sixties, that this has, as Tom Wolfe says, been the freest period ever in any society; that Americans are more free than any other people. But that in a political sense this freedom is meaningless—no matter how much personal prosperity it brings them, as you've just said—it's meaningless politically because a corporate structure, private and public power, so dominates the landscape that it dictates the options from which people can choose and those options are not really that much contrasting. And therefore the personal freedom can be spent on trivial things, but is lost on political things. What do you think about that?

Wolfe: Well, in short, I think it's absolute rubbish. Marcuse invented the marvelous term "repressive tolerance." And this is what is known as abjectival repression. And his idea was: these people are so free it's an instrument that the masters use to repress them. And so it's abjectival fascism. In this country there's always abjectival fascism; usually concocted by writers and thinkers. I think what happened to Marcuse, was here's a guy from Europe, he ends up in La Jolla, California—that's where he did his deep thinking—he walked along the beach, he comes to Wind and Sea Beach. And here were these fabulous-looking young men and women, and they're bursting with vitality and power. They look like the people that Marcuse as a young man saw on the strike posters in Europe, the proletarian breaking the—Prometheus breaking the bonds of capitalism. And he looked at them as the young rebels. Instead they were surfing. And he said, "They're free, they're strong, the masters have ruined them, they wanted to go surfing and smoke a little dope." He says it's a repressive time. That's absolutely rubbish. This is the old cabal theory that somewhere there's a room with a beige-covered desk, and there are a bunch of capitalists sitting around, and they're pulling strings. These rooms don't exist. I mean, I hate to tell Noam Chomsky this.

Moyers: You don't share that—

Wolfe: I think it is the most absolute rubbish I've ever heard. This is the current fashion in the universities. I mean, a lot of it is at—you find it at places like Harvard and others; the notion that the masters—

and this is a term you'll hear, the masters. It's another term for the establishment, the cabal, which is never located, incidentally, but that's the term—controls us not through military power, police power, and the obvious means, but by controlling the way we think. Frankly, I can't remember a period in which politics were more removed from corporate influence. Corporations are pussycats right now in the political arena, they're terrified.

Moyers: They give equally to both parties.

Wolfe: Yes, I mean, they—

Moyers: Protecting their bet.

Wolfe: When's the last time you heard an American capitalist— another rather antique phrase, to tell the truth—make a political statement? Now, they would answer that with, "Of course they don't make a statement, they control the way we think." It's patent nonsense, and I think it's nothing but a fashion. It's a way that intellectuals have of feeling like a clergy. I mean, there has to be something wrong.

Moyers: One of the things I see wrong is that we don't have two parties, that we have two factions of the business party, and that it is wealth and power and privilege that both parties serve, although they may strike a different posture with their rhetoric in the course of a campaign.

Wolfe: I'd love for them to give an example. I don't think they can. You'll notice how abstract these people become when they get into this area. Because you know, it's simply not true. I mean, does anyone think that Kennedy won under such circumstances? They obviously do, they obviously do think that, but I think to prove that point you'd have to hire the whole team of medieval Rosselinos and all the medieval scholastics to find the angels dancing on the head of the pin. I mean, it's rubbish.

Moyers: [*voice-over*] From his home in Manhattan, this has been a conversation with Tom Wolfe. I'm Bill Moyers.

The Book on Tom Wolfe

John Taylor/1988

From *New York Magazine*, 21 March 1988, 46-58. Copyright ©
1989 News America Publishing, Inc. Reprinted with the permission of *New York* Magazine. All rights reserved.

The Isle of Capri, on Third Avenue at 61st Street, is a dark, old-fashioned Italian restaurant right around the corner from Tom Wolfe's house. When I call him about getting together for lunch, he suggests we meet there. "The food is good," he tells me, "or at least *I* think it's good." A nice touch, that, and a characteristic one, too—the self-deprecatory, but-then-what-do-I-know note being very much in keeping with the courteous Virginia-gentleman manner Wolfe likes to assume.

The following week, Wolfe pushes through the restaurant's paned-glass doors and is effusively greeted by maître d' Angelo Sciavette, who takes Wolfe's enormous wide-brimmed hat and his fitted gray herringbone overcoat. Underneath, he is wearing the obligatory white suit—one of seven he owns—with the real buttonholes on the jacket sleeves and a lavender silk in the breast pocket.

Wolfe is now 57. The lank hair he tucks behind his ears is graying, and his eyebrows are starting to spiral out the way eyebrows do when men hit their mid-fifties. A certain wrinkly slackness is developing in the neck. It's not that Wolfe looks old, or is old; it's just that his writing is so irreverent, so mischievous, so frisky—*The Bonfire of the Vanities*, which *Harper's* magazine said has 2,343 exclamation points, employs that same hyperthyroid prose style Wolfe concocted when he was 32—that it is easy to forget he's been on the scene for more than a quarter of a century.

Wolfe has had a lot of successes in those years, but *The Bonfire of the Vanities* is of an entirely different order. It climbed to the No. 1 slot on the *Times's* best-seller list eleven weeks after its publication in November and has been nailed there ever since. To date, 625,000 copies have been printed. There's been a paperback sale of $1.5 million, and producers Jon Peters and Peter Guber bought the movie rights.

255

But the book has had an impact far beyond what its sales figures suggest—impressive though those are. Although set exclusively in New York (except for one brief scene in Southampton), *Bonfire* has proved even more popular around the country than either *The Right Stuff* or *The Electric Kool-Aid Acid Test,* both of which were also best-sellers. Indeed, *The Bonfire of the Vanities* has become a sort of Rosetta stone, a reference source for deciphering the eighties. You can hardly discuss any aspect of life in New York today without someone's invoking the book. As Joseph Heller did with *Catch-22,* Wolfe has created a vocabulary that captures the spirit of an age in all its excesses and contradictions.

It is difficult even to pick up the New York *Times* without coming across some echo of the book. The Reverend Al Sharpton has seized control of the Tawana Brawley abduction-and-rape case in much the same way as *Bonfire's* Reverend Reginald Bacon takes charge of the hit-and-run murder of a black Bronx teenager. In January, Mayor Koch was jeered on a Harlem stage in a scene that seemed to duplicate the book's prologue. Even John Mulheren, the arbitrageur who allegedly stalked Ivan Boesky with a gun, seems to be acting like Sherman McCoy, the bond salesman in *Bonfire* who is driven to desperation when his life collapses around him.

"There have been a lot of resonances," Wolfe says, "but I believe that if you make it your point to describe what's actually out there, this is what will happen. Two things that are so much a part of the eighties—and I couldn't believe nobody else was writing about this in book form somewhere—are the astounding prosperity generated by the investment-banking industry, and the racial and ethnic animosity."

The book, however, has not been received without reservation. Many critics are of the opinion that it is, of course, a great read, impossible to put down, hilariously funny, and indisputably on target, but still, in the end, somehow disappointing. One objection is that the book lacks Psychological Insight. Wolfe, the critics say, is preoccupied with all these superficial matters, like clothes. Some were outraged when *Bonfire* came close to receiving the National Book Critics Circle Award. "That the bailiffs almost gave their bauble to Tom Wolfe's catalogue of shoes—electric blue lizard pumps! snow-white Reeboks!

bench-made half-brogued English New & Lingwoods!—is scary,"
John Leonard wrote in *Newsday.*

Wolfe has encountered this sort of criticism before and over the
years has proved himself a master at turning it to his advantage.

"I take great solace in the fact that Balzac, who is my idol, was
constantly criticized for the enumeration of status details," he says,
pointing out that Balzac was never admitted to the French Academy
while many of his now-forgotten contemporaries were. "There was a
great debate in the nineteenth century between observation and
imagination. Observation was seen as tainted, and Balzac was
dismissed as a mere observer."

Wolfe, who has been heavily influenced by the German sociologist
Max Weber, describes himself as "a status theorist." He argues that
the status group—be it the Army platoon or the Park Avenue charity
establishment—is the paramount social unit. In *Bonfire,* Wolfe refers
to the Bororo Indians of the Amazon, who "believe that there is no
such thing as a private self." Wolfe, too, maintains that individual
identity is largely defined by the status group. In *Bonfire,* he quotes
the Spanish brain physiologist José M. R. Delgado, who studied the
Bororos. "For nearly three millennia, Western philosophers had
viewed the self as something unique, something encased inside each
person's skull, so to speak," Wolfe writes. "Not so, said Delgado.
'Each person is a transitory composite of materials borrowed from
the environment.'"

According to Wolfe, the task of the status theorist—and the
novelist—is to analyze the composite of materials that form the status
structure.

"I think it's a literary fashion, but there's a great emphasis on the
emotional life, the inner psychological life, of characters," Wolfe says.
"It's considered much more elegant to stay on the psychological
terrain than to get on the social terrain. The idea is [to reach] a higher
sensibility [by examining] the torture in our souls. The setting is a
given."

A delicate study of exquisitely tortured souls was not what Wolfe
was interested in writing.

"I wanted to do a big book about the city of New York in the same
way my idols, Balzac and Zola, had done big books about the city of
Paris—my contention being this was the second great era of the city."

The first, he explains, occurred in the 1800s with the development of the modern industrial metropolis. The second era emerged by virtue of the extraordinary wealth generated since World War II.

"We've been living in a 45-year boom with little dips up and down that people call recessions," Wolfe says. This second era has also been marked, he says, by "license, and I'm talking about license in the sense of licentiousness, primarily in the sexual area but also in the break down of conventions, of manners and respect for authority."

The most recent stage in the second era of the city has been the flowering of New York's New Society. Wolfe expends a considerable amount of time in vivisecting its milieu, and New Society, in return, has expended time and energy on trying to figure out who's who in *Bonfire*. It has been said that the Bavardages, who give the frightfully lavish dinner party, are based on John and Susan Gutfreund; but then it has also been said that John Gutfreund is the model for Eugene Lopwitz, the head of Pierce & Pierce. Arthur Ruskin, the septuagenarian whose wife is Sherman McCoy's mistress, is rumored to be based on John Kluge or Alfred Taubman. But Wolfe insists that all the characters are composites. "It's not a *roman à clef.*"

Balzac and Zola wrote extensively of the clash between old money and new, and Wolfe was also drawn to the subject, largely because of its rich ironies. Both in Paris a century ago and in New York today, older families recoiled at the newly rich but found themselves unable to withstand the lure of their wealth. "Old money has its standards," Wolfe says, "but it can't resist going to the new parties."

Even Wolfe has felt the pull. "Writers all tell themselves they're just going to get material; then—*wow!*" While at just such a party, he came across the phenomenon that sums up the feverish pursuit of social ambitions: "I discovered the laugh, the excessive, compulsive laughter."

To describe this era, Wolfe adopted the same panoramic technique that Balzac and Zola had used to depict Paris in the nineteenth century. "I wanted to prove that it was not only possible but desirable to write the kind of novel that had been classified as dead for the past 40 years," he says. "The big naturalistic novel of contemporary life."

It is, as Wolfe loves to point out, a form that the literary establishment has generally dismissed. Ortega y Gasset has argued that the novel is a quarry that has been exhaustively mined. After Proust, Joyce, James, Flaubert, and Virginia Woolf, nothing was left, he says, but "narrow and concealed veins."

"That's what our best young writers coming out of the universities have been working for the past 30 years—narrow and concealed veins," says Wolfe, who believes that the theory is responsible for the current glut of etiolated minimalist fiction. "That's why we journalists had a field day. When I wrote *The Electric Kool-Aid Acid Test*, I honestly thought it would stand up only until the highly educated people who were really involved—as I wasn't—in the psychedelic world wrote their big novels. When I wrote *Radical Chic*, I thought it would only stand up until, again, the highly educated people in the New Left wrote their books. Then I was going to be in trouble competitively. Those books were *never* written. That's what's astounding. Not that they were written and weren't very good but that they were *not* written. And it's all due to intellectual fashion, which has said that if you have talent, then you direct your energies to the narrow and concealed veins, whether it's the absurdist novel, the fabulous novel, the meta-fictional novel, whatever. It was happening in all the arts. You had to move in an arcane direction to gain recognition."

Since the late sixties, Wolfe had been planning to do a book on New York, a book of scope and breadth, a book that would be— even though he didn't advertise this—Balzacian. The success of *The Right Stuff* in 1979 provided him with a certain financial cushion. In 1981, he published *From Bauhaus to Our House*, and with that out of the way, the time had come to give the big one a shot.

"I knew if I didn't do it now, I'd never do it."

Wolfe knew also that it had to be a novel.

"I didn't want to reach the end of my career and look back and say, after all this theorizing about fiction and nonfiction, 'What would have happened if I had tried a novel myself? What if this theorizing was an elaborate screen I've constructed so I don't have to face the challenge?' "

Most writers start a book with a theme and one or two characters. Wolfe approached it from the opposite direction.

"I decided first on the setting. I figured the characters would walk into the setting once I had it framed in my mind."

He had originally envisioned a book patterned after Thackeray's *Vanity Fair* but then realized that that would neglect the poor. "If you're going to do New York today, you have to do New York high and low." And the only place where the paths of high and low cross as equals, he felt, was the courts.

In 1981, Wolfe began getting up in the morning, putting on a suit and tie, though not the white rig ("I wasn't trying to be the star of the show"), and heading down to the Manhattan Criminal Court building at 100 Centre Street. He knew Burt Roberts, who is now the chief administrative judge in the criminal division in the Bronx. Roberts, upon whom Wolfe loosely modeled the character of Judge Mike Kovitsky, was at the time a trial judge at 100 Centre Street. Wolfe started watching one of his cases, at one point even sitting next to him on the bench during a calendar session.

Wolfe's cream-colored townhouse is in the noisy, exhaust-befumed district north of Bloomingdale's. After soaking up material for a year or so, he sat down in his second-floor study.

"I'm an outline man. I think spontaneous writing is a waste of time." He endured many false starts. At first, he envisioned a big art-world motif and sketched four chapters ("not bad chapters") that he later deleted because he thought the book was getting too long. "Maybe it was a mistake to cut it out."

Wolfe also continued to do research. He had struck up acquaintances with several court stenographers, and it was from them that he learned details about the hair-raisers at Bronx County Supreme Court.

"They would say, 'Things are much wilder in the Bronx.' "

In early 1984, Wolfe ventured up to the Bronx himself. His friend Edward Hayes had once worked as an assistant district attorney in the Bronx homicide squad, and he opened doors for Wolfe.

"It was directly through Eddie, for example, that I was able to go down to the detention pen," Wolfe says.

After a few such experiences, Wolfe relocated *Bonfire's* action to the Bronx. That decision helped him complete an outline. But after investing almost three years in the project, he had yet to start writing—and it was beginning to worry him.

"I finally decided, 'I've got to get this book out; I can't afford to be blocked. It's so stupid to be blocked.'"

Balzac, Dickens, and Zola had all written great books on deadline, and Wolfe felt (O Vanity!) that maybe if he were under similar pressure, he would have similar results.

"I really thought I could get it up. I knew I could meet the deadlines if I had to."

Thus it was that in the spring of 1984, he took a 100-page outline and individual chapter summaries to *Rolling Stone* publisher Jann Wenner, who agreed to pay around $200,000—the cushion from *The Right Stuff* was shrinking fast—to serialize the book as Wolfe was writing it.

Wolfe settled down to work in the white Victorian house in Southampton where, with his wife and son and daughter, he spends his summers. But even as he was submitting installments to *Rolling Stone,* he started spotting holes in his outline. To begin with, he had originally planned to have the central scandal revolve around the discovery of the rent-controlled apartment that Sherman McCoy's mistress keeps for her liaisons. That, however, was a rather limp pretext for ethnic outrage.

"I had racial friction but realized it wasn't making sense," Wolfe says. He had heard accounts of wealthy whites involved in hit-and-run accidents in the Bronx. "I decided this would make it much more plausible."

While that change solved one problem, it created a host of others. Wolfe had always been able to restructure his nonfiction work without too much worry, since the stories were held together by facts. The rules governing fiction, however, are entirely different.

"In fiction, if you start tampering with [events], like introducing an automobile accident, suddenly things are chaotic. You don't even realize how many loose threads you have created."

Because *Rolling Stone* appears every two weeks, he hoped no one would notice.

"One of the great things about journalism is, it's thrown away," he says. "I don't think many people were as aware as I was of how many times this thing was going offtrack in terms of structure. I was making mistakes. And I was acutely aware of it."

For example, he seized upon the idea of the hit-and-run accident at such a late date that he didn't write the scene until the book was half over—far too late to build suspense. But perhaps his largest problem was the occupation of Sherman McCoy.

"I'd made the mistake of making Sherman McCoy a writer, without having done any research about writers. I thought I knew it all, and I didn't. I hadn't even thought of myself in the role of a writer."

Assigning McCoy that particular career struck many as an odd choice. Wolfe did it "for convenience. I thought, 'I'm going to have to do all this reporting for all the rest of this stuff'; it was simply one less job to do. But [McCoy] was very boring. You never saw him sitting down at the typewriter. I can't stand novels or movies in which people have an occupation and you never see them at it."

At the last minute, Wolfe actually thought of changing McCoy's occupation. By the summer of 1984, he had started to hear stories about the gonzo atmosphere on Wall Street. Through a friend, he was able to spend a day on the government-bond desk of Salomon Brothers. Again eschewing the white suit ("I wasn't trying to attract attention"), he observed the firm in full deal-delirium, even listening in on the telephone conversations of traders.

The tumult of Salomon's trading floor fascinated Wolfe ("the sound of well-educated young white men baying for money on the bond market" is one of *Bonfire's* more memorable images). But he felt it was too late to introduce Wall Street into the *Rolling Stone* serialization. That would have required more reporting, and he was already engaged in the other huge changes even as the biweekly deadlines rolled toward him.

Given all the changes Wolfe did make, it is no surprise that the serialization—what he calls "a very public first draft"—was such a dud.

"I had the distinct impression the population was not thronging the docks waiting for the next issue, the way they did with Dickens," he says. "No one was rude enough to say, 'This isn't the hottest thing in history,' but I was beginning to feel that's what the verdict was."

In fact, for a while, he was convinced he had an outright disaster on his hands.

"I started thinking, 'What the hell have I done? I'm a lunatic. Why didn't I write a sequel to *The Right Stuff*, stick to nonfiction?' It really got to me. The first couple of months, I could hardly sleep. Or, rather,

I'd go to sleep immediately; then, about two and a half hours later—
thwock!—the eyes would open; I'd start worrying more."

Wolfe spent almost two years rewriting *Bonfire*. In addition to
changing Sherman McCoy's occupation and thereby introducing the
world to the Masters of the Universe, he made innumerable minor
adjustments, such as reducing the role of McCoy's wife, Judy, and
turning her into a more sympathetic character. In the first draft, he
says, she was "more bitchy. I didn't think I did it successfully."

He admits that *Bonfire's* females are a weak point. "I think I need
to learn a lot more about women."

This brings up another of the critics' complaints: that none of the
main characters is terribly sympathetic.

"I think that's one of the most truthful things about the book,"
Wolfe says. "Think about your own experience of New York. How
many Chuck Yeagers are flying around? There are people in New
York driven by principle, but they don't dominate."

The book's treatment of race, however, is probably its most controversial aspect—some people have actually called *Bonfire* racist.
Wolfe has said that he had a journalistic obligation to tackle the issue
directly and that he would find it easier to live with himself if he did
that and then took the heat than if he ducked the matter.

"Still," I tell him, "a lot of people are saying, 'Jesus, *Bonfire*
contains every stereotype imaginable.'"

"Well, I frankly don't know of any stereotypes," Wolfe answers a
bit testily. "Name one."

"The way black kids walk—the pimp roll."

Wolfe takes this opportunity to explain that "stereotype" is a word
originally used by typesetters to describe a word or phrase repeated
so often that they created a special plate for it. "It refers to something
that's used over and over. Who has ever mentioned the pimp roll in
all of American literary history?"

You can't argue with that.

"See, it's not a stereotype," Wolfe continues. "And the term is not
my invention. It comes from the streets. 'Pimp' is not a derogatory
word, if spoken by the right person. I wouldn't say it, but if you live in
these areas and you say, 'Hey, pimp!' with a smile on your face, it's
an ironic compliment."

Wolfe's attitudes on race have been questioned before. He says he provokes people because he refuses to treat controversial subjects with the conventional shibboleths and piety. For example, although his wife, Sheila Berger, a former art director of *Harper's* magazine, is Jewish, some have detected a strain of anti-Semitism in *Radical Chic*, his send-up of rich liberals, and in *The Painted Word,* his look at intellectual fashion in the art world. Christopher Hitchens has argued in *Mother Jones* that "Jousting With Sam and Charlie," Wolfe's story about Navy pilots in the Vietnam War, and "Mau-Mauing the Flak Catchers," a piece on San Francisco welfare programs, have racist undertones. He concludes by calling Wolfe "a moth-eaten court jester" for the Reagan administration.

"I think what I do sets people's teeth on edge because it's something of a gaffe—and we're talking about etiquette, not about anything else—to raise the issues so frankly," Wolfe says.

He points out that *Bonfire* explores friction not only between blacks and whites but among blacks, Jews, Italians, and Wasps as they jostle for power in the city. It is not always a pretty sight, and when a particular conflict is concluded, it is not always on an upbeat note.

"There's a [literary] convention that says you can bring these topics up so long as the tension is resolved in the end," Wolfe explains. "Well, the tension isn't resolved in New York in real life—or it hasn't been yet."

What annoys so many people is that the man who turned journalism into an experimental, avant-garde art form refuses to count himself among the politically progressive as well. Instead, he pals around with George Will and William F. Buckley Jr., and the Reagans have invited him to the White House for dinner.

Liberals feel betrayed by all of this. They love Wolfe's writing—or many of them do, anyway—but they're infuriated that he doesn't embrace the leftist political doctrines that constitute intellectual orthodoxy in the literary establishment.

To liberals, Wolfe's politics are a sort of faux pas. The kind of reaction liberals have to those who are not liberal is wonderfully captured in a scene in *Bonfire* in which Lawrence Kramer, an assistant district attorney in the Bronx, attracts the attention of two women only to have them discover his political beliefs: "Suddenly it

dawned on Kramer that they were all looking at him in a funny way,
all of them. Rhoda . . . Mary Lou . . . . They were giving him the
look you give someone who turns out to be a covert reactionary."
    I ask Wolfe about his conservative tag.
    "That's crazy," he says. "That's not even an issue. I'm a writer. I
can be backed up against the wall like anybody else. At that point, I
would have to make a lot of political decisions and would become
politically motivated. Right now, I'm not."

    Other things about Wolfe annoy people as well. The clothes, for
starters—those irritating white suits. They're a swishy pose, it's been
said, a throwback to the era of Oscar Wilde and Algernon Charles
Swinburne, of effete fops mincing around in spats.
    Wolfe's friend Ed Hayes explains that Wolfe is "a very macho
guy." The clothes, Hayes says, reflect the southern and English
tradition of "the warrior aristocrat." Wolfe, according to this theory, is
like the nineteenth-century cavalry officers who wore silk-lined capes
and stuck ostrich plumes in their hats and then gaily rode out into the
valley of death.
    Still, the fact remains that Wolfe does not dress like a modern
writer is supposed to. A tradition starting with Hemingway and
extending through Mailer holds that the task twentieth-century
American writers face is not just to produce books but also to seek
Existential Authenticity in their lives. This may at times require the
author to join the military, go on safari, or confront the fascistic
powers of the state. At the very least, it demands that the author shed
any concern for superficialities like appearances and, if possible,
retreat to a rural area, there to wander the pastures, brow creased in
serious thought. Wolfe's gaudiness, which he calls "counterbohemian," is an affront to this tradition.
    "In the literary world, there are certain patterns of consumption
that are demanded," he says. "It annoys me—the notion of
conforming to this."
    Thus, it can be argued that Wolfe's clothes are actually (to use the
rhetoric of the left) a subversive political gesture.
    "When you start off with the idea that you're going to write, you
think of yourself as some kind of rebel," he says. "Then you get to
New York and you see there is as much conformism within the

literary world as there is in the military world or business world. The rebel in a free country is the rebel within the status group. [Clothes] are a way of treating the literary-status world as cavalierly as I or any other writer would treat the outside world."

But for all Wolfe's posturing as the amused observer, the Virginia gentleman just in town to observe the follies, he has always been as ambitious as any of the people he ridicules in *Bonfire*.

"I am," he says as lunch draws to a close. "I don't like to spin theories from which I'm exempt. The money fever gets to writers."

Wolfe says he began to notice in the sixties that reaching the best-seller list had become one of the certifications of great writing. Once *Giles Goat-Boy, Gravity's Rainbow,* and *Mr. Sammler's Planet*—all indisputably literary books—made the list, writers of every persuasion began to lust after financial success.

"It got to us all," Wolfe says. "And we all said, 'Okay, the judgment of peers is the main thing, but I've also got to get on the goddamned list, and I've got to get a big advance.' "

It is by now late afternoon. Angelo waves to Wolfe and holds up the telephone. Mrs. Wolfe is on the other end, he says.

"It's after four?" Wolfe says into the receiver. "I'll be right there."

Apologizing profusely, he calls for his herringbone coat and his huge hat, slips through the doors of the Isle of Capri, and, confident in the knowledge that he is indisputably on top of the heap, heads up Third Avenue.

Cosmo Talks to Tom Wolfe: Savvy Social Seer

Pat Sellers/1988

From *Cosmopolitan*, 204 (April 1988), 186, 189-90. Reprinted with permission of *Cosmopolitan* and Pat Sellers.

A visitor to Tom Wolfe's Upper East Side Manhattan town house is greeted by a boisterous Jack Russell terrier named Raspberry and by the author, dressed in one of his trademark white suits and *faux* spats and looking remarkably trim and youthful at fifty-seven. Wolfe's wife, Sheila, and children, Alexandra and Thomas, are also in residence though not in view as he leads the way upstairs to his studio, decorated "during a period of yellow mania." Books and paintings line the walls; two high windows are binoculars trained on the city that he has faultlessly skewered and mounted in his latest book, *The Bonfire of the Vanities*.

His previous books, most familiarly *The Right Stuff* and *Radical Chic and Mau-Mauing the Flak Catchers*, were nonfiction works as entertaining as any novel. *Bonfire,* his first work of fiction, is as rich in authentic detail as any reportage. It's also enormously wicked fun.

In it, Wolfe leads the reader through vastly disparate levels of New York—first, the glittery, brittle upper crust and, then, the detention pens and criminal courts of the darkly forbidding slums. These two milieux seem many safe zip codes apart until they collide in the misfortune of Sherman McCoy.

Sherman is a blue-blooded bond salesman who becomes involved in a hit-and-run incident in the Bronx. The criminal-justice system, tired of grinding up and spewing out minority offenders, clamps over this temptingly rare morsel. Sherman soon becomes fodder for the ambitions of every corrupt politician, DA, and yellow journalist in the city.

Having sated his own ambition to write a successful first novel, Tom Wolfe temporarily relinquished his role of reporter in order to be interviewed by COSMO.

Q: What does the title *The Bonfire of the Vanities* actually mean?

267

A: In the late fifteenth century, Savonarola, a priest who ran Florence for about three years, had bonfires in which people's vanities—which meant anything from false eyelashes to nonreligious portraits—were put into pyramid-shaped heaps and set afire. He had these little Red Guard units of young Catholic zealots whom he'd send into people's homes to drag things out. And finally, the guard had about enough of this, and they burned Savonarola in the last one. In the book, money fever really started the flames of vanity in each one of these characters.

Q: You seemed to be making the point that everyone in New York is motivated by vanity in one form or another. Do you think of *yourself* as vain?

A: I don't construct theories that don't apply to me. Yes, I am vain. I mean, who else would pay as much attention to clothes as I do?

Q: When did you first start wearing your white suits?

A: It was when I came to New York in 1962 to be a reporter for the *Herald Tribune.* I went by a tailor shop to get a white suit made for the summer, which wasn't all that big a deal, as far as I was concerned, because I had grown up in Richmond, Virginia, and a lot of men wore white suits. The material I picked out was too heavy to wear in the summer, so I started wearing the suit in the fall, and it annoyed people enormously. Why I enjoyed that, I don't know. But after that, it became fun dressing every day. People were easy to disturb through dress in those days, not so easy today.

Q: You worked for ten years as a newspaper journalist, and yet, in your book, every print and electronic journalist comes off as pretty unsavory. Were you sleazy too?

A: I certainly did some sleazy things. The sleaziest thing I remember doing is going into the house of the parents of a teenage girl who had died in sordid circumstances and persuading them that it was in the interests of humanity that they surrender a picture of this girl to me to be printed in the *Washington Post,* which they finally did. The *Post's* interest was sheer prurience, the way every other newspaper's is.

Q: Besides journalists, many groups come in for a trouncing in your book—politicians, do-gooders, high society, low society. Don't you like *any* of these people?

A: Actually, I like them all. And I never thought of it as a trouncing.

Not for a moment did I say, Well, I'm going to *get* the press and the activists, I'm going to *get* the district attorney's office. To me, that's just the way they are.

Q: What about New York itself? In spite of all you said about it, you still live here.

A: And I still get a tremendous kick out of it. This really is the capital of the western world in the last days of the twentieth century. There was a time when Rome was the place everyone went who wanted to be where things were happening. And then there was a time when London was that, and then Paris certainly was. New York happens to be that particular spot right now. And it's exciting and awful, wonderful and dreadful. I mean, nobody lives in New York for the quality of life unless one's head is not screwed on tightly.

This is the city of ambition. People are always talking about the wonderful energy of New York; they mean ambition and greed. People who are not ambitious—even people who already have it made but are not doing anything, people who aren't working—find New York a bit alien. The Duke and Duchess of Windsor never felt comfortable here. They were just wealthy celebrities who did nothing.

Q: Your book is also very concerned with status. What does determine status in New York these days—money, power, lineage?

A: Among educated white people, the most crucial thing would be money, because today if you have money, you can become a socialite in two years no matter how crude you are. The magic ticket to making it socially in New York is to support the Metropolitan Museum of Art or the Museum of Modern Art. And the reason is that if you give a lot of money to a museum, they want to get more, assuming you have more, so they will put you on the party circuit. I would say this is the biggest change of the past decade in that particular social world.

Q: In the book, you have two scenes in which you depict the private parties of the rich and famous with scathing humor. Aren't you yourself very much a part of this scene?

A: I guess so, yes. I have been to many parties. I call them the boldface parties, where most of the people there are people whose names appear in boldface in gossip columns. But I had always gone just to wallow in the scene. So when it came time to write about it for the book, the next few of these parties I was invited to I didn't

socialize, I just shut off and listened, which of course makes you a
wonderful guest. I think the reason I'm not invited to these things
anymore is not that I've written a book, but that I didn't speak for
about a year.

Q: Do you mean the social doors have been closed to you as they
were to Truman Capote after he wrote about some of these same
people in all their absurd glory?

A: I'm exaggerating. I haven't felt the cold wind of ostracism. But
time will tell.

Q: You were the premier chronicler of the sixties in such works as
The Electric Kool-Aid Acid Test, and you designated the seventies for
all time as the Me Decade. Have you pinpointed the lavish eighties?

A: The one word I've come up with is plutography. It's the age of
plutography, meaning the graphic depiction of the acts of the rich in
magazines like *House & Garden, Architectural Digest, Art and
Antiques;* and in television shows like *Lifestyles of the Rich and
Famous.* The current restaurant fever is part of the same thing.
People go to them to breathe the air of the rich and famous.

Q: With all the lavishness and big-bucks spending going on, do
you think we're living in an age of decadence, like Rome before the
decline and fall?

A: This is certainly an age of decadence, there's no question about
that. That doesn't mean it's the decline and fall of the empire though.

Q: But it is the decline and fall of the stock market. Was that a nice
coincidence for you, having Black Monday fall right around the
release of your book?

A: I wouldn't necessarily wish that on the country, but as it turned
out . . .

Q: The scenes and dialogue in Sherman's brokerage house are
very authentic. Do you have a knowledge of high finance?

A: No, I spent a lot of time at those brokerage houses to get
information for the book. I took notes on what they were saying, and
after a while, I began to learn a little bit of those things. But some of
the things in the book . . . to this day I don't know what they mean.

Q: How do you answer certain reviewers who have accused you of
being racist because of the way you portrayed black and Hispanic
people in the book?

A: There have been a couple of reviews which, in fact, are worded rather curiously: "Well, I don't consider it racist, but a lot of people are going to take it this way. . . ." Now, I frankly have never seen an example given of anything in the book that could be taken that way, and I think the reason is that one cannot be found. I think what these particular reviewers are really reacting to is the fact that I am frank about the subject of racial friction in New York. I was convinced from the beginning that you could not write a big book about the city without including that part of it, the racial and ethnic animosity. It's so much a part of contemporary New York.

Q: At the outset, you were much more familiar with the high life than the low. How did you familiarize yourself with this aspect of New York?

A: Both areas involved a lot of reporting, although I was in a way much prouder of what I did with the Bronx. That was really unknown territory. I started sitting in on cases at the criminal court, and I got to know a judge. I went down to the detention pens. I needed that interior reporting to find out the feeling, the fears.

Q: After all these years and all your success, what made you attempt the transition from nonfiction to fiction?

A: Well, when I was in college, it was assumed that if you were serious about writing, you would write a novel, and one way to go about it was to work on newspapers first, to work some of the fat off your style and off your soul. And you'd quit the business one day and move into a shack somewhere and write a novel. That's what I fully intended to do when I started working in newspapers. But then I really began to be interested in journalism as a literary form, and it became my main interest.

This book was going to be a one-shot thing. It was not a new direction for me, it was a detour. I was going to do this one thing to prove whether I could or couldn't do it, then return to nonfiction. But it actually began to be fun toward the end—it wasn't fun at all at the beginning when I was very blocked—and so I'm very much tempted to write another novel.

Q: Do you have any advice for readers who feel they might like to write a book?

A: There are no special techniques to reporting, no tricks. It's so much easier than anyone would think. I mean, anyone could have done what I did if they wanted to. If you hang around the courthouse, people will wonder who you are, and as soon as they wonder, you introduce yourself. As soon as you introduce yourself, you have a chance to make a friend. And once you make a friend, that friend can introduce you to someone else.

Q: How do you feel about the state of fiction writing today?

A: It's improving slightly as young writers begin to discover that the future lies in realism and not in magic realism [books like *One Hundred Years of Solitude,* by Gabriel García Márquez] or meta-fiction [plotless stories] or any of the other nonrealistic fashions of the past twenty years.

Q: Which present-day fiction writer do you admire?

A: Richard Price, who did the screenplay for *The Color of Money,* is the writer I watch most closely. He has written four novels: *The Wanderers, Bloodbrothers, Ladies' Man,* and *The Breaks.* My favorite was his first, *The Wanderers,* a realistic novel about growing up in the Bronx. To me, it's one of the greatest coming-of-age novels written by an American since the Second World War. He has a tremendous amount of talent.

Q: Reverting to your role of reporter, if you were to interview Tom Wolfe, what would be at the top of your list of questions?

A: The question would be, What makes you want to live by your wits this way? Writing is a very risky way to live. You can't found a company, and then if you get hit by a panel truck, the company keeps chugging along. I don't even have anybody to transcribe my tapes. It's a one-man band. And I have no answer to my question. I don't know *why* I like it, but I do.

Tom Wolfe

Bill Moyers/1988

This is the transcript of an interview broadcast on *Bill Moyers'*
World of Ideas, 27 October 1988. Copyright © 1989 by Public
Affairs Television, Inc. Used by permission of Doubleday, a divi-
sion of Bantam, Doubleday, Dell Publishing Group.

Bill Moyers: [*on camera*] Good evening, I'm Bill Moyers. Just about
the time you think this is the best of times, something happens to
remind you it's also the worst, or vice versa. So, the opening line of
Dickens' *Tale of Two Cities* has become the cliche of each era: things
are never what they seem; on the other hand, they could be. We
don't often know what to make of our times until some writer informs
us, and no one has put more labels on more decades than my guest
tonight. Join me for a conversation with Tom Wolfe.

[*voice-over*] Tom Wolfe dresses like a dandy from the 19th century,
but his beat is the popular culture of the 20th, the follies of modern
times. With *The Kandy-Kolored Tangerine-Flake Streamline Baby,* his
first collection of essays, Wolfe, in the 1960s, helped to invent a new
journalism. It snapped, crackled and popped with exclamation marks,
word pictures and dialogue that bounced and cavorted like some of
the exotic characters Wolfe found growing in liberated America.
Other books followed: *Radical Chic,* with its unforgettable portrait of
piety on Park Avenue; *The Right Stuff,* and why America's space-age
test pilots had it. For a year now, Tom Wolfe's novel *Bonfire of the*
Vanities has been on the bestseller list, carrying readers into the
depraved, amoral and absurd life of New York City in the age of
acquisition. Wolfe has eyes like blotters, soaking up what others look
at, but do not see. And like the 19th century novelists who are his
literary heroes, he is first and foremost a reporter of the life around
him. We talked at his townhouse on the East Side of Manhattan.

[*interviewing*] The picture you paint in the book is one of utter
depravity in our society. The politicians are helpless. The clergy are
either charlatans or marginal. The police, the judges, the lawyers are

all cynical or sold out. Everyone's isolated from everyone else. There's not a significant likable, sympathetic person in the whole book. You get the picture that this is a society at the end of its period, at the end of its life, about to fall like some giant old building that has long ago lost its foundation.

Tom Wolfe: Well, if I may quote that famous philosopher, Goodman Ace's wife, Jane, you have to take the bitter with the better. There are two sides to the coin, and the coin glitters. Prosperity and freedom can lead, in the same moment that it shines this brilliant light, to tremendous excesses and to extreme forms of individualism, one form being vanity. Now, the book, *The Bonfire of the Vanities,* is about New York City in the 1980s in a period of money fever. I mean, there has never been such wealth as that generated in New York chiefly by the investment banking industry.

Moyers: White young men baying at the—

Wolfe: Baying, yes, baying for money on the bond market. Right now we're in a postal zone, 10021, in which the annual income is— personal income, I'm not talking about companies—four billion dollars.

Moyers: I didn't know your book had done that well.

Wolfe: I just added a drop in the bucket, but—

Moyers: Four billion?

Wolfe: Four billion, and that's—I mean, just think of all the countries in the world that don't have a budget of four billion dollars. What I'm saying is there's been tremendous, enormous wealth, that's part of prosperity and freedom. This leads to extreme forms of—to use an old-fashioned word, which I seem to be doing all the time this afternoon, vanity—and I've seen it in the '80s go right from Wall Street, all the way from Wall Street, to the South Bronx where I did a lot of my research. I'll never forget walking through the South Bronx doing research for this book and seeing these boys, thirteen, fourteen years old, with these necklaces on. And hanging as pendants from the necklaces were steel, or silvery anyway, rings. And in these rings were upside-down "Y"s, which I thought were peace symbols. And I said, "Isn't it interesting that these boys here in the poorest part of New York are so civic-minded. They're concerned about the threat of nuclear destruction and so on."

Of course, I looked more closely and they were Mercedes-Benz

hood ornaments. They knew what a Mercedes-Benz was. They knew
how much it cost because they knew that all hot-shots drive them.
The drug dealers drive them. And they wanted theirs. And they were
taking the only part that they could now get, which was the hood
ornament. This was the money fever spreading right down to the
bottom rungs of the social ladder. Now, this is New York. This is
vanity operating on all sides.

Moyers: But it's more than vanity, and it's more than money. It's
utter amorality that pervades that picture of New York. Is that true to
the way you see the city?

Wolfe: Oh, sure. But, now, in *The Bonfire of the Vanities* there is
no corruption in the broad sense of people being bribed.

Moyers: That's the old-fashioned kind.

Wolfe: It's corruption from within. You know, Sartre was famous
for the statement, in the play, *No Exit,* "Hell is other people." To
which Claude Levi-Strauss said, "No. Hell is ourselves." And the
inferno that I try to present in *The Bonfire of the Vanities* is internal.
I'll just cite one example from the book, probably the key example. I
present a young assistant district attorney named Larry Kramer. He
has gone into public service as a young prosecutor in the Bronx, on
purpose. He wanted to go into public service. He wanted to feel he
was doing something that was both real and important and good for
the city he lived in, as opposed to his classmates at Columbia, who
were going to go down to Wall Street and make a ton of money
shuffling papers and protecting the interests of perfume franchises
and leveraged buy-out kings and the rest of them. And that's exactly
the way it has worked out for him. His classmates have done that,
and he's done exactly what he set out to do. And yet, one morning
when he sees one of his classmates he hasn't seen in years coming
out of a terrific apartment house, heading for a car and driver,
beautifully dressed, carrying a $500 attache case, no doubt heading
down to Wall Street, he can't stand it. He can't stand it. The money
fever's got him. He can't stand the contrast between his shabby get-
up, his $36,000 a year and what his classmates are doing. And that is
how the money fever gets to people.

But is it bad to have a city or a country in which there is that much
money around? I say no. I mean, just look back over the panorama
of human history. They are two sides to the same coin.

Moyers: It's certainly not a city that you'd want to leave your mother alone in.

Wolfe: No, I wouldn't. But I live here, and I intend to continue living here.

Moyers: With bars on your windows—on my windows? I live across the Park; bars on the windows. I had to warn you a minute ago you'd left the key in the back door.

Wolfe: It's quite true. You either find New York an exciting place to be. You either enjoy the level of ambition that exists here and the kind of people that that attracts, or you leave. Because it is not a place that ranks very high on the scales of quality of life.

Moyers: Why do you stay?

Wolfe: Because I love the city. I love the people who are here. I love the people it attracts. You know, when I say people of ambition, it's not just the perfume franchisers and the leveraged buy-out kings and their lawyers. Think of, today, all the Asians who are, by no means, from the top of the heap, who are coming to New York City, who are taking over the small candy stores, the grocery stores—I think particularly of Indians from India and Koreans—out of a sense of ambition. And many of them are making it. And they put up with a lot of the same things that you were alluding to, mainly crime.

Moyers: I'm alluding to them, but I read about them in *Bonfire of the Vanities*. One of the notions you strike so hard at in that book is that old American notion that, somewhere down there along the line, there's a system of justice, there's a rule of law. The system of justice and the rule of law do not exist in *Bonfire of the Vanities*. They are gone.

Wolfe: Well, there are certain figures in the novel.

Moyers: The judge.

Wolfe: Judge Kovitsky.

Moyers: Well, what happens to him?

Wolfe: He doesn't prevail. There's another figure, the head c˙ the homicide bureau in the Bronx, Bernie Fitzgibbon. All the way through he's the real voice of the law in the book. He keeps saying, "Wait a minute. We have to do this the right way. We have to have sufficient evidence. We can't cater to the mob," and so on. The district attorney keeps overruling him. He's determined to cater to the

mob, because he has an election coming up. Now, this is really
personal corruption, not the corruption of a system.

Moyers: But isn't that the worst corruption? You said a minute
ago, it's the amorality of the spirit.

Wolfe: Right.

Moyers: Buying politicians is an old art form, but this is kind of a
terminal corruption.

Wolfe: Well, it may not be terminal, but it's more an inner thing.
It's more inside the individual responding to the pressures of the
money fever. A lot of people, including some critics, said that *The
Bonfire of the Vanities* has no heroes. And I was reminded after that
of the—I hadn't thought about it—but the subtitle of Thackeray's
Vanity Fair is "A Novel without a Hero." And he was writing about a
similar period; flush times, there seemed to be no limit to wealth and
to indulgence.

Moyers: Do you really believe, as the book portrays, that the rule
of law is finished?

Wolfe: No, and I didn't intend to make that point. As a matter of
fact, when I was writing that book, it was with a spirit of wonderment.
I was saying, "Look at these people. Look at what they're doing.
Look at that one. Look at that one." It was only after I finished and
read it over that I see that there is a cumulative effect that leads to the
kind of conclusion you mention. The rule of law hasn't broken down,
it's in a place, a borough like the Bronx, it's swamped. There aren't
enough courtrooms to deal with the level of crime. And this is a
problem all over New York City, and I think a lot of major cities. So, it
isn't the system of justice; it's a) the sheer volume of crime, and b) the
vanity of certain sorts of figures who, as I suppose is natural up to a
point, are looking out for their own political careers.

Moyers: You said somewhere else that there are principled people
in New York, people who act out of principle, but they don't
dominate. Why don't they dominate?

Wolfe: I think that's part of the other side of a period of great
prosperity, and you have to keep telling yourself—I mean, look at the
history of humanity—prosperity is great. It's great, but there is hell to
pay now and again. And, I think, part of that is, if you've got this
much ambition geared to financial success, geared to fame, to the

things of this sort, it exerts a pressure so intense that self-abnegating, heroic figures tend to be shoved aside. I think it's a well-known fact in the realm of sociology that levels of crime—street crime, personal crime, muggings, this sort of thing—go down in bad times. The Depression was a rather peaceable time in terms of street crime. It's when times are good like they are now that the passion to get more is inflamed. There's a motto among the so-called "Wolf Packs" who come in from—not only from Brooklyn but that's the most famous— from Brooklyn into Manhattan to prey on people, pedestrians on the street. The motto is "Manhattan makes; Brooklyn takes." That's an awareness of the age we're in. These are mostly youngsters and they're saying, "Those people in Manhattan are making a lot of money. Times are flush—"

Moyers: Let's cross the bridge.

Wolfe: "Let's cross the bridge." I think that's what goes on rather than any breakdown of a system, or justice.

Moyers: What surprised you the most? You've been around a long time, been around this city a long time, but there's a sense of wonderment in your reporting which becomes the fiction of *Bonfire of the Vanities*. What surprised you most?

Wolfe: Well, one of the things is what I would call "media ricochet," which is the way real life and life as portrayed by television, by journalists like myself and others, begin ricocheting off of one another. That's why, to me, in *The Bonfire of the Vanities*, it was so important to show exactly how this occurs when television and newspaper coverage become a factor in something like racial politics. And a good bit of the book has to do with this curious phenomenon of how demonstrations, which are a great part of racial and ethnic politics, exist only for the media. In the last days when I was working on *The New York Herald-Tribune*, I'll never forget the number of demonstrations I went to and announced to all the people with the placards, "I'm from *The New York Herald-Tribune*," and the attitude was really a yawn, and then, "Get lost." They were waiting for Channel 2 and Channel 4 and Channel 5, and suddenly the truck would appear and these people would become galvanized. On one occasion I even saw a group of demonstrators down in Union Square, marching across the Square, and Channel 2 arrived, a couple of vans, and the head of the demonstration walked up to what

looked like the head man of the TV crew and said, "What do you
want us to do?" He says, "Golly, I don't know. What were you
gonna do?" He says, "It doesn't matter. It doesn't matter, you tell
us."

Moyers: I was astonished. I read *Bonfire* before the Tawana
Brawley case broke, and then it broke. And I thought, "Wait a
minute. They set this up to confirm his book." You anticipated that. It
was right out of the book.

Wolfe: I was called prophetic after that. Although if you think
about it, the real life story made my story look rather tame by
comparison. I didn't dare go that far. But I think, in fact, it's not in the
matter of being prophetic. I think if you're willing to go out as a
reporter, whether you're writing in fiction or non-fiction, and try to
understand the mechanisms of the particular society we are in, and
look at them without an hypothesis. Particularly without an ideo-
logical hypothesis, which is the great bane of writing in our period. If
there were some way that you could remove ideology from writers
for about a five-year period, it would be the best thing that ever
happened. Then they'd just look. You know, they'd see.

Moyers: But this is another trembling venture that one takes in
reading *Bonfire of the Vanities,* particularly if one comes out of a
liberal background as I do. Many conservatives have praised the
book for speaking frankly about the failure of liberal pieties toward
race. But I was one who argued in the '60s for integration, because
the other side of integration is disintegration. And reading your book
confirms me in that. The book is about disintegration, and that's the
opposite side of integration.

Wolfe: I would agree with you.

Moyers: Has it come to this? Are we a disintegrating society
racially?

Wolfe: I think what has happened is that we've reached a particular crossover point politically in which, finally, a lot of the have-
nots, a lot of people who are not of white European background, are
coming into their own politically, out of sheer numbers if nothing else.
And this inevitably heightens the tensions that have been there all
along. And now, you can see it in New York every day. I mean,
politicians all over the City are beginning to think about the racial
component of anything that they say. And, actually, that's not all bad,

at all. But it's a very tense period because the crossover is beginning. New York has always had waves of immigration, and the most famous waves were white and European; first, the Germans and the Irish, then Italians and Jews. And these groups all came to power. The heads, politically, in this City today are Italian and Jewish politicians. Their constituency, though, is leaving them. And the waves that have come in since then—which is mainly the wave of black immigration from the South, waves of immigration from the Caribbean, from South America, and now from Asia and, for that matter, North Africa—are coming into their own. Does this lead to an absolute disintegration? Not at all. New York has been marvelous in accommodating these shifts. It's a little tougher when the shift involves a change in skin color. That makes it tougher. But you'll notice, you know, there's no pattern of bloodshed in the streets. It has never come to that, and I don't think it ever will.

Moyers: Conservatives have claimed you. They have claimed you for a long time because, in part, you find a lot of liberal pieties insufferable, and in part because your own journey has led you to some conclusions that, politically, they embrace. But are there conservative pieties that you find as insufferable as you do some liberal pieties?

Wolfe: You know, I really haven't been thinking in those terms. I really haven't. I hear myself called a conservative, both by conservatives and by liberals. It doesn't bother me. It usually means that I've been unorthodox in some way. I haven't gone along with the reigning intellectual line. My own politics, incidentally, since you've brought this up, are right here in this block. I happen to be president of my block association. This is not a hotly contested job. Nevertheless, I'm in my second term as president of the block association, and to me, this is real politics. I go down to City Hall and testify and meet with city councilmen. I go to community board meetings and that's the politics that really engages me. I'm interested, the way everybody is interested, in national politics, but I don't have any national agenda. I have a terrific agenda about developers coming into the East 60s. If you want to hear about that I can go on about that.

Moyers: Well, I'm interested to hear you say that, because the greatest joy I've had in politics, and I've been in and around it for twenty-five years now, was getting involved on my side of Manhattan in a quasi-successful effort to slow down the development of Columbus Circle. And testifying at the Board of Estimates, and organizing people in the blocks, and taking part in those activities was the real joy of politics to me.

Wolfe: I think that's where political ideas should begin, and I wish—I'm going to say something I shouldn't say—I wish my fellow writers would approach politics that way. I'm tired of hearing from writers whose knowledge of the world, and for that matter the political world, consists of what they see in their apartments and the taxicab that they take to work—they don't go on the subway—and the magazine office. You know, for God's sake, fellas, let's get out and look at something for a change and stop breathing the same ideas.

Moyers: You think the City could, this city, be turned around from the blocks up?

Wolfe: I mean, nothing's going to happen soon, but, you know, all this talk about the system, for example, and the masters. Block politics do work, and I'll give you a gigantic example. I had never seen such a coalition of forces—talk about the system and masters and the establishment—as came together in the City for the Westway project. Everybody from the revered, much-respected Senator Jacob Javitts to all the leading banks in this city, to all the leading labor unions, down to the small ones. Every financial interest you can think of was behind Westway. This colossal project to, not only rebuild the West Side Highway, but to build gigantic real estate complexes down through half of Manhattan, down to the Battery. I mean, gigantic— billions and billions of dollars at stake, and a lot of it already committed. It was stopped. It was stopped rather easily by a coalition of neighborhood groups who were against gigantism in their neighborhoods, with a little help from the Army Corps of Engineers.

Moyers: And the snail darter—

Wolfe: And the snail, and—

Moyers: —or some little fish.

Wolfe: —we were concerned about the fish in the Hudson. Stopped it absolutely cold. Where was the juggernaut in that case? That was democracy.

Moyers: You'll be reporting on it, perhaps. Nat Hentoff says reporting is the highest form of journalism. I think it's become the highest form of fiction, as well.

Wolfe: I just think it's indispensable now, in a period like this. This is a period of thresholds, of tremendous changes as we come to the end of certain experiments and as new people come to this country from all over the place. This is an amazing, wonderful period to be a writer in. And I don't see how a writer can operate without going out as a reporter. I don't care if you're writing plays, movies or even if you're a poet. I don't see any other way to do it. And yet so many writers are, at this moment, turning inward. I don't get it. Think of the feast that's out there.

Moyers: [*voice-over*] From New York City, this has been a conversation with Tom Wolfe. I'm Bill Moyers.

Master of His Universe

Bonnie Angelo/1989

From *Time*, 133 (13 February 1989), 90-92. Copyright 1989 The
Time Inc. Magazine Company. Reprinted by permission.

Tom Wolfe, a journalist and novelist with a keen eye for
society's foibles, looks back at a decade of greed and
foresees a cooling of the national lust for money and
license.

His novel, *The Bonfire of the Vanities*, spent 56 weeks
on the hard-cover best-seller list, and currently leads the
paperback list. He pioneered a kind of journalism that was
remarkable for its vivid verisimilitude and its unflinching
dissection of characters. In a conversation with New York
bureau chief Bonnie Angelo, Wolfe predicts that the nation
will seek a new moderation in its ways.

Q: Decades are artificial measures, but that's what we use, and you
have a flair for defining them. You called the '60s "the whole crazed,
obscene, uproarious, Mammon-faced, drug-soaked, Mau Mau, lust-
oozing '60s." The '70s were "the Me decade," "the sexed-up,
doped-up, hedonistic heaven of the boom boom '70s." As we close
out the '80s, how do you define the decade?

A: It is the decade of money fever. It's almost impossible for people
to be free of the burning itch for money. It's a decade not likely to
produce heroic figures.

In a way it's been an extension of normal human behavior, more
than the '70s and '60s. Then there was a reluctance among educated
people to show their affluence—it was the time of the debutante in
blue jeans who worked in a child-care center.

In the '80s people of affluence returned to the more normal thing:
they had it, they showed it. And that radiated throughout society.
When I was spending time in the Bronx, I saw young black men
wearing chains with what I thought was the peace symbol. I thought,
how interesting that these young men, living in such difficult cir-

cumstances, would still be concerned about such issues as world peace. And then I came to realize that these weren't peace symbols—they were the hood ornament from a Mercedes. And they knew everything about a Mercedes, how much it cost, how fast it would go. They knew Mercedes as the car of choice of the drug dealer. Money, greed, reaches all through society.

Q: For 25 years, as a journalist and author, you have been a commentator on life-styles and mores in this country. What's happening to American society?

A: I wouldn't presume to call myself a commentator. That suggests having answers.

Since the 1960s we have had extraordinary freedom in this country, and we are seeing the good and the bad sides of the same coin. We've had tremendous prosperity. In many ways we have fulfilled the dream of the old utopian societies of the mid-19th century. But the other side of the coin of prosperity is money fever and the vanity that is the undoing of all the characters in *Bonfire.*

But I for one would not want to change this country. When you think about conditions across the long panorama, the poverty—there's never been anything like this country, no parallel for what money and freedom have brought to Americans.

Q: Yet you seem pessimistic about our society. Is America going the same road as Rome at its height?

A: No. That's what is called the organic fallacy: countries are not plants, they don't have life cycles that mean there is a time to die. There's no reason we should be on a downward course.

Q: In a speech at Harvard, you were concerned about the fifth freedom—freedom *from* religion and ethical standards.

A: After you've had every other freedom—the four that Roosevelt enunciated—the last hobble on your freedom is religion. We saw it in the '60s in the hippie movement, when tens of thousands of young people quite purposely emancipated themselves from ordinary rules.

In the '60s Ken Kesey told his merry pranksters, Be what you are. It didn't matter what, as long as it was what they really felt they were. Being what you are was a revolutionary, radical notion then. Now it is pretty much accepted.

That's particularly true in sexual issues. The sexual revolution—

such a prim term—was a tremendous change in the '60s. Now we almost don't include it in discussions of morality. We don't think of it in moral terms.

In many ways this new freedom has been a marvelous experiment, without parallel in history. But part has gone to an excess.

Q: Where do you see excesses?

A: The '80s are wilder than the '60s. Rock music is much wilder. Just think how tame the Beatles' music is today: it's almost Muzak. And the sexual revolution—in the mid-'60s the idea of a coed dorm, putting those nubile young things and these young men in the season of the rising sap in the same dormitories, on the same floors! Now the coed dorm is like I-95. It's there. It hums. And you don't notice it.

Q: An erosion of standards?

A: Erosion, no. It's been much faster than erosion. There's been a sweeping aside of standards. Every kind of standard.

Q: What does a seer of the American scene expect of the '90s?

A: The '70s were almost over when I called it the Me decade. I don't deal in predictions, but you appeal to my vanity, so I'll talk about it anyway. I think that in the '90s we'll probably see a good bit of relearning, even though it might seem boring. It's in the attitudes of college students now. I sense they are already voluntarily putting the brakes on the sexual revolution—not screeching to a halt, and not just because of AIDS.

I think there will be a lot of discussion in the '90s about morality. It has already begun. I pick it up in talking to college students. I expect a religious revival. We already see an awakening: the new interest in the Evangelicals, charismatic versions of established religions, and new religious forms such as est and channeling. That fifth freedom excites some and upsets others.

When Nietzsche said that God is dead, he said there would have to be created a new set of values to replace the values of Christianity. God was dead, but guilt was not, and there was no way to absolve it. That, perhaps, is exactly the period we are in. No use saying we are going to return to the dissenting Protestant view of sexual morality at the turn of the century. We won't.

Q: These views have marked you as a conservative.

A: When I'm called a conservative, I now wear that as a badge of honor, because in my world it really just means you are a heretic, you've said something unorthodox. You are supposed to conform to certain intellectual fashions, and if you don't, they say, "That's heterodoxy!"

Q: Reading *Bonfire,* one felt you were writing about the things going on around us now. Did it give you a jolt to see those things and say, "Hey, that's Chapter 7"?

A: Philip Roth said that we live in an age in which the imagination of the novelist is helpless before what he knows he will read in tomorrow's newspaper. And it's true! No one can dream up the things that pop up in the papers every day.

At one point I was a little worried about having my main character, Sherman McCoy, losing $6 million for his firm in about 15 minutes. I thought, "Well, this is fiction. I'll go ahead and do it." My typewriter had hardly stopped moving before I picked up the New York *Times,* and there on Page One was an account of a young investment banker, about the same age as my character, 38, who lost $250 million for his firm in a week. I felt like Alice in Wonderland, running as hard as I can to stay in the same place.

Q: *Bonfire* has received great critical acclaim, but critics have also called it cynical, racist, élitist.

A: That's nonsense. I throw the challenge to them: if you think it is false, go out and do what I did. Go beyond the cocoon of your apartment and taxicab and take a look. Take notes. Then let's compare notes. I'll bet your picture of New York is not very different from mine.

What they are really saying is that I have violated a certain etiquette in literary circles that says you shouldn't be altogether frank about these matters of ethnic and racial hostility. But if you raise the issue, a certain formula is to be followed: you must introduce a character, preferably from the streets, who is enlightened and shows everyone the error of his ways, so that by the time the story is over, everyone's heading off wiser. There has to be a moral resolution. Unfortunately, life isn't like that. I felt that if you are going to try to write a novel about New York, you cannot play falsely with the issue of ethnic and racial hostility. You can't invent implausible morality tales and make it all go away in some fictitious fashion.

Q: How did you tackle the task to get the texture, the sound of every layer of New York?

A: I'm a journalist at heart; even as a novelist, I'm first of all a journalist. I think all novels should be journalism to start, and if you can ascend from that plateau to some marvelous altitude, terrific. I really don't think it's possible to understand the individual without understanding the society.

Q: *Bonfire* portrays New York at its worst, a city consumed by greed and corruption.

A: I never thought of it as a bleak picture. My feeling was wonderment—this amazing carnival was spread out before me. I really love New York. It attracts ambitious people, not just at the top. Think of all the Asians who have come here and have the newspaper stands and candy stores and grocery shops. New York is the city of ambition.

Q: Americans seem obsessed by the quest for status, and certainly the characters in *Bonfire* are, which suggests that you are.

A: Status is an influence at every level. We resist the notion that it matters, but it's true. You can't escape it. You see it in restaurants—not just in New York. People seem willing to pay any amount to be seen at this week's restaurant of the century. It's all part of what I call plutography: depicting the acts of the rich. They not only want to be seen at this week's restaurant of the century, they want to be embraced by the owner. But status isn't only to do with the rich. Status is fundamental, an inescapable part of human life.

Q: In your books you pay meticulous attention to what people wear, as signals of status.

A: Clothing is a wonderful doorway that most easily leads you to the heart of an individual; it's the way they reveal themselves.

Q: Some critics say you judge a man by the shoes he wears.

A: I take some solace in knowing that Balzac was criticized the same way—he was obsessed with furniture. Details are of no use unless they lead you to an understanding of the heart. It's no mystery; it has to do with the whole subject of status.

Q: What would you say about a character who wears a handsomely cut vanilla-colored suit on a winter day in New York, with a lilac tie and matching striped shirt with a collar seven stripes high, and shoes custom-designed to appear to have white spats?

A: I was afraid you might mention that. I suppose I might say, "Here's somebody who's trying to call attention to himself." But I leave that to others to interpret. It's always hard to describe yourself.

Q: Does it bother you to be called a "dandy"?

A: Not at all. Writers, whether they want to admit it or not, are in the business of calling attention to themselves. My own taste is counter-bohemian.

My white suits came about by accident. I had a white suit made that was too hot for summer, so I wore it in December. I found that it really irritated people—I had hit upon this harmless form of aggression!

Q: Is America becoming too homogenized? Is individualism in danger of being lost?

A: No. I think this is a very wild country. Ever since the '60s there has been a moving off dead-center. I see a lack of inhibition. Look at international travelers. I used to think in terms of Adolphe Menjou in his cloak, arriving on a ship, with 42 pieces of luggage. Now the international traveler comes into Kennedy airport in a summer football sweatshirt and running shorts, and his wife is wearing shorts and a T shirt and high heels. And they are flying first-class.

Q: Did you always want to be a writer?

A: I decided at five or six that I wanted to be a writer. My father was an agronomist and the editor of a magazine called *Southern Planter*, in Richmond. I always thought of him as a writer. And I wanted to write.

Q: When you were a small child, there was another famous Southern writer named Thomas Wolfe. Was that a subliminal influence?

A: I love his books. As a child I couldn't understand, since his name was the same, why we weren't related. He was a maximalist, and that's what I admire. Somebody once told him to take out all that was not necessary. And he said, "No. I'm a putter-inner." And that's what I am, a putter-inner.

Q: Critics compare you with Dickens, Balzac, Zola. Pretty good company.

A: They were my models. Particularly Zola. It's the idea of the novelist putting the individual in the setting of society at large and realizing the pressure society exerts on the individual. This is something that has been lost over the past 40 years in the American novel.

Q: An assessment of yourself as a writer?

A: I am just the chronicler. My passion is to discover, and to write about it.

Index

A

Abstract Expressionism, 79, 89, 90, 91
Ace, Goodman and Jane, 274
Addison, Joseph, 220
Adler, Renata, 136
AIDS, 238, 247, 251, 285
Aldrin, Buzz, 138
Alfie, 52
Algren, Nelson, 12
Ali, Muhammad, 111
All the President's Men, 101, 203
Alsop, Joseph, 26, 183
American Spectator, 202
Apollo 17, 31
Aragon, Louis, 124
Architectural Digest, 226, 270
Armstrong, Neil, 125, 137, 139
Arnold, Matthew, 174
Art & Antiques, 226, 270
Art Forum, 92
Art in America, 91, 92
Art News, 89, 92
Ashton, Dore, 94
Astronauts, 31, 103–5, 109, 111, 118, 125, 135, 137–39, 164, 182, 231
Auchincloss, Louis, 67
Auden, W. H., 31

B

Balzac, Honoré de, 36, 37, 39, 41, 43, 60, 63, 64, 72, 96, 134, 156, 179, 187, 220, 227, 257, 258, 259, 261, 287, 288; writing technique, 64
Barth, Frances, 88, 93
Barth, John, 37, 39, 61, 112; *Giles Goat-Boy*, 266; *The Novel Since World War II*, 38
Barthelme, Donald, 167; *Snow White*, 47
Beatles, 235, 236, 285; *Revolver*, 235
Beckett, Samuel, 33, 178
Bellow, Saul, 65; *Mr. Sammler's Planet*, 266

Bennett, Arnold, 183
Berger, Sheila. *See* Wolfe, Sheila Berger
Berkeley, George (Bishop), 46
Bernstein, Carl, 185, 233
Bernstein, Felicia, 213
Bernstein, Leonard, 45, 73, 76, 96, 121, 135, 213
Best Little Whorehouse in Texas, The, 119
Black Panthers, 29, 76, 96, 113, 121, 135, 213, 237
Bladen, Ronald, 90
Boorstin, Daniel, 141
Boston, 141
Brautigan, Richard, 39
Breslin, Jimmy, 66, 100, 132, 136, 137, 209, 230, 241
Breton, André, 124
Brokaw, Tom, 238
Brown University, 61
Bryan, C. D. B., *Friendly Fire*, 179
Bryan, William Jennings, 176
Buber, Martin, 84
Buckley, William F., 264; *Firing Line*, 70; *God and Man at Yale*, 144

C

Caine, Michael, 52
California, 22, 23, 27, 32, 252
Calverton, V. F., 159
Cambodia, 113, 192
Cannon, Jimmy, 231
Capote, Truman, 25, 142, 209, 270; *Answered Prayers*, 51, 66; *In Cold Blood*, 51, 64, 66
Carter, Jimmy, 103, 128, 145, 154
Casals, Pablo, 85
Céline, Louis-Ferdinand, 48, 50
Chekhov, Anton, 41
Chicago Daily News, 100
China, 119
Chomsky, Noam, 253

290

APPOMATTOX REG. LIB.

8202 9100 014 917 3

APPOMATTOX REGIONAL LIBRARY
HOPEWELL,VIRGINIA 23860
07/90

818
Con
c.1

Conversations with
Tom Wolfe

89025046

APPOMATTOX REGIONAL LIBRARY
HOPEWELL,VIRGINIA 23860
07/90